ARSENAL ALL 4–1

Acknowledgements/Credits

When it comes to gratitude, I guess it would be fitting to start with Arsène Wenger, his toptastic team to whom I am eternally indebted for the most amazing memories of all my many years of watching the beautiful game (not to mention the fact that their incredible endeavours have our pitiful pals down the road even resorting to supporting Chelsea and absolutely anyone one else with the slightest chance of putting the mockers us).

With thanks to Bill Campbell, Graeme Blaikie, Debs Warner and everyone else at Mainstream Publishing who've had the misfortune to have their patience seriously tested by my pedantry and perennial tardiness.

My long-suffering 'skin and blister' Debbie, her hubby Si and my ma, who have all gone hungry awaiting my arrival at the dinner table. The colleagues of my sibling at Pentagram, Angus Hyland and Sharon Hwang, without whose artistic inspiration this book wouldn't have such a wonderful cover. Kevin Whitcher, whose scything editing skills ensured that there weren't too many pages to fit in between.

Mike Winnett for the many hours spent maintaining the Arsenal mailing list and all the listees who put up with my constant queries. In particular John Wilson, Ben Dimech, Ian Good, Stuart Singer, Trevor Granger, Ronnie and Renata, Sameer from India, Markus Franke, Stefan and John from Hamburg, and all those who were kind enough to forward me their photos. If I'd had my way, there would be more pictures than words, but there was only a limited space. Not forgetting Raffi Ouzounian (raffi@myway.com).

A big shout to Brian Dawes and his detailed match reports and Chris Parry for his efforts with www.arsenal-world.co.uk.

Heartfelt thanks to Con Murphy for being the catalyst in starting all this writing malarkey; and Brian, Patricia and all in Dublin who are so diligent in posting me a copy of my column every week. Tony Leen, Colm and Declan at the *Irish Examiner* in Cork for not giving me the 'tin tack' when my copy is late and invariably twice the required length.

Last but not least, Nell, a mine of useful and useless information. And my missus with whom I've been able to share so many magical Arsenal moments.

ARSENAL
ALL 4-1

A guidebook to an historic season straight from
highbury's gooner grapevine

Bernard Azulay

MAINSTREAM
PUBLISHING
EDINBURGH AND LONDON

For my missus, Róna, who, for all the
aggravation she suffered, might as well have
written this book herself. And for my mum
because she is the best.

First published in Great Britain in 2004 by
MAINSTREAM PUBLISHING COMPANY (EDINBURGH) LTD
7 Albany Street
Edinburgh EH1 3UG

ISBN 1 84018 916 9

A catalogue record for this book
is available from the British Library

Typeset in Garamond and Univers

Printed and bound in Great Britain by
Creative Print Design, Wales

Contents

Introduction
Reasons To Be Cheerful (Part Two)

I've been writing my weekly column for the *Irish Examiner* for more than five years now. In addition to forwarding my Gooner's Diary for my good mate Chris Parry to put up on his Arsenal World website, I also email my missives every week to a couple of hundred Gooners dotted around the globe. These unfortunate, geographically challenged Arsenal fans appear to appreciate the flavour of being present at the live games which they can't get from the usual media sources. Several times over the years it has been suggested to me that I should compile my pieces into a book. Each season, I threatened to do so but if procrastination was an international sport, I would be England captain and so I never got past talking about it. However, after the Gunners' glorious Double season in 2002, I thought if I don't do it now, I never will. I was under the misapprehension that I had already done all the hard work. Róna, my missus, and I had slipped away the day after the Town Hall parade for some much needed R&R in Sardinia. We were sunbathing on the beach when I received a call with the offer to publish *Arsenal On The Double* and I made the fairly typical mistake of setting a totally unrealistic deadline.

Since my work appears in the Arena, the *Irish Examiner's* Wednesday sports supplement, long after everyone has picked the bones of the weekend's footballing battles, and based on the fact that my column is likely to be read by football fans of all sorts of persuasions, I tend to make it largely anecdotal, in the hope that anyone can enjoy it, not just us devoted Gooners. So, from the moment we returned from our holiday, I was sweating over the arduous process of not only stitching my weekly pieces together but also having to write from scratch details of what actually took place on the pitch. I've such a dreadful memory that I am often left having to ask my missus who scored the goals before we've even reached the bottom of the stairs of the West Upper. As a result, this proved to be such a troublesome task that I found myself swearing that this was the first and last time I would commit to such an undertaking.

I actually ended up sitting at my desk long past several deadlines, trying to finish the book on the very day that England were playing Brazil in the World Cup. I detest watching football on the box when I can't give the game my full concentration – that's why I prefer not to watch matches in pubs (aside from the fact that I'm one of the few non-conformists to the football fans' obligatory beer gut, alcoholic beverages are not my particular poison). Instead of trying to write and watch the game simultaneously, I thought I would enjoy the football that much more if I recorded it to watch later, when I could relax, having finally forwarded my finished work to the publishers. What a big mistake! Most footie fans can relate to the ridiculous lengths they've gone to in an effort to try to reap maximum enjoyment from the delayed transmission of a match by avoiding prior knowledge of the result. Who hasn't answered the phone on a Saturday evening with the stern pronouncement, 'Please don't tell me the score!'? How naive was I to think that I could get away without knowing the outcome of the most important England match since '66?

Even with the TV turned off, and all the doors and windows shut on that warm summer's day, it was downright obvious what was going on in the game. Our entire block of flats vibrated to the sound of the celebrations when Owen scored. Consequently, if you are looking for a culprit for England's ignominious exit from the 2002 World Cup, look no further. The game was up and England's tournament was over the moment I gave up and turned on the TV halfway through!

I guess a couple of years was just long enough for me to forget all the tribulations of my first book. I would be lying if I said that the welcome surprise of a totally unexpected royalty cheque had nothing to do with my decision. It was just before Easter when I first started getting the jitters about how I was going to juggle our credit-card balances. I was already fretting about creating sufficient credit to cover the astronomic cost of rapidly looming season-ticket renewals. Yet while any advance would be better than a poke in the eye with a sharp stick (as my missus would say), it wasn't my primary motivation.

To the contrary, I had a contract for this book lying on my desk for a couple of weeks in March and I was terrified of signing it. Superstitious sod that I am, I convinced myself that the Arsenal's season was going so well that the very millisecond I attempted to exploit it for my personal pecuniary gain, Sod's law would guarantee that I would be putting the complete kibosh on the Gunners. But as week by week we equalled and then surpassed all the records previously set and as this Arsenal side inched their way towards immortality, I became increasingly certain that we were witnessing a feat which might never again be repeated. I therefore felt obliged to offer my individual account of our historic achievement.

I might never have been so presumptuous as to let the 'T' word fall from my lips but I have to admit there was a point just before Easter when it was hard not to be taken in by all the tabloid hype. The hacks were raving as if all the trophies were already won, when, in the space of four days, instead of collecting all the pots, our season was suddenly in danger of going completely *to* pot. I was just relieved that I hadn't signed the contract before our defeats to Man United and Chelsea, otherwise I would have felt singularly culpable for our FA Cup and Champions League exits. Oh, me of little faith! I was bloody quick to get it signed and returned before we played Liverpool on Good Friday, in case we got beat and the collapse of our Premiership challenge coincided with the publisher changing its mind. In fact, if I'd been clever and written the necessary match-day notes alongside each of my weekly pieces, this book would have been virtually ready for publication the day after Martin Keown's testimonial. I was certain that such premeditation on my part was destined to result in a season that wasn't worth writing about so the upshot was that I was faced with the dreadful déjà vu which I'd been desperate to avoid. While everyone else was settling down during warm summer days to savour the feast of football from Portugal, I was distracted by the task of digging up the details of our goalie's gaffes on a gloomy autumnal evening in Eastern Europe.

During my summer of cogitation about the Arsenal's amazing conquest, I came to the conclusion that in some respects we would have been left with nowhere to go but down, if we had actually fulfilled last season's Treble promise. It's true that the Champions League trophy has become something of a Holy Grail for most Gooners but even if we'd won the European Cup, it wouldn't have had anything like the same kudos in years to come compared to the feat we've achieved, which will stand out like a beacon in all the record books. It is often said that you don't fully appreciate something when it is happening around you. We were like a bunch of morose Humpty Dumpties when our Easter eggs came crashing down around us. At that time, the undefeated record felt like a consolation prize which certainly couldn't put us back together again.

For those who witnessed the Arsenal's exploits week by week and who care to look beyond the lavish plaudits of the media bandwagon, we know that in truth the Arsenal were far from the all-conquering Premiership kings who nonchalantly swept aside all comers. In most games, we were a long way from the swaggering side which positively steamed through opponents early in the previous season and, in matches against the likes of Pompey and Man United, we were only a whisker away from our assault on the record ending before it had really begun. Yet, in my warped mind, this is what makes our achievement all the more remarkable.

If we had simply blown away all our opponents, there would be nothing particularly fantastic about our feat. However, it was the grit and gutsy determination we displayed in grinding out many of our results which makes me so proud. It meant that unlike Chelsea's team of all-stars, the Arsenal demonstrated the tight-knit team spirit of a collection of players prepared to sweat blood for one another. In coming from behind to rescue a result in nine League games, we showed the sort of resolve of never knowing when we were beaten, and never laying down and accepting defeat. These are the sort of traits which only develop between a group of players who have lived in one another's pockets for a period of time. It is only by enduring the bitter taste of defeat together that they know the extent to which they have to perform to avoid it.

The pressure for immediate success in the modern game is so great that the opportunities to develop young home-grown talent are becoming increasingly rare. As a result, many of the top teams prefer to cherry pick new players every season from the merry-go-round of intercontinental mercenaries. Consequently, the charismatic collective team spirit witnessed within the Arsenal squad last season is likely to become the exception rather than the rule amongst the Premiership elite.

In fact, if it wasn't for the financial constraints faced by Arsène Wenger as a result of the club's efforts to fund the new stadium, our manager might have introduced three or four new faces last summer who could've had a detrimental effect on the delicate chemistry within our camp. There's no denying that with a stronger squad overall, we might have had the resources to rest players over the congested Easter period and have still brushed aside both Man United and Chelsea. But who knows if the squad would have retained the same sense of togetherness which enabled them to triumph in several other tight League games when the chips were down.

It is this incessant demand for a conveyor belt of talent going in and out of the top clubs every summer which means it will be all the more unlikely that squads will contain a majority of players who've been together as a unit for more than a couple of years. Apart from the very long odds of any team not suffering one bad day at the office amongst all 38 in a season, this is the principal reason I am fairly certain in my conviction that we will never see the likes of the Arsenal's undefeated season again.

If you'd asked Arsenal fans at the start of the season to choose between winning the Premiership or the Champions League, there would have been many who would have chosen European success because it is the one trophy that has eluded us and the one competition which can confirm to the rest of the footballing world what we already know to be true. However, in retrospect, there will be many Gooners who, along with Arsène Wenger, would rather have achieved our astonishing record, with the exquisite title triumph at White Hart Lane as the icing on the cake. Especially when any old team appeared capable of putting together the 13-game run necessary to rule the European roost. In the words of our manager, 'Every year, there is a team that wins the Champions League but it is not every year a team sets a record like that . . . This is something unique, especially in a difficult championship in England. So, would I swap it for the Champions League? Not really.'

As for myself, I am as desperate as the next Gooner to see the single missing honour included in the front of our match-day programmes, if only so that I might give up on this crazy and far-too-costly quest of following the Arsenal to the far-flung corners of the Continent. If/when we finally achieve our Champions League ambitions, assuming I am not bankrupt beforehand, I think I'll be forced to join the majority of Gooners in being more selective, only choosing the tastiest trips abroad and stopping at home to watch the remainder from the comfort of my armchair. Nevertheless, despite my misapprehension (along with thousands of others) that our name was on the Champions League trophy last season, I also wouldn't swap what we achieved for the world.

The fact that we were forced to fight it out for the vast majority of the 3,420 minutes of League football meant so much to me. It proved that the special 'Arsenal spirit' was alive and well, and in evidence every single week amongst this particular squad of Gunners. I grow increasingly concerned as each season passes for the demise of this *je ne sais quoi*, the certain quality which distinguishes the Arsenals from the Chelseas of the footballing world. My concern is in no small part due to the decreasing percentage of players from these shores year on year. As a result, there was nothing more reassuring than the proof positive that we've been watching a group of players who perform with the same passion expressed by those of us on the terraces.

That the majority of them are primarily playing for their teammates and their manager rather than the Arsenal cause per se, doesn't detract from my appreciation. You can't expect an Edu or a Gilberto to be imbued with the same feeling for the club after only a couple of seasons, compared to the likes of Ashley Cole. Ashley has been at Highbury since he was in short pants and I would therefore assume his very blood runs the red and white of the Arsenal, just like those of us who've supported them our entire lives. But in an age when we've grown accustomed to seeing selfish players with overblown egos blame anyone else but themselves for their mistakes, not to mention glory-hunting fans whose only fervour is for the 'next big thing' bandwagon, the 'all for one, one for all' spirit coursing through this Arsenal squad is a joy to behold.

To my mind, the most conclusive proof of the all-pervasive musketeer mood at Highbury came with the arrival of Jose Reyes. As our most-expensive-ever signing and aged only 20, it would have been perfectly understandable if Reyes had arrived at The Home Of Football (THOF) with a bit of a swollen head. We might not have been surprised to see him standing around for the first couple of games waiting for the ball to arrive at his feet, until he realised from watching Thierry Henry that it is beholden of even the world's very best to have to graft along with all the Gunners. However, Jose immediately threw himself into the fray with the fervour of a man possessed.

I can rarely recall being quite so impressed by the debut of an arrival from abroad. His dazzling ability was undeniable from the moment he first touched the ball. Yet it was the way in which Reyes was prepared to run his socks off from minute one which made many Gooners warm to him so quickly. I am not sure how good his grasp of French is, but Jose certainly didn't need to speak English to pick up on the Gunners 'defend as a team, win as a team' vibe. Who would have thought it, but with a work ethic to match his wonderful skills, Jose has so rapidly endeared himself to Arsenal fans that when the new home strip made its debut in the Arsenal shop, Reyes was an even more popular choice of name to have printed on the back than Henry!

Personally, I value Jose's industry almost as much as his ability. It gives me the same 'warm all over' feeling that I get when I see Titi lose possession up front and tear virtually the length of the pitch to put in a tackle on the edge of our own area to try to win the ball back. It's not something you necessarily want to see because you would rather they conserved their energy for where they can do most harm, but it is certainly the sort of donkey work that you don't expect these days from players of their calibre. It is the definitive answer to all those cynical critics who contend that all modern-day stars only play for financial gain and personal glory.

Having used this 'all for one' musketeer theme on the cover, I've been waiting to write this introduction these past couple of weeks, hoping that the long-running soap opera about our very own Porthos – club captain Patrick Vieira – might be resolved. I should have known that the saga would reach a surprising climax within hours of writing these words and, as of this moment, it would appear that the Arsenal have survived yet another Spanish attempt to steal our prize asset.

Considering that it is almost inevitable that Paddy will eventually want to take his turn on football's gravy train whilst his star is still in the ascendancy, most Gooners were convinced our captain was a goner this time around. It seemed as if our recurring nightmare of the past few summers was finally going to be a reality and that Patrick would be joining the Galacticos at Real. Yet, while the rain in Spain still stays mainly in the plain, it would seem that the grass is not any greener. It is a massive relief that this summer's saga is over at long last and that our captain is staying at the club. We proved in almost a quarter of our League games last season that we could cope without him but Paddy's transfer would have been a bitter psychological blow for his teammates.

Patrick was probably the original inspiration for the musketeer spirit in Wenger's squad and we've enjoyed eight incredible years of his loyal service to the cause. However, there are many who feel that he only performed at 75 per cent of his capability last season. So, if Paddy has only decided to stop at Highbury because they weren't offering sufficient money in Madrid, there will be Gooners who are bound to have some qualms about his continued commitment to the Arsenal. Even an under-par Paddy is probably still better than most midfielders on the planet but our club captain is going to have to prove that he's still hungry for success at Highbury. As they say, 'talk is cheap' but it is on the pitch where he will have to quash all our concerns by demonstrating his continued motivation.

It is a mark of Wenger's amazing success on a relative shoestring that our players are constant targets for those teams with backers who have, by contrast, bottomless pockets. Our main-man musketeer has eventually pledged his future to the club and escaped the clutches of the leeches who constantly prey upon the individual's selfish commercial instincts. Hopefully, Vieira's decision will dissuade his French compatriots from getting itchy feet and all the Arsenal's stars will be encouraged to avoid the lure of filthy lucre.

Meanwhile, in some respects, Ray Parlour's departure is no less disturbing. Obviously, you can't compare the two in terms of natural ability but in all honesty I believe Parlour's exit could prove particularly detrimental to our squad. With Parlour and Keown gone, Sol Campbell and Ashley Cole are the only two players from these shores currently playing in the regular first-team squad and, of these two, Cole is the sole home-grown player. When Arsène originally arrived at the Arsenal, he immediately earned my respect by stating that he recognised the need to maintain the correct balance if we were to retain that special 'Arsenal spirit'. I've always believed that we've reaped the benefits as our foreign players have fed off the passion of players like Parlour, Keown and Cole. This has inspired the Continentals to play the sort of committed football which might otherwise not have come naturally to them. Far be it from me to second guess our great leader but despite the obvious enthusiasm of the likes of young Kolo Touré, I fear for the future if Wenger doesn't redress this balance by bringing on some home-grown youngsters.

Arsène faces a bit of a catch-22. It seems the youngsters are too inexperienced to risk throwing them into any matches other than the Carling Cup because we can't afford for them to learn by their mistakes on the job. Yet without a decent run in the first team, we're never really going to discover if they can cut the mustard. So, invariably, these days they end up learning their trade out on loan at another club. However, without a sufficient number of players to set the example of the sort of high standards of commitment expected at Highbury, I'm constantly terrified by the thought that we could turn into another Chelsea, where on an unglamorous miserable winter's night up north, our players might all be standing around waiting for one of their teammates to roll up his sleeves and dig us out of a defeat.

It must be hard work for the likes of Liam Brady, trying to entice the cream of the schoolboy crop to the Arsenal's Academy, with Ashley Cole as the only example of what they might achieve. What's more, it must be soul destroying for the academicians who are frequently taking a step forward to find themselves on the fringes of the first-team squad, only to be forced to take two steps back as Arsène introduces another experienced foreign player in their position because he's too afraid to risk the Arsenal's season on their young shoulders. In this respect, with Sol Campbell out injured, the Arsenal will be starting the season with Ashley Cole as the only British player on the pitch. I would be a whole heap happier if, instead of all the talk of the possibility of bringing in Trabelski from Ajax, Wenger would redress the balance slightly by allowing the home-grown likes of Justin Hoyte an opportunity to prove himself as cover at right-back.

It is ironic when you consider that we started lasted season surrounded by gloom and doom. Our squad was supposedly too thin to offer a serious assault on the Championship and the drain of the new stadium on the club's finances meant that we were left with nothing more than a plot to piss in. This summer we've seen Kanu,

Wiltord, Parlour and Keown exit Highbury (from the main protagonists) to be replaced only by Van Persie and Flamini, and yet somehow suddenly we have the strongest squad in the land, according to all the pundits. I assume the redoubtable Jose Reyes and the emergence of exuberant youngsters like Cesc and Pennant are the main reasons for the change in attitude. Meanwhile, any of my Vieira-related anxieties seemed fairly ridiculous whilst watching a ten-goal romp on a warm summer's afternoon at Underhill. In what's become the traditional pre-season curtain-raiser against Barnet, Reyes was in such heady hat-trick form, as if he was on a mission to show his countrymen the sort of magic they missed by omitting him from Spain's Euro 2004 squad. My pessimism resulting from Paddy's saga soon passed and I was left with good cause to be looking forward to another sensational season.

A short snooze to the soporific sound of wood on willow and that was the sum total of football's summer break. What's more, the Arsenal's new stadium seems to have sprung up whilst I was dozing. As I drive past the gargantuan building site of Ashburton Grove almost daily, the rapid progress suggests it might be finished long before the August 2006 moving-in date. Considering the site lay fallow for so many months, it's astonishing to witness the quantum leap since the turn of the year as the stadium and the surrounding high-rise edifices are erected before my very eyes. I fully appreciate all of the advantages to the Arsenal of the increased capacity at Ashburton Grove and the fact that thousands more Gooners will be able to watch live games, when so many currently can't obtain tickets. Yet as our new ground gradually takes shape, I can't escape my feelings of personal dread. The higher the stadium reaches towards the sky, the inevitable day draws ever closer when we will finally have to leave our Highbury home for the last time.

Most football fans are creatures of habit. Apart from the fact that I now walk to Highbury instead of driving from north London, and I no longer have to be dragged kicking and screaming past the hot-dog and burger stalls because I've long since learnt that you have to be really starving for them to taste anywhere near as good as they smell, I follow the same match-day rituals today that my old man introduced me to some 30-odd years ago.

Sadly, the designs of all modern stadia suggest that we are unlikely to find anything comparable to our fabulous West Upper pitch in the new ground. The equivalent seats are bound to be a lot further away from the action. What's more, it will be almost impossible to recreate that wonderful aura of football history that one feels the moment you enter Highbury's portals. I am sure there will be many advantages to our brand spanking, state-of-the-art, new stadium. The PA system might be more audible and there will be a myriad of choices for those half-time hunger pangs other than just bagels and hot dogs. But such trifles are all likely to be small consolation for losing the footballing home in which I have lived and loved (and had the odd cross word with) the Arsenal for most of my life. Watching football will indeed be a 'whole new ball game'. I fully appreciate the club's intentions to safeguard the Arsenal's long-term future as a major force in both English and European football but for purely selfish reasons, I couldn't be more content with the old one!

However, the knowledge that we have a finite amount of time left to luxuriate in the comfortable familiarity of our Home Of Football means that I will be sure to savour every single match between now and the doubtless tearful last clunk of Highbury's turnstile. As I write at the beginning of August, Róna and I are both at the letterbox first thing in the morning, eagerly awaiting the delivery of our season tickets. It's crazy to think of the struggle involved in stumping up the money for something so small but which is our passport to so much potential pleasure.

After last season's amazing exploits, I think I am even more desperate than usual for the day when we can get back up on our Highbury horse. I can't wait to head out of our flat in Highbury Quadrant for the short walk to our first home game. Out of the Quadrant, into a Blackstock Road positively buzzing with optimism about the new season, everybody sporting their new replica tops with a whole new rash of 'Invincible'-type epithets printed across the back. Then, past the throng outside the Gunners pub, where you catch the first whiff of football's peculiarly distinctive airborne bouillabaisse of beer, fried onions, sweat and hors d'oeuvres.

There's always a small frisson to see a rapidly filling North Bank (or usually already full in my case) looming large, occupying the entire vista at the end of Elwood Street. Then it's a quick dash around the ground, weaving our way through the waves of the East Stand's incoming tide of Gooners, only stopping to satisfy my superstitious need to purchase a programme from the same seller, and hesitating just long enough to hail my good mate Kev at the bookstall near the Tube station, before he responds with the obligatory raised-eyebrow exasperation at my habitual tardiness, as he hollers for me to get a wriggle on. Turning left at the station, as I pass the entrance to the North Bank and Lower West I will usually pat my pocket for the umpteenth time for confirmation of the reassuring feel of my red booklet of coupons. Finally, I reach one of my favourites of the Arsenal's art deco aspects, the relatively small facade of the West Upper, squeezed in between the Victorian terraced gaffs on Highbury Hill.

A quick fumble for some loose change to throw in the bucket of whichever charity happens to be collecting (for good luck rather than an act of conscience) and then for the first coupon in my booklet, always taking care not to tear out two. Amongst all my Highbury hocus-pocus, I have to enter via the same turnstile, unless they are all closed and there's only the one left over for latecomers like myself. As a slower walker, Ró might often leave home before me or I might have hurried on ahead of her but for the first game of the season, we will usually walk around together, splitting up at the foot of the stairs once inside. Ró makes the most of her asthma to save her from the slog up the stairs by heading into the Exec to use the lift. We meet up again at the top with me the one breathing heavily, cursing my 40-a-day Camel habit after I've tromped up all those steps.

Then it's along the corridor, past the bagel counter and the other food and drink outlet, and finally up the last flight of stairs to the top of the bulkhead for Block X. The thrill never diminishes as I step out into the sunlight and my field of vision is filled with the bright green perfection of the Highbury pitch. It's all downhill from there in the physical sense. Halfway down the steps, I'll linger to catch the eye of Nell, my long-suffering partner in awayday Arsenal crimes, and a brief bit of lip reading to suss out if he's prepared to miss the start of another match by accompanying me on our next sortie. Turning right three rows from the front of the West Upper, I will apologise as usual for forcing everyone to their feet as I shuffle along to my seat.

There are a few seats near us with an obstructed view which don't belong to season-ticket holders, where the faces might change from match to match. However, the occupants of the seats in our immediate vicinity are forever constant and so the first game of every season feels more like a family homecoming. There's the eternal fixture of the two elderly gents behind us, whom remind me of the two old men in the balcony of the *Muppet Show*. Ray, whom I bump into all over this country and Europe, since he follows the Gunners as religiously as myself, sits in the adjacent seat on my right and Simon sits on Ró's left, or sometimes he wangles a seat in the Exec and we have his son beside us.

Sitting in front are Joe and Nick, two very old mates who were responsible for me obtaining my seat in the first place. I originally agreed to lease the season ticket from a pal of theirs who'd moved to Hong Kong and eventually I was fortunate enough to inherit it for good. When the adjacent seat came up for grabs a few years back, there was no way I was going to let it go, even though the price of two season tickets leaves us permanently up to our eyeballs in debt. I am forever indebted to Joe and Nick as a result and I express my gratitude at every game, regularly bestowing headaches on them both with my incessant hollering. Nick's fitting claim to fame is that he is the creator of the 'George Knows' and 'Arsène Knows' banners, which many will have seen hanging from the front of the West Upper and, more recently, in the background of those magical photos of Arsène Wenger at White Hart Lane. Having introduced you to my Highbury cast of characters, all that remains is for me to ask if you are sitting comfortably, then let the sensational story of the Arsenal's historic season begin.

1

Friendly: Friday, 11 July (A) Arsenal 0 Peterborough 1

Friendly: Saturday, 19 July (A) Arsenal 0 Barnet 0

Friendly: Tuesday, 22 July (A) Arsenal 2 Ritzing 2 Cygan (60), Ljungberg (85 pen)

Friendly: Friday, 25 July (A) Arsenal 2 Austria-Vienna 0 Bergkamp (29), Jeffers (44)

Friendly: Tuesday, 29 July (N) Arsenal 1 Besiktas 0 Bergkamp (48)

Friendly: Thursday, 31 July (A) Arsenal 3 St Albans 1 Volz (19, 51), Halls (60)

Friendly: Saturday, 2 August (A) Arsenal 1 Celtic 1 Kanu (71)

Friendly: Tuesday, 5 August (A) Arsenal 3 Rangers 0 Edu (31), Lauren (47 pen), Campbell (59)

Community Shield: Sunday, 10 August (N) Arsenal 1 Manchester United 1 Henry (20); Utd win 4–3 on penalties

Cup-final triumph followed by news that Thierry Henry has signed a new contract with a three-year extension; keeper Jens Lehmann is signed from Borussia Dortmund for £1.5 million; Arsenal's proposed move to Ashburton Grove is still in limbo due to financial uncertainty; Russian billionaire Roman Abramovich buys Chelsea; customary doubts whether Patrick Vieira and Robert Pires will follow Titi by putting pen to paper; Arsenal send Van Bronckhorst and Jeffers on loan to ease the wage bill; Dennis Bergkamp is offered a further year at Highbury on vastly reduced terms; the club is so hard up that the players travel to Austria for pre-season preparation on an economy flight; Gael Clichy signs from French Second Division AS Cannes for £250,000 and Philippe Senderos from Servette for an undisclosed fee, rumoured to be worth around £2.5 million; Kolo Touré plays at centre-back in the pre-season friendlies.

Downhearted? Despondent? Do Me a Favour!
11 August 2003

It is that time of year when I lie awake in the mornings, eagerly awaiting the familiar sound of the postie's trolley trundling along the pavement outside Highbury Quadrant. I get more anxious as each day drifts by, hoping that the rattle of the letterbox will signal the arrival of the small, brown envelope which contains the key to another season's worth of heart-stopping thrills at The Home Of Football.

With each passing season, our two little red booklets of vouchers are turning ever more into the torment of Tantalus, priced so far beyond our means. If it wasn't for a Premiership Barclaycard stumping up all £3,300 at 0 per cent interest, this term we would certainly have been up shit creek without the proverbial paddle. And with only beer money to service our champagne tastes, it is becoming increasingly inevitable that Róna and I will eventually have to throw in the sponge to our privileged posh pitch. Perhaps it won't be such a wrench when – if? – our new stadium becomes a reality. Yet, sadly, I will be most surprised if we are able to obtain season tickets at the sort of football-fan friendly £400 paid by the inhabitant of the Stretford End who was sitting next to me on the train to Cardiff on Sunday. Perhaps those prices don't include seven Cup games, but it remains less than a quarter of the cost of our seats and a third of a comparative pitch in Highbury's Clock End or North Bank!

However, at t'other end of the value spectrum, it might be a first for Highbury prices to have edged above those charged at the wrong end of the Seven Sisters Road, but you have only to look at the paucity of entertainment on offer from Hoddle's assorted has-beens to appreciate that our Arsenal pleasures would appear cheap at twice the price.

No, this is not a memo to Messrs Dein and Fiszman, implying that they might take even more advantage of our limitless loyalty to dig the club out of our Ashburton grave – we have already seen some not-so-poor punters prepared to stump up five grand for a bond which seems to promise nothing more precise than a seat, somewhere, at some point in the future. I am certainly no expert on the subject, but even to my commercially callow ears, it sounded like the board were building bricks with straw. In the light of events, or the lack thereof, during the summer, the scheme to create a separate company to oversee our ambitious building project and to ensure that it doesn't have a detrimental impact on either the playing side of the Arsenal plc or Arsène's ability to challenge for trophies, would on the face of it seem somewhat naive.

Nevertheless, the sole purchase of a bargain-basement replacement for Spunky in the Arsenal onion bag, a middle-aged keeper who, according to Sunday's Grobbelaar impersonation, might be more suited to the Edinburgh Festival than a footie pitch, hasn't left me feeling like the harbinger of doom and gloom that's been heard from some Gooner quarters. To the contrary, I am quite optimistic about starting a season where, for once, the insatiable expectation levels are slightly less than usual, and I'm looking forward to laughing at the absolute lack of impact of all the 'show me the money' mercenaries elsewhere.

It is indeed ironic that some pundits are suggesting that Abramovich's millions will allow Chelski to usurp our capital crown, when, last season, they were writing about the best team spirit seen at the Bridge in more than 30 years, engendered by the club's very lack of summer spending. I am hoping that the external problems, along with the absence of any divisively large egos arriving in the Arsenal dressing-room, will foster that famous 'us against the rest of the world' spirit which was sadly lacking when the chips were down last season.

A dour 0–0 at Underhill did little to inspire such faith. In fact, seeing a strikingly similarly built Yaya Touré attempting to fill Vieira's vast shoes, I couldn't help but wonder if we were about to cash in on Patrick and hope that no one would notice. Still, any fears I might have felt about the Arsenal's future were soon dispelled as Martin Keown came off the pitch displaying reassuringly familiar pride in yet 'Another clean sheet!'

Moreover, there might be a silver lining to our prospects for the Premiership poorhouse, if it proves to be a platform for our home-grown youngsters and the sort of scintillating skills seen from Aliadière at Celtic Park. Having witnessed Volz bag a brace against St Albans, I only hope there will be room for a couple of Brady's boys from slightly closer to home to redress the cosmopolitan balance. Meanwhile, Patrick Vieira's impact in the second half of the first of our Glasgow friendlies put me in mind of the 'wherever he wants' punchline about where the 20-stone pet gorilla sits. The Arsenal were a completely different animal once our captain came on the pitch, Patrick's presence seeming to transform the entire team from timid lemurs to tenacious lions. As infuriating as the incessant conjecture about Vieira's contract may be, if I drew one conclusion from his contribution, it was that the club should pay Paddy absolutely whatever he wants.

Whereas, there were several conclusions to be drawn from Sunday's game. The Millennium Stadium would be a wonderful stage for football – if they upped and moved Cardiff a little closer to home. After travelling to Wales for the FA Cup final only a couple of months back, there was little enthusiasm for the trip to Sunday's friendly. Two of Róna's sisters are visiting from Dublin, but I couldn't persuade any of these Gooner gals (nor anyone else for that matter) to give up their seat on the sofa and sweat it out on an eight-hour slow coach to Cardiff and back.

I think Franny Jeffers' petulant red-card reaction was perhaps inspired by his frustration at his abysmal first touch. I am convinced there is something awry with Jeffers' persona which suggests he will never quite gel with the sophisticates in this Arsenal squad. We were more than patient with Pires's last season, as we waited for him to recover fully from the effects of his injury. Yet if we are to mount a serious challenge, both he and Ljungberg will need to prove they aren't one-season wonders. I hope to see the two of them firing on a few more cylinders this term, while Bergkamp serves up the ammunition as his flame burns bright on one last burst of glorious Gooner oxygen. With Titi Henry sitting pretty atop this tree, winning friends as one of the few players who hasn't been blinded by the roubles in Abramovich's apparently bottomless pockets, there can be few more potent strike forces.

Along with everyone else, my greatest fear is for the Arsenal's defensive frailties. Considering there was a German goalie, who has just been introduced to the Arsenal's defensive system, a right-back from Cameroon, who has only recently begun to learn his trade, and a young centre-back from the Ivory Coast in Kolo Touré, who has to date played in virtually every position on the pitch, they weren't the only ones who were apparently nervous every time United stormed forward on Sunday. It remains to be seen if Wenger can mould the resources at his disposal into a solid defensive unit.

However, the Gooner bellyachers don't know they are born. We are slap bang in the middle of an era that many of us wouldn't have dared dream about only a few years back, privileged to be watching football artistry which might not be bettered in our lifetimes. Instead of counting down the days, searching for signs of the almost inevitable cyclical decline, put away your prematurely drawn knives and just enjoy! All the pressure is on the proliferation of prima donnas, stepping on each other's toes as they trot off down the Kings Road, and if watching them fail is not sufficient fun, we can always laugh at Tottenham.

2

Premiership: Saturday, 16 August (H) Arsenal 2 Everton 1 Henry (35 pen), Pires (58)

Ten man Arsenal secure maximum points despite Sol Campbell red card.

Absence does indeed make the heart grow fonder and, after being deprived of my beloved Highbury home during a couple of long summer months, I never tire of the terrific thrill of trotting around for our first home game of the season. I get no less excited now than I did when I was only six years old. A few more years towards the infirmities of old age and I will probably have to start worrying about pissing my pants again! I know we Gooners are fortunate that our silverware fantasies are not as fanciful as all those fans whose teams are forced to compete on an increasingly uneven playing field, but, starting from scratch, I continue to cling to the romantic idea that, up and down the country, fans are arriving at their particular places of worship with all of us united. No matter how unrealistic a notion it might be in the heads of some, our hearts are all full of hope that this might be our season.

I had the wind knocked out of my sails on opening day before I'd even entered the stadium and it was straight round to the box office on Monday after an embarrassing incident. I am not proud to admit that I tend to look down my nose at anyone who dithers at the turnstiles, tentatively handing over their ticket, unsure whether they are at the correct entrance. I automatically assume that the fact that they aren't a member of our far too exclusive season-ticket club means they can't possibly be as faithful a follower of my religion and therefore have little right to be holding me up (as I'm always late and hurrying to make kick-off). However, on Saturday it was me who felt like folks behind in the queue might mistakenly assume it was my 'first day at school'. I even overheard someone tut-tutting with a 'schoolboy error' snipe as I was turned away.

I was told to go round to the East Stand because my booklet had pink vouchers instead of yellow. I just stood there in a state of shock. I certainly didn't fancy missing much of the first half of the opening game whilst running round to the box office to resolve the mix-up. Thankfully, I gained admittance at the second attempt, after showing the geezer at the turnstile the ticket in the front of my little red booklet which showed the details of my West Upper seat. Having swapped my booklet over for the correct one on the Monday, I was a happy bunny walking home with a whole season of guaranteed football pleasure in my grubby little hands.

Hail to the Grief
18 August 2003

The press haven't finished pontificating about the opening games of the Premiership and already the Arsenal face the prospect of losing two of our best players to suspensions. As one of the least mercurial members of our squad, it was surprising to see replays of Campbell's uncharacteristic reaction to Djemba-Djemba's tackle at Cardiff. I can't recall the last time Sol let an opponent get under his usually stoic skin. Additionally, anyone who has ever had a kickabout in the park will know how hard it is to resist the temptation to hack away the legs of an opponent who has just taken advantage of your statuesque defending, leaving you for dead, staring at your shoelaces, hoping there are no spectators. I can only imagine that such feelings must be far more intense when one is burdened by all the optimism for the forthcoming season of 30,000-odd baying Arsenal fans (although I couldn't help but wonder if Campbell would have been quite so quick to clip Gravesen and prevent an attempt on goal if the reassuring frame of Dave Seaman was still standing between the sticks).

As for Thierry Henry, I could see the charge of disrepute descending on the club from the second he started prancing towards the wrong corner of the ground on Saturday after sticking away his penalty. However, what Henry does with the ball at his feet is usually a big enough outrage for opposing fans. He has rarely resorted to Robbie Savage-style roguery to raise the temperature a few notches. Nothing will convince me that his inadvertently triumphant teasing of the Toffees fans was anything more than an act of gross stupidity. If it hadn't have been the first game of the season and we had been away from home, where Henry might have been reacting to the remorseless badinage from the Blues fans, I wouldn't have been so certain. Although there would be no mileage for the tabloids in cutting Henry some slack and, as a result, I have a feeling that, since it's the Arsenal, the FA will relish this 'early doors' opportunity to set such a high-profile example.

As with Arsène, my paranoia meter might already have been piqued by the media. I can immediately recall several instances where opponents have been equally irresponsible and their actions haven't even rated a mention (considering the passion this sport arouses, I personally think it is ridiculous to always expect players to have the patience of Job in the face of intense provocation). Moreover, if incitement is a hanging offence, I can think of several officials who should long since have been hung, drawn and quartered as the lead instigators of several incidents of wholesale mayhem!

As far as I am concerned, it is no coincidence our players' actions are regularly subject to far more intense scrutiny than teams located in the North. If you heard the way they moaned about having to traipse to Wales, you would realise that the majority of the tabloids' principal panderers of tittle-tattle rarely roam beyond the boundaries of the M25. One of the privileges of their seniority is that they can bag Highbury at the weekend, sacrifice an Arsenal lamb (lion!) on the altar of their asinine headlines and still be home for tea. (Please, forgive me, but I have to blame the press for perpetuating the myth of our disciplinary problems by planting subconscious seeds into the minds of the officials. While I am fully aware that we are no angels, I know full well that we are far from being the worst offenders.)

Perhaps I am no better. I've spent the weekend whinging about the media's failure to focus on the football being played, as they constantly nit-pick at the periphery (do we really give a monkey's how the Russian mogul chooses to celebrate the evidence on Merseyside that he hasn't entirely wasted a couple of hundred million quid?). Yet here I am, spouting from my soapbox, after less than a week of the season because Róna and I had to scrimp and save (more like beg, borrow and steal) over three grand for the scrumptious prospect of Highbury's high-class entertainment. If only we could demand a refund for some of the sixty quid it cost us for our seats when deprived of our favourite stars when they're suspended on the sidelines as hostages to their misfortune! The senseless punishment doesn't fit the crime. Everton certainly didn't benefit on Saturday, but it is their immediate competitors who might end up profiting from Sol's suspension.

Sol didn't leave his stud marks on anyone's shin. In fact, Thierry was probably the most injured party and I doubt he'll be in a hurry to do it again. He looked disgusted as he subsequently brushed himself down having been showered in a hail of coins, spittle, ale and anything else that came to the berserk Blues fans' hands. No malice or harm was intended or caused by either Campbell or Henry. Compared with the antics for which the game was once renowned, the likes of Peter Storey and 'Chopper' Harris must be laughing their heads off over the innocuous incidents which result in early baths in contests up and down the country today. As ever, it will be us poor punters who'll end up being punished.

Halsey is as popular as Gollum to most Gooners after sending Sol off for the second time in successive appearances at Highbury, but perhaps Campbell's favourite compadre has done us a great service. While I am quite confident that the Arsenal first eleven are capable of frightening the life out of any opposition going forward, listening to the pundits on the radio rave about United's Portuguese prodigy or considering the collection of tried-and-tested talent queuing for a place in Chelsea's team, I am concerned that our squad might begin to look a little stretched (sadly, it appears, somewhat sooner than expected).

However, I am hoping that the hard-learned lessons of letting a somewhat-arrogant eight-point grip on the title slip through our grasp will inspire a greater determination this term. What's more, we now have one of the most settled squads in the League. This should ensure that we outshine our opponents in at least one extremely important department: team spirit. If there is one positive aspect to the repercussions from Cardiff and Saturday's contest, it could be the immediate inspiration of a 'backs to the wall', 'Arsenal against the world' sense of injustice. Previously, this hasn't materialised until at least midwinter, after some months of mauling by the media, when we've become well and truly demented by a multitude of diabolical refereeing decisions.

When Everton conjured up a consolation goal with five minutes on the clock, recent memories of late goals conceded and points carelessly wasted resulted in plenty of worried faces in the West Upper, especially with Rooney on the pitch. However, someone should have warned young Wayne that it was his ball skills which were being compared to Gazza's. It wasn't an invitation for an identical battle with the bulge (song for the day: 'Salad for Rooney!').

Meanwhile, it is onwards to Boro with three points in the bag, which is all that matters at the end of the day. Yet if suspensions are the source of a 'fortress Arsenal'-style resolve which ensures the end of weekly last-minute white-knuckle rides, I guess I should be grateful to Halsey for a heart that will still be ticking in the weeks ahead and which will be able to cope with all these Gooner collywobbles!

3

Premiership: Sunday, 24 August (A) Arsenal 4 Middlesbrough 0 Henry (5), Gilberto (13), Wiltord (22, 60)

Arsène finagles 16-year-old 'Cesc' Fábregas Soler from Barcelona; Gunners go top of the League after Riverside romp.

I am renowned for my rotten recognition skills, but ever since the Cellnet Stadium opened, my pal Nell and I have grown accustomed to seeing the same two huge police horses outside the away fans entrance, with the same particularly sociable copper in the saddle of one. He'd trained his mount to entertain the punters and, in return for a titbit, this splendid creature would tap its hoof and nod its head. This season, we saw the same rozzer but, sadly, he informed us that his old companion had been retired. I like to think that this lovely animal's lifetime of service was rewarded and it was seeing out its days in a luscious meadow. Yet the cynic in me imagines that, in light of the prohibitive cost to the police force, it is perhaps more likely to have ended up in a tin of our pooch Treacle's pet food, turned into the same mincemeat that we were about to make of Middlesbrough.

Slow Boat from Cairo
25 August 2003

There's nothing like driving 500 miles in one day to serve as a reminder that the season has started in earnest. That and the sight of the Arsenal strikers putting a sock in the mouths of all those in the media who have focused on anything other than this football side's fabulous ability to frighten the life out of the opposition's defence. The line might read, 'one of those smiles', but I would walk a million miles for some of those skills and, with the Champions League draw this Thursday, I will doubtless end up doing so once again this season.

Mind you, my aching back is grateful that the demise of the Black Cats means one less trek to the Northeast this term. Although, the trip to Teesside was a mere trifle for my passenger: he'd travelled all the way from Cairo on a pilgrimage to watch his beloved Gunners. Amr must have thought all his Christmases (Ramadans?) had come at once, as we Gooners sat there gobsmacked by the glorious way in which the Arsenal tore the Teessiders to pieces in those first 20 minutes.

Despite this country's ridiculously inept rail network, the predicted meltdown on the motorways on Sunday mercifully never materialised. I imagine many must have heeded the scaremongering headlines since we positively sailed all the way North on a relatively traffic-free road. Nell and I were both shocked to arrive with over two hours to spare. While I grieved for the extra two hours' kip I might have enjoyed, my Egyptian pal pondered on the question of his safety as he proposed to strut around on enemy soil in his brand-new, bright-yellow-and-blue replica shirt.

No matter what high-tech, heat-dispersing disguise they dress it up in, I have never been able to wear the synthetic shirt material next to my skin and so this has never been a question I've had to concern myself with. Not that I bury my loyalties under a bushel (apart from our annual sortie into Spurs territory), but I lean towards wearing somewhat more discrete cannon logos. I told Amr that he was unlikely to get any grief because, by and large, Boro fans are a friendly bunch. However, wearing a replica shirt to away games can be a somewhat risky business. It is an open invitation to the inevitable over-inebriated idiot, offering an outlet for them to express their bitterness about the Arsenal being the better team.

I told Amr that if the result should go our way, he might be wary of keeping his head down on the way back to the car. Laughing, he suggested he'd be safe in our company, but I couldn't resist pulling his leg, warning him that we would be making like the traditional Islamic couple, with him walking five paces behind! Occasionally, during the course of a game, the home fans will get stoked up by bad decisions and unfortunate incidents, and you have to be cautious on the way out to avoid being a target for their ire (as much as I love animals, I would rather their cat got a 'good kicking' than me!).

However, in all our travels, watching Premiership football across the length and breadth of this country during the course of the past decade, the nearest we have come to being victims of any football hooliganism was when unruly Foxes fans threw some coins in our direction. Thankfully, altercations between sets of supporters these days are certainly the rare exception, rather than the rule. I am aware that the problem is more prevalent outside of the Premiership, at clubs with a history of hooliganism, where bored bovver-boys think they have a reputation to protect; with only a weekly walk to the dole office, the kids' favourite distraction is causing chaos at their weekend contretemps.

Yet the disproportionate amount of media coverage given over to what I imagine are really only minor altercations, drives me absolutely potty. No one seems to accept their responsibility for perpetuating any such problems, or perhaps even creating trouble where there's been none previously by encouraging impressionable youngsters who might want to imitate their peers.

As far as Arsenal fans are concerned, we couldn't possibly want for any antisocial distractions from the dazzling skills of Henry, Vieira et al. If the purveyors of tabloid poppycock don't possess the imagination to fill their column inches with insightful comments about the entertainment on the pitch, perhaps they could concern themselves with the important question of why the prospect of being present to witness such wonderful football wasn't enough to attract anything like a full house to the Riverside. I was stunned to see so many thousands of empty seats for Boro's first home game of the season. I imagine it won't just be on the pitch that Gaizka Mendieta (and Mills) will be expected to produce a return on Steve Gibson's money, but also in attracting a few more bums on Boro seats.

A couple of racist scum wasted their unsavoury abuse on Amr. He either didn't hear their disgusting drivel or didn't understand their Teesside drawl. However, the majority of the home fans' misery was directed towards their own team's dismal effort. Like any genuine football lover, most Boro fans were gracious in showing their appreciation of the Gunners' awesome attacking display in the opening period of the game and were just gutted to have been on the wrong end of it. Amr almost disappeared in the crowd as a Boro fan, whose merriness suggested he must have started drowning his sorrows sooner than most, with his plastic pint pot still in hand as proof, regaled our Egyptian pal with his reaction to their drubbing by saying how they'd been undone by the better team and a striker who is undoubtedly one of world football's greatest talents.

Amr actually turned down a seat on the halfway line with the suits in the directors' box so that he could wear his new away shirt, and sing and shout (and swear, in Arabic!) with all us Gooners behind the goal. He certainly wouldn't have been able to wave his Egyptian flag in those more-sterile surroundings, on the off chance his Arsenal-supporting compadres were watching the live broadcast back home. I was only being funny when I suggested that my old man (who fought in the Israeli army) would be turning in his grave at Amr's suggestion that he might leave his flag in my car, ready for next week's rendezvous in Manchester. I hope he didn't take me seriously.

After such a fabulous first awayday of the season, superstition decrees that I alter none of the circumstances of the outing for fear this might affect our fate. I am certain Amr would love to stay, but failing being able to keep him in this country to accompany us all season might mean I have to requisition his flag. It would present a delightful dichotomy with my cannon-crest embroidered skullcap that sits amongst the mishmash of Arsenal amulets which, unlike my completely tapped-out credit cards, I can't leave home without.

Each season, I become more certain that, according to the law of averages, we must eventually be presented with an opportunity to watch the Arsenal play in the Bernabéu (it being one of the few great stadiums I have yet to visit). However, it is in keeping with the sadistic laws of Sod and Murphy that I am convinced my chance is bound to come now, only because I might not be able to afford to take it!

4

Premiership: Wednesday, 27 August (H) Arsenal 2 Aston Villa 0 Campbell (57), Henry (90)

Draw for Champions League groups: Thursday, 28 August, Lokomotiv Moscow, Dynamo Kiev, Inter Milan

Premiership: Sunday, 31 August (A) Arsenal 2 Manchester City 1 Wiltord (48), Ljungberg (72)

Little fluency, but an obdurate three points against O'Leary's Villa is all that matters; not-so-Safehands earns some Gooner gratitude in scrappy win at City of Manchester Stadium.

For every previous Champions League draw, I've been sitting in front of my laptop ready to bag cheap, no-frills flights because it's the only way I can justify the cost of following the Arsenal abroad. I blame the early onset of Alzheimer's but I was up at the box office on Thursday because our tickets hadn't turned up in the post. It was a complete shock when a fellow Gooner shouted out the result of the Champions League draw. I freaked, realising I'd forgotten all about it. Usually, it is only a matter of a few minutes between the draw being announced and any chance of cheap flights disappearing: either all the lowest fares are bagged by those who are quickest off the mark or the airlines suddenly twig and take advantage of the sudden increase in demand by withdrawing all their loss-leader fares.

The Easyjet and Ryanair empires have yet to reach Eastern Europe and with all the travelling Gooners focusing on flights to Milan, I was convinced I would have already missed the bargains boat. I was absolutely gutted and didn't even bother hurrying home. However, there's always a delay between the draw being announced and the actual dates of the games being confirmed and it must have just been my good fortune to walk in the door and turn on the computer literally moments after the match schedule had been finalised. 'Surely some mistake,' was my immediate response when flights for only £3.99 flashed up on my screen. Nevertheless, I couldn't hit the 'confirm' button quick enough.

Believe the Hype
1 September 2003

The bedlam in the Arsenal box office ensured that our tickets for the City game never turned up, so we faced a disconcerting drive to Manchester to collect duplicates. However, Nell had his unusual credit-card-sized ticket for the City of Manchester Stadium and, on the way down, we speculated on the absence of any barcode (I suppose they are all at St James' Park) which might be required for automated turnstiles.

It was when we joined a queue outside the ground that the wonders of this new stadium's technology were revealed to us. It turns out that, as with almost everything these days, there is a chip contained within the ticket and when you hold this up against a gadget at your designated entrance, you have 20 seconds to get yourself through the turnstile. The bloke in front was explaining to us that, apart from all the other potential problems related to people pushing buttons on the computer that governs this system, there were many instances where punters were turning to their pals to marvel over the technology and missing out on this 20 second window. I suppose you can't provide for human inefficiency within this automated system without offering an open invitation to wily Mancunians to attempt to defraud it.

Consequently, there is no second chance and, as a result, the majority of the large queue was made up of irritated City fans waiting to have their tickets 'reactivated' for one reason or another. Moreover,

I don't imagine that City's newfangled system will have made any great saving. In the absence of turnstile operators, they will still have to employ staff at every entrance to explain to us idiots how to use it!

Nevertheless, their modern new stadium is a magnificent place; a fitting stage for the Premiership's glamorous product. It may lack all of the history and a little of the intense atmosphere attached to the dilapidated Maine Road, yet the designers are to be congratulated because, in an arena originally built for athletics as the centrepiece of the Commonwealth Games, there is absolutely no evidence of any compromise as far as playing and watching football is concerned. Considering the Arsenal's ongoing struggle to meet the spiralling costs of our new stadium project and its impact on our now non-existent spending power (despite the fact that the board continue to have the brass to deny it!), I am sure the likes of David Dein covet the considerable advantages to City of being the benefactors of the local authorities' impressive cast-off.

My biggest gripe with many modern grounds is that the fans are too far from the pitch to have much of an influence on affairs. I've a great aversion to the detached atmosphere of grounds on the Continent, where fans are separated from the action by running tracks, nets, glass and moats. I would hate to see British football go this way and lose its distinctive flavour – the intense fervour seen in our stadia when the fans are sitting or standing right on top of the pitch. I was pleasantly surprised to find my binoculars were somewhat superfluous on Sunday. Sitting six rows from the front, I could almost reach out and touch Jens Lehmann.

'Sea-man, Sea-man.' 'Lee-man, Lee-man.' The Gooner choristers must have sounded a little confused, but it was obvious that our affections for the big Yorkshire galoot remain undiminished. The press made a big deal of his indecisive part in Freddie's points-winning strike, suggesting that Spunky had been allowed to leave the Arsenal because he was past it, but I am certain if our coffers weren't quite so dry and our manager had been able to make more than a derisory offer, both big Dave and Wenger would have been more than happy for him to have remained at Highbury.

It was events at St Mary's that were interesting us en route, as we listened to the radio commentary of the match involving the other Mancunian team. Any doubts I had about the outcome disappeared just before kick-off. The huge roar that went up in the stadium could have meant only one thing. You would struggle to find supporters of two other teams who would have been happier to hear that Man Utd had conceded an 88th-minute match-winner. Wenger and his side would all have to have been deaf, dumb and blind not to be aware of Southampton's late strike. I didn't believe a word of it, when he and Keown suggested the same afterwards. It seems to be an unwritten code of practice to avoid giving the competition the satisfaction of knowing that you care about their results. Who are they kidding?

I was tempted to have a bet at the start of the weekend. With Chelsea and United facing awkward opposition, I had a feeling in my water that both would drop points. However, as has often been the case when we've played later than our immediate competitors, I fully expected the Arsenal to fail to take advantage of our opportunity. To my mind, the news of United's loss might subconsciously allow for a little complacency within the team, in the knowledge that they could afford to slip up without losing ground. The evidence of our abysmal first-half performance hardly contradicted my conjecture.

It was fairly typical of the bashful big keeper that he turned down the opportunity to captain the City side on the day (in contrast to Schmeichel, who couldn't resist Keegan's similarly kind offer last season!). As I said to a steward at the break, I fancied it might already have been written that it was to be Seaman's day, where absolutely everything would stick in his Safehands.

I guess that one of the advantages of a manager who is prone to a naturally reserved disposition is that when he does eventually lose his rag, it is not without good reason. It happens so rarely that he has a fair chance of making some impressions. Mind you, if there was indeed a well-deserved half-time haranguing, it wasn't like it produced a performance which was unrecognisable from the first-half rubbish. It might have been a different story if we hadn't managed to score so soon after the break. The belief we've become accustomed to seeing Keegan instil in his sides, and which was evident early on, began to melt away the moment we equalised.

Yet I am glad I went to the post-match press conference, if only to confirm to you the utter codswallop touted by the tabloids. There was absolutely no 'fury' about a downbeat Keegan afterwards. In fact, he was quite impressed that City had been more than a match for us in the first half and merely expressed his disappointment that their determination diminished after the break, as if they expected to be beaten by the mighty Arsenal. As for Arsène, his unflinching loyalty to his players, past and present, was evident in his reluctance to discuss any details of his dressing-room dressing down and in the regular 'didn't see it' refusal to apportion any blame on Seaman for our second goal, before going on to give us a detailed, step-by-step account of how the hapless Lauren managed to stick the ball in his own net.

I also find no end of amusement in the fact that, before the season started, we were already being written off as also-rans because of the Arsenal's penny-pinching in the transfer market. It was in complete contrast with Man Utd's multi-million-pound investment in new players and Chelsea's prodigal Russian son parting with more than £100 million. Suddenly, after four straight wins, everyone is singing from a different songsheet; the fact we're a settled side, undisturbed by any oversized egos belonging to new arrivals, makes us firm favourites. Can anyone see the parallels with Chelsea last season, where their best League finish since the old King died was a result of their lack of summer spending? 'Logically', according to Wenger, if our undefeated start to the season stems from the side's stability, we shouldn't be surprised if Chelsea finish strongly. Such sensible theory rarely applies to our illogical sport.

A similarly timed international break last term was seen as a minor disaster because it interrupted some of the best football we Gooners have ever seen. This time around, we have scraped six points from our last two encounters with entirely sloppy performances by comparison. Perhaps the only positive has been our defensive displays, where Kolo Touré and our new keeper have been the most pleasing constant. Sitting pretty atop the pile with a three-point lead after the Arsenal's best League start in fifty-six years, the media are bound to 'big us up' during the two-week break. I am hoping that we will come back having swallowed plenty of the hype, breeding the confidence that will result in a return to our imperious best. We have got away with it against the likes of Villa and City, but we will need to hit top form if we aren't to be found out by the fixtures soon coming thick and fast!

5

Premiership break for internationals on first Saturday of September.

No Substitute for the Real Thing, but Hopefully the Calm Before the Storm
8 September 2003

I am probably spoilt by being privileged to watch the likes of Henry and Vieira perform each week. When the Ireland starting eleven was announced on Saturday afternoon, I was struck by the thought that, aside from Damien Duff and John O'Shea, there wasn't one of the remaining nine I'd fancy in my team (OK, possibly Shay Given). Whatever your thoughts on Brian Kerr as Ireland manager, it is no mean achievement for a squad sadly wanting in genuine world-class players to be punching well above their weight. All square against Russia, in the absence of Robbie Keane, it seemed that too much was resting on the diminutive shoulders of young Damien – and didn't the visitors know it!

The prospect of watching encounters involving journeymen like Breen and Carsley might not have me jumping around the living room for joy. Yet at least there remains some intrigue about Ireland's attempts to recover from the disastrous start to their qualification campaign. Could they slip under the wire, as we have come to expect over the years, on little more than terrific team spirit? In contrast, my waning interest in (what to my mind is) Sven's bunch of overpaid wasters ensured that the England v. Macedonia game was already 20 minutes old by the time I remembered to turn the telly over. I assume the FA must have wheeled Sol out for the waiting media the day before because the Saturday papers were full of 'England's rock ready to roll' type headlines. *The Guardian* picked out five of Sol's England performances which stood out for various reasons. Talk about tempting fate!

Although, considering the circumstances, perhaps Sol's embarrassing 'stoops to failure' slip-up was not so surprising. By half-time, England's indifferent efforts on the pitch left me so unenthused about the second half that I decided to take the dog for a walk over Hampstead Heath instead. At least an early evening stroll while listening to the commentary on the radio would mean that it wouldn't be a total waste of time. I was listening in the car en route when Radio 5 Live's microphones picked up the heinous monkey noises directed by some Neanderthal Macedonians at Emile Heskey. The commentator, Alan Green, was duly disgusted since the racist scum responsible were standing right in front of him, along with some comatose Macedonian coppers. It's one thing to read about these shocking incidents, but much more horrifying to hear it with your own ears.

It is outrageous in this day and age that sporadic fighting between supporters sees England threatened with the possibility of having to play behind closed doors, while the game's authorities lack the gravitas to do anything more than scratch the surface of a far more serious problem with their paltry fines. UEFA must start handing down far more draconian punishments if they want to prove that there is a real desire to stamp out such overt displays of racism, at least within our football stadia.

According to my radio, Wales were holding their own in the San Siro by the time Treacle and I had finished our walk and reached my favourite café for some refreshment. I was tempted to tease the Italian proprietor, but I didn't want him doing something nasty to my plate of lasagne. I should have lingered over my latté until full-time, when I might have inveigled a free dinner by informing him of his country's 4–0 victory. Still, I was keen to get home to collapse on the sofa and savour a recording of the Arsenal . . . sorry, France, demolishing Cyprus 5–0.

Poor Ashley Cole came in for some stick from a few of the moaning minnies in the media on Sunday with them questioning his defensive capabilities at international level. However, I have some sympathy with Cole since it couldn't have been easy for the black players in Skopje – especially playing out wide where it must have been impossible to ignore the odious insults. Moreover, how can you possibly justify praising young Ashley for the attacking potential he offers down the left flank in one breath, then slaughter him for getting caught out occasionally as a result in the next? I was just grateful that the feats of young 'Roonaldo' saved both Arsenal players from a fate worse than Seaman's and the savage mauling he suffered after his Macedonian mishap.

The first break for internationals last season did the Arsenal absolutely no favours. We were flying at the time, unbeaten away from home for an eternity (well, since the season before last) and playing some of the best football we'd ever witnessed. We came back to see our amazing away record fall to the wondrous last-minute strike that introduced Wayne Rooney to the world and were beaten at home by Blackburn the following week.

With a bit of luck, following their imperious performance in Paris and, hopefully, another high in Slovenia on Wednesday, our French contingent will come back having forgotten the fact that we were fairly fortunate to scrape all six points from our previous two matches. Buoyed by that winning feeling (and after four wins in four when our form was fairly mediocre), just imagine the possibilities if/when they start producing some of the prodigious football we know them to be capable of.

6

Premiership: Saturday, 13 September (H) Arsenal 1 Portsmouth 1 Henry (40 pen)

Pires's party piece earns a penalty and the twice-taken spot-kick preserves a fortunate point.

Can-a-Baloney
15 September 2003

I should have known our 100 per cent record was about to come a cropper the moment I realised Wenger had received the accursed manager of the month award. Arsène may undoubtedly be the dog's proverbial whatsits, but that does not make him immune to dropping the occasional clanger. The rigorous demands of international call-ups on a crowded fixture list have been a fairly regular theme of his in recent times. Perhaps Arsène is hoping that the authorities will eventually heed his plea for those who pay the performing pipers to be able to call the tune with regard to the all-too-common conflict of interest over international encounters. Or his reflections on this matter in Saturday's match-day programme notes might merely have indicated that Wayne Rooney's wonder strike, and the resulting demise of our undefeated away record after a similar intermission last season, was as much on his mind as it was on all of ours. Whatever the case, Arsène appeared to have made a ricket by raising the topic. It was as though he was responsible for putting thoughts of fatigue inside the heads of our foreign contingent.

Our fab four Frenchmen returned from Slovenia in fine style. An Arsenal director sent his private jet over to fetch them back as fast as possible. I could have accepted the subsequent excuses if some of our players had begun to fade towards the end of the second half, yet from the leg-weary look of our lot right from the first whistle against Portsmouth, one could be forgiven for wondering whether they had pedalled their way back on a push-bike!

The gaffer's word is gospel and his disciples were unlikely to make a mockery of his grievances. Auto-suggestion alone didn't account for us giving away a couple of points which were ours already, according to many presumptuous pundits. Yet it certainly didn't encourage the Gunners to gallop onto the pitch and promptly put Pompey to the sword with a 'fresh as daisies' performance.

The fact that this was probably Teddy Sherringham's Highbury swansong didn't help either. Having taken so much stick from our supporters as the butt of so many Arsenal anthems, it is obvious that Teddy gets untold pleasure from putting a sock in Gooner gobs. You only had to see his last-ditch tackles in the unfamiliar territory of Pompey's own penalty area to know that he was determined to do his level best to leave us with a parting gift. An addition to all the other unpleasant 'made by Sherringham' memories which have haunted us over the course of his long career.

He was ably assisted by his strike partner, Yakubu, who, according to Redknapp, had been a doubt during the week when he came down with malaria. If this is an example of how much of a handful the Nigerian is when he's under the weather, I eagerly await an opportunity to witness what a nightmare he can be when he's 100 per cent fit! Mind you, if the forward fails to prove quite such a problem for other opposing centre-backs, it will be further confirmation of the fact that this was probably Sol Campbell's most error-prone performance for many a moon.

I'd been particularly impressed by Pompey's Amdy Faye prior to our encounter. Patrick Vieira spent most of the afternoon in Faye's pocket, a feat rarely accomplished by any world-class opponent, let alone a relatively unknown midfield lieutenant from lowly Pompey. Considering our captain's Senegalese compatriot was in the Auxerre side that hindered our progress in Europe last season, it again remains to be seen whether he's one of the few players to slip under Arsène's ubiquitous radar. Then again, maybe Faye was flattered by Paddy's particularly bad day at the office.

Nevertheless, in this instance it is not like we can blame the break since our weekend encounter was equally as lacklustre as those which came before it. According to the law of averages, the lack of inspiration in the Arsenal's efforts to date meant that without a marked improvement, our luck was bound to run out sometime soon. What's more, we must acknowledge the fact that the fickle finger of fortune didn't exactly desert us when Pires managed to finagle a penalty with his much-maligned pratfall.

I am no fan of football's con artists, Arsenal or otherwise. When Henry was asked to re-take the penalty, I wondered whether bad karma was about to cost us. Having equalised, I was praying for another Arsenal goal, primarily because I would have much preferred that any points were earned honestly. Perhaps 'le garcon qui a crié loup' is not such a popular parable across the Channel. Pires might otherwise have been more aware that his crime would probably condemn the Arsenal to any number of genuine penalty shouts going against us! However, I am not nearly such a hypocrite as all those tabloid hacks who took Pires to task, as if being hung, drawn and quartered would be far too good for the joker who was personally at fault for the jiggery-pokery which now permeates the game at every level.

These are the same *slieveens* who sniggered smugly when their blue-eyed boy bit the duplicitous dust for Queen and country during a World Cup quarter-final (now, if he'd been biting a pillow for some old queen . . .). Maybe, like Sol, I am suffering from a severe case of paranoia, or perhaps his sly shenanigans are so common that they don't merit such malevolent comment, but I am sure Van the Manchester man's dastardly deeds aren't received with quite so much rancour by the red tops (if he wasn't Dutch, doubtless I'd be spouting off about their dogmatic, anti-frog agenda).

Talking of which, I know that much of the sporting media struggles to speak ill of our northern nemesis, their tongues stuck so far up Fergie's backside for fear of offending him. Yet when our whimsical football wunderkinder are playing with plasters on their conks, tape on their ears, Vicks on their chest and heaven only knows what pierced, doesn't it strike you as odd that the disseminators of such serious details haven't satisfied their discerning public with an explanation as to why the Mancunian's new Portuguese starlet insists on playing with spaghetti on his head?

Meanwhile, it is the Milanese pasta eaters on the Arsenal's plate this week. With our somewhat fragile defence, most of the Highbury faithful are focusing on the threat of Vieri. With his sexy, long hair, the Inter centre-forward suddenly looks more of an Italian than an Aussie and seems to be playing with the style of one. Myself, I am more worried about the lessons learned by any of our European opponents who watched us play Ajax last season. They proved it was eminently possible to prevent us from scoring on our narrow playing surface.

On the assumption that a clean sheet is hardly likely to be on the cards, victory will require a whole lot more vim and verve than has been evident to date. We Gooners have our own sex god in the form of Freddie Ljungberg. Let's hope the Calvin Klein model and his compadres can catch Inter with their pants down since we all know how vital home victories are if we have any aspirations of Champions League success.

7

Champions League: Wednesday, 17 September (H) Arsenal 0 Inter Milan 3
Premiership: Sunday, 21 September (A) Arsenal 0 Manchester United 0

Calamitous start to European campaign, but back to battling best in spite of Vieira dismissal as Van Nistlerooy misses injury-time spot-kick at Old Trafford; Martin Keown cements cult status as Arsenal legend in post-match 'handbags' with Ruud van Sh*t Himself.

The Usual Suspects
22 September 2003

Many of the journalists gathered around the TV monitor in the Old Trafford press room, including myself, burst into laughter on seeing a replay of the shenanigans that occurred after the final whistle. However, the majority of them would go on to slaughter the source of their amusement in the Monday morning papers, as they described the 'disgraceful scenes' that took place in 'the Theatre of Dreams'.

I have to tell you that I, along with 3,000 other Gooners massed in what is fast becoming quite a welcoming little corner of Mancunian turf, all thought we were dreaming when Van Nistelrooy's venomous penalty rebounded off the crossbar. Considering his customary clinical finishing, we all had hearts in mouths, assuming that any hope of a humble point had walked the plank the moment ref Bennett pointed towards the penalty spot. One might have thought we'd just won the Premiership itself, the way we celebrated.

In view of the underlying tension which must have been present in players who were going into a game where defeat might have been the death-knell to an entire season, where their confidence would have required a Lazarus-like comeback, is it that surprising that their feelings found some expression at the final whistle? Naturally, I would have much preferred for them to have vented their emotions in a more responsible fashion than their display of playground posturing around United's whiter than white Van man.

I doubt it would have occurred to our lot that they played a direct part in raising the temperature on the terraces beyond boiling point. I was standing outside, waiting for admittance into the press facility, when I watched, with horror, as some harmless-looking Gooners made the fatal mistake of heading against the tide of departing United fans. Sadly, with a few wearing colours, they were sitting ducks for some dirty Red Devils, who expressed their disgust with a similar lack of self-control. I was just grateful that I'd had the sense to be more anonymous, but was relieved to see them escape from getting a 'good kicking' as they sought sanctuary in the stands.

Nevertheless, in an age when our sport has become plagued by far too much apathy, there was some part of me which couldn't help but feel quite proud. We regularly have cause to question the hunger of players who pick up their substantial pay packets win, lose or draw. So, I was pleased in one sense to witness such overt proof of some of our players' passion, although I very much doubt this thought will be to the fore when I am cursing the foolishness which is likely to see them sitting out vital encounters, suspended as a result.

The replay I am looking forward to seeing is the one which shows our goalie's very amateur dramatics when he threw himself to the floor in a manner which Norman Wisdom himself would have been proud of. We were all laughing our heads off at Lehmann's antics. I find all talk of points being deducted as our punishment just as laughable. Compared with the infamous mass brawl, this was pure handbags stuff, the sort of which has now become the norm as the intense rivalry between these two great sides has developed over the years. These are human beings we are talking about and until such time as there are 22 insensitive robots involved in these encounters, they are bound to boil over occasionally. Thankfully, the only thing hurting on the pitch was pride and for those poor Gooners who were left nursing their bruises a points deduction really would be adding insult to their injuries.

As for the game itself, I felt the fear of losing was such an inhibiting factor that both sides failed to produce the sparkling football we know them to be capable of. A policy of hanging on to what they had was probably the reason Wenger didn't introduce Pires and Wiltord late on, when Arsenal fans were hoping we might take advantage of tired legs. It was obvious from the way United were fired up for the second half that Fergie must have got his hairdryer out at half-time. Replacing O'Shea with Forlan was further indication that he wasn't happy settling for a draw. After Wednesday's woeful result against Inter, I imagine Sir Alex would have been absolutely desperate to take advantage of this opportunity to kick Wenger's side whilst we were down.

Mercifully, they didn't manage and I am hoping that, having got this game out of the way, whilst at the same time re-establishing our right to challenge for the title, with all the tabloid coffin-chasers already reading our defence their last rites, we can use what, without doubt, felt like a moral victory (in footballing terms, at least!) as a springboard for further success.

Meanwhile, it took us two hours crawling along in traffic before we even reached the motorway on our tortuous six-hour drive home. However, our load was lightened by news of the lamentable goings on at White Hart Lane. I never fail to be amazed by the foibles of football. What other enterprise in the world would give a man so many millions to spend a mere few weeks before sacking him? Still, it was comforting to know that Hoddle's departure had been perfectly timed to deflect some of the tabloid attentions away from their relentless efforts to remind us about the Arsenal's disciplinary dilemmas!

8

While I continue to search for that dramatic turning point, where the Arsenal were transformed from misfiring hostages-to-fortune into that indestructible team of crack troops at the very top of their form, it is beginning to dawn on me that there was no overnight miracle. The following piece represents an oft-repeated plea from a sentimental old bugger, who fears for the eventual demise of that distinctive Arsenal spirit if Arsène doesn't make more of an effort to maintain the balance between

Continental flair and home-grown grit. However, it appeared in an issue of The Gooner which was on sale for the period between the Pompey match at Highbury and our annual trip to Anfield. Its inclusion, therefore, seemed appropriate because this was the period where we witnessed a gradual change: incremental improvements in a defence that was rapidly developing an intuitive understanding, a squad which was beginning to defend as a team and, above all, a striker who was fast becoming the greatest entertainer on a football pitch on the entire planet. The culmination of our mutation wouldn't be seen until everything came right on that magical November night in Milan when Arsène Wenger's 'New Invincibles' were born. In the mean time, in the typical tradition of us Gooner ingrates, what better way to celebrate than with a mealy-mouthed moan.

Temps, Monsieur, S'il Vous Plaît
The Gooner, Issue 137, 22 September 2003

It is no exaggeration to say that all Arsenal fans worship at the altar of the enigmatic Arsène. No matter their sexual proclivity, I am sure that there are some who wouldn't think twice about slipping off to Brazil to have their balls chopped off if they were so summoned for the purpose of bearing Wenger's babies. Even his less extreme admirers wouldn't dream of denigrating the Gallic demigod whose eventual departure from Highbury will doubtless signal the demise of the Arsenal's ability to corner the market in the cream of his compatriots.

Without enduring endless months of miserable Arsenal mediocrity at the latter end of the management eras of the likes of Bertie Mee and George Graham, you might not fully appreciate our fabulous fortune. We've witnessed a total transformation during Wenger's tenure, as the Arsenal have turned into one of the most entertaining football teams on the planet. And of those poor masochistic buggers who were present every week when we were plumbing the depths of the bottomless pit of 'Boring, boring Arsenal', many of us struggle to believe our luck.

On an almost weekly basis, I find myself sitting in the West Upper with my jaw on the floor, dumbfounded by the wonderful footballing feats taking place before my very eyes. According to Buddhist principles, I cannot imagine the number of reincarnations it must have taken for us to attain our Arsène-inspired nirvana (not to mention the dreadful deeds which must have condemned our colleagues down the road at White Hart Lane to their lifetime of suffering!). By comparison to the relative dross that went before, why not a Wengorian calendar with everything that occurred AW (After Wenger) dated from the arrival of the footballing Buddha who is responsible for our current state of sporting enlightenment?

Arsène's Gooner account is in such credit with the entire Highbury co-op that even the most obvious cock-ups with calamitous consequences (e.g. Stepanovs, Upson) appear to have an insignificant negative impression on a balance bulging with Wenger's not so filthy 'feel good' lucre. However, as disinclined as we might be to do it, I've actually lost count of the number of times I've heard the most faithful of Wenger's followers register the one persistent criticism about Arsène's failure to further the careers of some of our home-grown youngsters.

At the start of every season we always hear wishful whispers, wondering whether this might be the moment for the 'big time' arrival of the latest in a long line of eagerly anticipated 'great white hopes'. In truth, Wenger has been in an invidious position in seasons past, damned if he does and damned if he don't, where the Worthless Cup is the one competition without the pressure cooker circumstances which permit a punt at the unknown. Even then, should we progress in this tournament, there comes a point where Arsène is obliged to bring out the big guns. Elsewhere, absolutely every bloomin' encounter has become so crucial that he's invariably forced to count on less inspiring known quantities. Their deficient killer instincts don't often achieve the comfort zone necessary to offer the young bloods a brief opportunity to shine on the big stage. What's more, without the cushion of at least a couple of goals, a sink or swim chance to impress for some might be a career wrecking occasion for others, carrying with it the risk of a ricket that might haunt them to the grave (as in Igor getting hung, drawn and quartered at Old Trafford).

As the club strives to fly the Ashburton Grove kite (where currently only the sky-high costs are soaring!), there was one silver lining to the resulting lamentable financial climate. Wenger wasn't able to bolster our squad during the close season with the usual assortment of Garde and Grimandi-type 'does a decent job' journeymen. He assured us that this would be the ideal carrot for the kids. As the season progresses, and injuries and suspensions begin to take their toll, our financial circumstances should present a fillip for us all, as for the first time Wenger is forced to plug the gaps with some home-grown Gooner protégés. Perhaps there will be nothing more for us to moan about (although, true to type, I am sure we will find something).

Possibly a mite misleading, but Mihir Bose's maths in *The Telegraph* were nonetheless mortifying. According to him, from our squad of thirty-one players, six are out on loan, including Jeffers, Pennant and Volz, to Premiership sides. There are four goalies in the remaining twenty-five and five who've never played a first-team game, which leaves a scant-looking squad of only sixteen!

After Aliadière's impressive pre-season outing in Scotland, I had hoped to see the likes of him, or David Bentley, on the subs bench from the start of this season. Three–nil up after only twenty minutes on Teesside, I am sure there won't be many better opportunities for giving them a risk-free run-out than at Boro. However, if the strict hold of the Highbury purse strings has prevented Wenger replenishing the squad with the odd million-pound purchase of ageing but reliable pros, it hasn't put the kibosh on him pilfering the odd prodigy or two from across the Continent.

With Fábregas Cesc joining the Swiss centre-back Senderos, someone of whom I've heard so much without having seen hide nor hair, my biggest concern is that there might be quite a bit of consternation amongst the home-grown ranks should they see their big chance given to a couple of new queue jumpers! When Wenger was questioned as to the opportunities he'd spoken about for Arsenal's own academicians to shine, he rightly set us straight. Both Pennant and Volz are being given a chance to prove themselves at the highest level every week and what is Kolo Touré if not an Arsenal youngster? Moreover, unlike some of his contemporaries, Wenger said he doesn't feel it's appropriate to begin meddling with our winning formula. As we stride along the opening steps of another marathon, it is more than evident that Wenger will have to call on the kids during the course of a long winter 'when the time is right'. I only hope that some of Brady's bairns are included in this number.

The inevitable day of Martin Keown's retirement draws nearer every time he mows down another number 9, while poor Ray Parlour seemed to be proffered as the makeweight in all the tabloid transfer tittle-tattle throughout the course of the summer. Unless Liam Brady's esteemed efforts bear fruit in the immediate future, there could conceivably come a time when Ashley Cole remains the sole surviving home-grown representative amongst the regular first team. Heaven forfend!!

Suppose the Spaniard, Cesc, is all he's cracked up to be and Senderos the best thing since sliced Gouda, there remains absolutely no substitute for several years as an Arsenal apprentice, the drip-fed daily influence of having the heroes of yesteryear staring down at you from the walls every time you walk through the hallowed Marble Halls, daring you to show the spirit and desire to deserve the honour of wearing the same shirt.

If/when we move home, the hardest task will be to recreate the tangible taste of history which assaults the senses on entering the Marble Halls. In the days before the depth of the digits on a contract cheque decreed whether a club was worth signing for, impressionable youngsters knew that they had 'arrived' the moment they entered The Home Of Football. It wouldn't matter how many other clubs were courting them, all most apprentices wanted to know from the moment they walked into Highbury and were enveloped by the distinctive atmosphere within those walls, was 'where do I sign?' There is an instinctive desire to be associated with this ancient bastion of British football which bears so little resemblance to the bland concrete lobbies of many modern clubs.

However, in the current mercenary era, most young prodigies are undoubtedly prone to becoming prima donnas from a very early age. They all have a phalanx of agents, managers and advisers feeding their egos from the moment they managed more than three keepie-uppies. Personally, I would confine all new arrivals at the Arsenal to the cinema in the museum, preventing them from leaving until they've learnt the club's history by heart. How can we possibly expect today's teenage millionaires to trot out in an Arsenal shirt with their efforts meaning anywhere near as much as it does to those of us on the terraces?

People respond to my prissy complaints about Robert Pires

shirking a challenge by skipping up in the air in anticipation (leaving the ball behind) by rightly pointing out that Wenger doesn't play (pay!) him to take and make tackles. Mind you, I am concerned that it might be his half-hearted tackles and his obvious tension when being tackled that could well be the most likely cause of another awful injury! Although it is not just the conservation of Pires's cruciate ligaments that has me concerned about his occasional lack of commitment. I remain the sentimental sod who hopes (mostly in vain these days) that while they are wearing an Arsenal shirt, our players' priority first and foremost is winning the ball for the cause. As far as I am concerned, self-preservation should be nothing more than an incidental afterthought.

There are obvious exceptions to my outdated rules. For example, Henry and Vieira didn't have to imbibe the Arsenal spirit over a period of several seasons to produce performances of true Gooner passion. Additionally, in a team of eleven you can afford to carry a couple of talented selfish stars with a preponderance for putting themselves first. Nevertheless, in British football, grit and determination can be such a leveller that the only teams to win a championship are those with a central core of players prepared to roll their sleeves up and get down and dirty when ability alone just ain't gonna win the day.

I am afraid that we soon won't have enough players within the Arsenal squad to set the example to the others of the commitment expected from them. And if Ashley Cole doesn't get some company quickly from one of the kids who has grafted his way through the ranks and whose appreciation is reflected in his work rate, who will our prospective stars have as their role models? Who will help to rein in the temptation for excess and prevent them from painting the town red in preference to earning their massively inflated salaries and pleasing us Gooners with an insatiable greed for medals?

Whether it be the French Aliadière, the Irish Bradley or the English Bentley, it doesn't matter where they originate from, so long as wearing the red and white of the Arsenal means as much to them as their efforts do to us. There is nothing more demoralising than doubting whether one of our own is quite so devastated as we Gooners when a game doesn't go our way. Similarly, we desperately need to see credible signs of some Brady-schooled successors if Ashley

Cole isn't to become the solitary home-grown standard-bearer of the future of the famous Arsenal spirit. Otherwise, future Gooners might come to know of it only as another tacky product, bottled and waiting to be sold alongside the Arsenal champagne in the event of us ever having anything to celebrate.

9

Premiership: Friday, 26 September (H) Arsenal 3 Newcastle United 2 Henry (18, 80 pen), Gilberto (67)

Jenas thinks Fridays are for Crackerjack! – not football – as he 'hands' us the points in the pouring rain.

No Miracles, Just a Little New Year's Resolution?
29 September 2003

I wish I could tell you that the missus and I will be winging our way back from Russia as you read, yet while those wonderfully generous credit card wallahs were happy to cough up nearly three-and-a-half grand for our season tickets, even they weren't about to countenance the folly of a five-hundred quid overnight trip to follow my team to Moscow.

The nip in the air the past couple of nights suggests it might soon be time to dust off the warm astrakhan titfer, a much-loved, well-worn memento from a miserable night in the Ukraine. In 1998, the Arsenal were undone by Dynamo Kiev's dynamic duo, Shevchenko and Rebrov. Mercifully, Mikhailichenko's modern-day Dynamo are supposedly a shadow of the previous collection of computer-generated Trons. This was a side synthesised in the laboratory by the leviathan mathematician/manager, Lobanovsky. During an amazing 25-year tenure, his team of statistically superior titans helped themselves to an assorted collection of Soviet, Ukrainian and European silverware.

Having already ticked off Kiev in my Champions League itinerary, I am not so concerned that I can afford the inflated cost of a return trip. Although, I have to admit that I am more than a little miffed about missing out on the opportunity of an introduction to Mother Russia.

I also owe a big debt of gratitude to Ryanair and the fleet finger-tapping on the net which dug up a dumbfounding £3.99 o/w flight to Milan. Otherwise, much like our own Dennis Bergkamp, I might have missed out on all the away matches in the group stage. Having followed the Arsenal over land and sea for so many years, with my presence on the terraces always assured, no matter what adversity fate threw my way (a lottery win notwithstanding), it might be hard to accept my almost inevitable admission into the legion of armchair Arsenal fans. It baffles me how those with apparently no greater means than myself manage to make it to every game, home and abroad.

Being in hock for our season tickets, I was actually hoping that we'd find ourselves accommodating UEFA's corporate partners for the European encounters at Highbury. Many Gooners grumble, but I always welcome our turn to be moved out of our regular seats because the club is kind enough to compensate us with an entire refund for the cost of these tickets. Annoyingly, the seats invariably end up occupied by Arsenal fans fleeced by touts, or employees of Ford and the like with little or no previous interest in the Arsenal.

Instead of moving us, it has always baffled me why the club doesn't save itself a small fortune and a lot of aggravation by allocating UEFA the seats which are apparently already available. You won't catch me complaining, though, their 300-odd quid refund for the two of us being perfectly timed in the past to pay for a European jolly or two, which might otherwise have been out of the question. Sadly, it wasn't to be this season. I therefore intended to forsake the group stage away games and keep some of my plastic powder dry in the hope of Arsenal progressing in the competition.

We usually justify our foreign jaunts on the basis that by grabbing bargain flights before they disappear, Róna and I can enjoy a two- or three-day break for about the price I alone would have paid on an official overnighter (that's assuming we are sufficiently humoured by the football and don't find ourselves flying back from Milan with a suitcase full of haute couture). Personally, I avoid these group excursions like the plague, but there will have been few other options for Gooners going on the first two exotic outings.

Aside from all the incidental costs, for the best part of the £1,500 it will cost to travel on organised overnight trips to all three games, the compact convoy of Gooners will 'enjoy' the pleasure of being chivvied across the Continent like cattle. Herded on and off planes, and in and out of stadiums with a 'hail fellow, well met' friendly welcoming committee of local militia with their water cannons, these loyal fans will have forked out for little more foreign flavour than that which they would have found on an awayday to Leicester! Or at least this will be my argument as I try to settle on my sofa on Tuesday afternoon.

If, true to form, I become frustrated by events in Russia being shown on the box, it probably won't take long before Róna is begging me to go to the Ukraine for the match in a couple of weeks' time. As Treacle runs for cover under the coffee table and the offensive smell confirms Liffey's feline fear, Ró is bound to be fretting that the neighbours think I am committing hara-kiri because I'm attempting to make myself heard in Moscow. Far more unnerving than my irrational concerns about not being present and unable to influence matters on the pitch is the angst I am bound to feel about much more influential absentees. In addition to Bergkamp, to date we've lost the services of Ljungberg, Campbell and, perhaps crucially, our captain.

Now, if not for our annihilation by Inter in the opening game, I would have been able to relax, put my feet up and watch as Wenger used this match against Lokomotiv merely as a proving ground. He could suss out his best potential line-up when the impending suspensions begin to bite. If we'd begun our campaign with three crucial home points, we could regard anything we achieved in Tuesday's encounter as a bonus. Instead of which, it is behoven of a severely depleted side to bring the Arsenal back from the brink of Champions League calamity. We can only begin to imagine the ripple effects of both the financial and footballing ramifications of a premature exit. All would be far from lost with four games still to go. But considering Kiev took all three points against the Russians, we really can't afford to come back to Highbury with bubkas!

I can envisage only two possible outcomes: a triumph in adversity, which would once again leave Wenger testifying to the remarkable spirit of this squad; or a bungling debacle, which would delight the vultures of the media because they'll be able to pick over the bones of a squad which they've all slated for its apparent emaciated appearance. We've witnessed some of the Arsenal's finest moments when their backs have been up against the wall in this fashion. It remains to be seen whether Wenger's stand-ins can step up to the plate. I just pray that they don't arrive in Moscow with any inclination about playing for a point!

Not that it was necessary, but Newcastle provided a timely reminder on Friday that the current team bears absolutely no resemblance to Arsenal sides of the recent past, which were schooled in the art of keeping clean sheets. One might think the rhythm method might be second nature to a squad with the capacity to seduce us with some of the sexiest football on the planet, yet such virile footie comes at a price. Arsène could have an army of family planning instructors and still be unable to ensure the sort of responsible football which might result in the occasional clean sheet. After our captain limped off on Friday, few could fathom why Wenger pulled off the Romford Pelé. To continue with my lurid analogy, Parlour was the only midfielder left on the pitch who knows how to cross his legs.

Thankfully, we were left lighting up and sighing with satisfaction after Henry finally brought the sweaty encounter to a consummate climax. Titi certainly didn't fake it! I couldn't help feeling sorry for all the Toons facing a long journey back to the Northeast with nothing to show for their efforts. The fact that it was impossible to get back home using public transport from the fixture, which had been scheduled with absolutely no thought for all the long-suffering fans, would at least have been some consolation for all those Barcodes who weren't able to attend. All three points were probably more than we deserved; most Gooners will confirm that we are still some way from hitting anything but the briefest bursts of form. Therefore, it is surprising to find ourselves still looking down on all our Premiership opposition. It's certainly not that we are playing better than anyone else; we've just managed to be a tad more consistent. At this rate, though, we'll be found out eventually, as Inter demonstrated with ease.

The G–d-fearing Arsenal fans of the Jewish persuasion might have thought this moment had come on Friday, the start of the Jewish New Year, when they could have provoked the wrath of their Lord by their failure to observe His festival. The sight of several empty seats suggest that the 'Yid Army' is far from being exclusive to Spurs. Perhaps the irreligious among us, who were at the game, owe a vote of thanks to people like Nell, who sacrificed his first home fixture in 12 years for our sake. All right, so perhaps he was motivated merely by his fear of being ostracised by his family, but as they say, 'the Lord moves in mysterious ways, his wonders to perform'. Considering how lightweight we looked in midfield without Vieira, I just pray he brings his boots on Tuesday!

10

Champions League: Tuesday, 30 September (A) Arsenal 0 Lokomotiv Moscow 0
Premiership: Saturday, 4 October (A) Arsenal 2 Liverpool 1 Hyypia (31, own goal),
   Pires (68)

A precious point in Europe, followed by three from fortress Anfield after surviving a profligate Scouse onslaught during the first forty-five.

Scourge of the Shareholders: Keown the Kop's Knight Errant
6 October 2003

Late as ever, I legged it out of the house at daybreak on Saturday morning, dashing to the Tube like a lunatic, desperately hoping to make Euston in time for the early-morning departure to Liverpool. Rudely stirred by a 6 a.m. alarm, it would have been easy to roll over and return to a beautiful dream about banging in a hat-trick at the Bernabéu. Neither the missus nor Nell were able to accompany me, so I was sorely tempted to stop in bed until noon then wake to a much gentler alarm with the dulcet tones of Andy Gray's live match coverage on TV.

Based on previous experiences of the Arsenal's lethargic Premiership efforts after a long trip back from a midweek Champions League encounter, along with no-shows from Vieira, Bergkamp and Ljungberg, rustling up any real enthusiasm for the long trip to Anfield at such an ungodly hour was a real challenge. However, the more games you go to, the harder it is to miss one for fear of copping out on the match of the season. Not only was I grateful to witness Pires's wonderful strike nestle in the net before my very eyes, but it is only by enduring such exhausting outings that one earns the right to slaughter shareholders without a scooby when they start having a dig at our marvellous manager's disciplinary dilemmas.

Every year, I announce to Róna my renewed desire to purchase a share in a concern which is so close to my heart and each year I end up kicking myself even harder as the price of a small piece of the Arsenal continues to soar beyond the pitiful reach of my penniless pockets. Nevertheless, profitability is not my principal motivation. Above all, it is not a financial, but an emotional investment which interests me. I am most grateful to various Gooner shareholders who have been unavailable for the Arsenal's AGM over the years and who've allowed me to attend as their proxy.

Prior to last Thursday, our double-barrelled, old Etonian chairman might have taken one look at me and assumed I was the representative of the Gooner branch of Al-Qaeda. With this in mind, I shaved especially for the occasion and dug out my most respectable looking strides and shirt. I might even have donned a suit in my efforts to achieve a sufficiently respectable mien to merit consideration for putting a question to the panel, but I couldn't face all the 'Where's the funeral?' or 'What are you charged with?' abuse.

Yet I was so keen that I turned up ten minutes early. Already, the seats laid out along the length of the North Bank's ground floor concourse were full. Not wanting to sit so far from the dais that I'd have to view proceedings on the screens set up for that purpose, I carried a chair from the back to a point near the front where I hoped the chairman wouldn't be able to ignore me during the question and answer session. Sitting there with my hand in the air for almost the entire hour, I grew increasingly frustrated at the folly of my efforts to jump through the hoops of social acceptability.

At least I was looking fairly buff for about the only result of the day

– yet another chance for shareholders to have their picture taken with some silverware. Compared to my last photo a couple of years back, where the men's and women's teams had amassed a plethora of shiny pots and plates, the solitary FA Cup in this photo looks a little forlorn. Nevertheless, I have given the Gunners such a vast fortune over the years that there is no way I will ever give up an opportunity to get something back, gratis.

I always eagerly anticipate the AGM in the belief that it will present a rare opportunity to dispel a year's worth of tabloid half-truths; where all the Gooner gossip will be dealt with as we discern Arsenal fact from 'red-top' fiction. In truth, as far as the board are concerned, it seems to be nothing more than a querulous necessity in the corporate calendar. The shareholders might be hoping for transparency, but the directors always do their level best to comply with the regulations whilst playing their cards as close to their chests as possible. Never has this been more apparent than in the current climate.

We were treated to a detailed presentation about the progress being made in the plans for our new stadium. I assume some of the intricacies and complexities of this ambitious inner-city regeneration project were addressed in an attempt to appease all those punters who have become impatient, perceptions being that the entire future of the Arsenal is up in the air whilst the stadium build stagnates. If you are to believe our board, construction itself is due to begin in the first quarter of next year.

Meanwhile, as always, I ended up feeling more than a little frustrated with more questions than answers. For the most part, there was an attempt to impart a mood of optimism about Ashburton Grove with the board's conviction that there was absolutely no doubt about it going ahead and that there would be minimal impact on the Arsenal's ability to compete on the pitch. However, we heard how the club has failed as yet to secure the all-important long-term loans necessary for the bulk of the project. Apparently, these remain the subject of crucial ongoing negotiations with overseas financial institutions. Yet, as with the premature announcements in the media concerning the birth of this Arsenal baby, I would have fully expected the entire board to bluff it out with assurances that their borrowing was already in the bag.

Our managing director had yet to be embarrassed by a shareholder who wanted to know how, in such hard times, with all the cost-cutting constraints, the club could justify our hard-earned cash going towards a £60,000 increase in this poor man's paltry £400k salary! So, there was little excuse for dropping what sounded like a 'far too candid' clanger in an 'off the cuff' comment concerning his disquiet about securing the finance. He divulged: 'Worried? It depends which week I'm asked!' Words which spoke volumes, in my opinion.

Nevertheless, I am fairly confident that by hook or by crook the new stadium will eventually happen. If only for the fact we can't afford otherwise, because we are already in the hole to the tune of £95 million. With all the bluff and bluster the board could muster, they steadfastly refused to entertain any suggestion of a 'Plan B'. Yet I can't help but wonder who exactly they are trying to kid with the outrageous assertion that the Ashburton Grove deal won't have a detrimental affect on our ability to compete on the pitch?

It might make sound economic sense to separate the property development so that it doesn't appear on the balance sheet of the club's regular activities, but it is plain to see that our precarious financial circumstances are forcing Arsène to skate on incredibly thin ice. Moreover, injuries and suspensions might have caused it to melt somewhat sooner than expected. I doubt the board could convince us that Wenger was delighted to deduct the veteran Gio van Bronckhorst's salary from the weekly wage bill when he found himself in Russia with almost his entire bench still wet behind the ears.

In a week when John Halls, another product of Brady's academy, has gone to Stoke for the guarantee of first-team football, no one is happier than me to see the youngsters thrown more frequent carrots. In fact, I believe it could have been the discontent that Wenger discerned from the floor at the AGM which might have resulted in Aliadière being included in the starting line-up on Saturday. After Arsène had explained his reluctance to risk the youngsters with the contention that, over the course of a season, their inexperience would cost us points, we might have expected him to wet their head at home to Wolves or Leicester, not a crucial 'top of the table' six-pointer away to Liverpool! An immediate understanding between Titi and Jeremie in such a competitive climate was unlikely, but Aliadière's inclusion was a blessing, if only to administer a much-needed kick up the backside to Wiltord, hopefully ensuring that he's not quite so comfortable about his first eleven place in future.

Considering we should have been 0–3 down at half-time, it felt like daylight robbery to be coming away from Anfield with all three points. A draw would have been generous and I would have gladly accepted a point as we entered the ground by a gate where a steward was offering free admittance to anyone named Keown! I adore the Scouse sense of humour. The hospitable welcome we usually receive in Liverpool often makes me feel that much closer to Ireland than bovine Britain. No matter the result, you can invariably guarantee a good *craic* – although that's probably due to the fact that Ryanair have flown half of Ireland over for the weekend.

It was teeming as I trotted out of the ground, hopeful that, for once, I wouldn't have to walk all the way back to Lime Street. Mind you, I was so delighted that, if I hadn't been so sensitive to the feelings of the locals, not to mention my own self-preservation, I might have broken into a Gene Kelly impersonation. I stared longingly at the occupants snugly ensconced in every passing cab and couldn't believe my luck when someone took pity on me. It didn't come as a surprise to find the cab occupied by two Dubliners on their way back to Manchester Airport via the station, as I wouldn't have expected such a kindly gesture from my own countrymen. Naturally, despite my protests, they wouldn't even let me contribute to the fare. I only hope their good karma ensures success for Ireland against Switzerland this weekend!

11

Another international Saturday sees England draw in Turkey to secure a place at Euro 2004, whilst France trounce Israel; Rio Ferdinand is pulled from Sven's squad after his failure to attend a drug test at Man Utd's Carrington training complex.

Can Titi and Co. Repel the Russian Tank?
13 October 2003

After watching three hours of tiresome footie without a single goal to celebrate and two Swiss strikes to mourn, five hours of channel hopping finally paid off on Saturday evening when I found France versus Israel being broadcast on French TV. The match in Paris proved a mere formality for the only side to secure maximum points en route to Portugal in eight straight wins. I had found watching Ireland and England so frustrating that an entertaining masterclass from Zinedine Zidane and his compatriots was most refreshing. It was football of the sort of supreme quality that bore no comparison to the disappointing dross televised earlier in the day.

I don't know what the mood was like over there in Ireland, but here in Highbury Quadrant we grew gloomier and gloomier as the clock ticked down towards the whistle and Ireland's ignominious exit. It would have been easier to take if the 'Boys in Green' had bowed out of the tournament in a blaze of 'hell or high water' glory, but it was the uncharacteristic way in which their involvement in the competition ended with a whimper that I found so utterly depressing.

There was a time when you could confidently bet your shirt on the Irish side's capacity to make up for any perceived deficiencies in ability with a strength of purpose that ensured they were incredibly hard to beat. For so many years, it didn't really make much difference who was wearing the green shirt, or that they were found wanting for true world-class guile up front; the sum of the individual parts was always so much greater than their apparent fallibility on paper. These days, with the exclusion of a couple of obvious names, I can't help but fear the worst when I consider an Ireland line-up made up from what looks to me like a motley collection of extremely mediocre journeymen.

Perhaps they've become victims of their own success, following an era when they've consistently overachieved? There was certainly little evidence on Saturday of the credo which has served so well; where success was based on working twice as hard as their opponents. Considering Brian Kerr's common-sense approach to what is, above all, a simple game, it was surprising to hear him explaining away such an abysmal effort with a load of baloney about Ireland's tactical naivety in dealing with the diamond formation favoured by the Swiss. Come off it, Brian. It doesn't matter if the opposition line up as a Christmas tree, a diamond or a lump of bleedin' coal, so long as you keep the ball!

Where once Ireland could be relied on to resolutely defend a clean sheet until the cows came home, in Basle they'd messed the bed within five minutes. O'Shea's fateful prevarication on the pitch had me contemplating calling Setanta to see if I could claim a refund, having paid the princely sum of eight quid to view the abysmal contest. We've just started taking Treacle to obedience training, but I will be very impressed if we ever get her to imitate Ireland's example of rolling over and playing dead.

In such circumstances, the burden of responsibility falls squarely on the somewhat slight shoulders of Damien Duff, as has been the case in most Ireland matches of late. Robbie Keane might be a proven goalscorer at the highest level, but no striker can do his stuff unless he gets given the ball in the final third. At this level, aside from a stroke of fortune at a set piece, Duff is the only player capable of the creative spark in midfield necessary to make something happen. The Swiss aren't exactly blessed with an abundance of ability, but they know enough to smother Ireland's solitary playmaker.

In days of yore, the close attention to Duff would have provided a perfect opportunity for one of his teammates to produce the sort of memorable contribution which would have meant he would never again be able to put his hand in his pocket in an Irish hostelry. Sadly, however, my abiding impression of this game was that there wasn't a single player in green capable of, or willing to, grasp the Man of the Match mantle. Worse still, the second we glimpsed a glimmer of hope, with the first sign of some concerted pressure around the 60-minute mark, it was immediately extinguished with Switzerland's second goal. This might have been the final nail in the coffin of Irish qualification but, in truth, they were dead if not buried when the Swiss first hit the back of the net only five minutes in. There was no shame in Brian Kerr's inability to inspire a comeback; even the great David Blaine would have struggled to bring this lot back from their funereal fate.

Now, if only Ireland matches were won and lost with the singing of the national anthem. This would have been a walkover as the team put their Swiss counterparts to shame with a hearty rendition of 'The Soldier's Song'. Regrettably, there was no such pride in their play. They were a pallid reflection of the patriots who wrote: 'We're children of a fighting race, that never yet has known disgrace.'

The involvement of Arsenal's Campbell and Cole might have meant that, like myself, Róna was hoping England would succeed against Turkey, or at least that neither would be responsible for a calamitous, career-threatening cock-up. If ever I wanted proof that she used to ride around on her bicycle singing rebel songs as a child, it came in her instinctive reaction to Golden Balls' pathetic penalty miss. With Ireland having failed the fans, her resentment towards England's qualification was reflected in a response which made Alpay's 'in yer face' tantrum look positively reserved. I imagine that most of Ireland and Portugal, and all the suits at UEFA, were praying for the Turks to triumph so that England's potential exit via the play-offs might promise a Euro 2004 without all the elaborate arrangements necessary to expunge the inevitable hooligan element.

After spending most of the Ireland game trembling under the coffee table, terrified by my tirade of abuse at the TV, Treacle was just getting up enough courage to emerge from her hidey-hole when Ró's howls of hilarity ensured the poor dog's nerves were shot anew. Mind you, her anxiety wasn't exactly helped by the sound of blaring horns. We live within a few hundred yards of The Home Of Football on one side and London's largest Turkish community on the other. What more could you wish for? Fantastic football and loadsa late-night kebabs! Apparently, as a result of their enforced absence, some England fans had decided the next best thing would be to watch the game in one of the many Turkish gaffs on Green Lanes. Despite the language barrier, I don't doubt that a kooky Turkish TV commentary was preferable to the somnolent punditry of Alan Shearer. Moreover, it was a symbolic gesture to all those who would prefer this was a safe, sanitised product and who are prepared to let the threat of the unruly few ruin it for the rest.

Perhaps you had to be there amidst the intense atmosphere in Istanbul to fully appreciate the Anglo-Saxons' achievements. Personally, I was less impressed by England's efforts than I was surprised by the Turks insipid showing. It was hardly the overthrow of the Ottoman Empire as portrayed in the press. With all the bombastic ballyhoo, you would never believe England were only a balletic David James dive away from drowning in the same dubious boat as Wales and Scotland.

Meanwhile, if the pain of Ireland's exclusion from play-offs struck home when the draw for Euro 2004 took place in Germany on Monday, Irish eyes will be anything but smiling as the build-up to next summer's Portuguese party begins to gather momentum. It will be all the harder to swallow if England, Scotland and Wales all end up being involved.

To be honest, I am glad that it is all over for the moment and that we can get back to more important matters. I pray that the Arsenal can improve on the dreadful form we've shown in the immediate aftermath of recent international adjournments. Saturday's London Derby could prove a defining moment in both teams' season. The players might not perceive the match in such melodramatic terms, but, as far as I am concerned, the Arsenal will be playing for the very soul of the English game.

To quote our vice-chairman: 'Abramovich has parked his tank on our lawn and is firing £50 notes at us.' The tabloids might have trumpeted our 'special team spirit', but avid Arsenal watchers know that we will need to see more tangible signs of the famed Arsenal spirit if we are to repel the Russian onslaught. Can Chelsea confirm they have true Championship credentials? Or can we prove there is a soupçon more to solving the Premiership puzzle than simply pouring a couple of hundred million pounds into the Blue brigade's quest for the prize which has eluded them for nearly half a century?

12

Premiership: Saturday, 18 October (H) Arsenal 2 Chelsea 1 Edu (5), Henry (75)

Points are priceless, even for Roman Abramovich, as Chelski come unstuck courtesy of a Cudicini clanger.

Despite the small fortune we pay for our Sky subscription and the additional amount squeezed out of us for our pay-per-view season ticket, mercifully I don't have to rely on Rupert Murdoch's mob for my Arsenal viewing. I couldn't possibly imagine missing out on the biggest home occasion of the season so far. For sentimental Gooners like myself, the distinctive rivalry of the north London Derby will always exist, in spite of the fact that Spurs seem destined to mid-table mediocrity for all eternity. Spurs fans will be 'pleased' to hear that for many other Arsenal fans the real enmity is reserved for our south-west London rivals. Saturday's match was definitely the hottest ticket in town. As the day drew nigh and the clamour for spare seats intensified, I realised that my guaranteed West Upper seat for just such a match is the reason why I suffer the struggle to finance my season-ticket renewals every year.

Love in a Cold Climate
20 October 2003

By the sound of the Blues fans in the corner of Highbury on Saturday, The Beatles were way off the mark when they said, 'Money can't buy me love'. Abramovich's couple of hundred million quid has bewitched the Kings Road crooners to the point where they are so full of Roman's romeo spirit that they were after enquiring, 'Shall we buy a ground for you?' The bloody cheek of Chelsea's Johnny-come-latelys provoked the obvious retorts of 'Where were you when you were sh*t?'

Possibly, a more poignant response from the Clock End came with a chorus of 'Shall we win a cup for you?' The amazing Chelsea experiment has ensured an array of endless, albeit interesting, conjecture. Perhaps the most moot point, though, is exactly when it will dawn on Siberia's wealthiest son that he cannot simply buy his way to the Championship; an honour which his new team have been struggling to achieve for nearly half a century. Surely, the law of diminishing returns will have been induced long before the January transfer window. So, will he continue to plumb the depths of his apparently bottomless pockets before he discovers the folly of his fruitless investment?

Following an interminable international break, I was truly thrilled to be returning to Highbury for such a mouth-watering match. Although my excitement was tempered with trepidation at the thought that Arsène's undefeated run against the Blues must eventually fall victim to another ubiquitous law, the law of averages, and believe me when I tell you that I would have gladly given up many of the victories against the Pensioners from the recent past to guarantee success on Saturday. The three points might prove just as crucial as any others but there were far greater implications to the outcome of this match. With Chelsea undefeated to date in domestic competition, it was down to the Arsenal to prove a point for the entire Premiership and everyone who values the principles of team spirit on which this great game was based.

Jack Walker might have similarly pursued a Premiership title for his beloved Blackburn (on a scale which, I imagine, must have been modest by comparison to the Russian's millions) but he was British and had been spunking his money in vain for years, so no one really blinked – apart from his heirs, I assume, when they saw their inheritance squandered on the likes of Shearer. I don't think many of us minded too much, as Jack managed to achieve his ultimate Championship ambition with his last major blow-out before he shuffled off this mortal coil. Especially since Blackburn broke Man Utd's monopoly on the title.

Meanwhile, there is something rather obscene about the Russian's ostentatious arrival on the football scene. Sure, I am jealous. I don't think there's a fan of any club who hasn't dreamt of such a wealthy sugar daddy fulfilling their wildest fantasies (naturally, football related rather than bacchanalian). Abramovich's arrival has provided an ironic contrast in an era of such severe austerity. Heaven only knows how many clubs would be going to the wall by now after billions of pounds worth of injudicious 'keeping up with the Joneses' spending, if he'd bought Chelsea a few years back.

However, if Chelsea's unabated expenditure proves one thing, it is quite what a miracle Wenger and other Premiership managers, like Bruce, Strachan and Souness, have achieved on a mere shoestring by comparison. No doubt they are all envious of Ranieri's ability to purchase any player he pleases, yet the Italian manager appears to be not the only person in the Chelsea camp who isn't overly enamoured with their Russian revolution.

From the boorish Ken Bates to their BNP bovver boys, I have always hated everything about Chelsea but it's difficult to dislike the endearing Ranieri, who comes across as a charming man every time he appears on television. To some, he may be Tinkerman, but, to me, he's become Joey Grimaldi, the famous clown, painting on his happy face for the public to try to hide the turmoil beneath. It would take a gallon of greasepaint to disguise the Italian's worry lines. He's a manager who knows that almost every match might be his last, being, as he is, at the mercy of Chelsea's capricious money man.

Most managers tell us that they are in their element when the whistle blows, when all the increasingly impinging nightmares on the periphery of their position evaporate and they can do the job they are paid for; on Saturday, Ranieiri's resistible force met the immovable object. Our inscrutable Arsène was, as usual, the epitome of equanimity, sitting stoically in his dug-out seat, rarely jumping up to remonstrate against a dubious decision, while Ranieri appeared to patrol the perimeter of his permitted area in a highly agitated state for the entire 90 minutes. It was exhausting just watching him mentally kicking every ball and making every challenge.

It was Damien Duff whom I expected to be their most dangerous threat down the flanks. I was dumbfounded, albeit delighted, that Duff's creative spark was completely cancelled out in the cramped conditions in the centre of the park. I just don't understand the sense in paying £17 million for a world-class winger, only to play him out of position. It is not as though they are short of a few midfielders (and without a single midfield substitute on the sparse Arsenal bench, it would have been sporting of them to lend us one).

Chelsea are brim full of the sort of talent evident in the quality of Crespo's strike, which might maintain their challenge. Yet assorted wayward passes were evidence that they are still some way from having the understanding of a team. In this respect, I am glad we've played them early in the season. However, lost somewhere amidst all the ballyhoo about their keeper's blunder (no doubt resulting in a collection of keepers replacing Rooney on the media's next list of Roman's 'most wanted'), the sleaze-pandering schlemiels of the press have patently failed to portray a one-sided second half which confirms you can't turn a collection of talented individuals into a team overnight.

Even another spending spree in the January sales won't buy them the sort of 'hearts of oak' obduracy of a squad prepared to roll up their sleeves at the sight of a substitute like Kanu. At the end of the day, resentment of Chelsea's fortunate circumstances will be the fuel that inspires each of their opponents to dig that bit deeper, ensuring their ultimate downfall.

My own determination to do my bit on Saturday had me hoarse before half-time. There is a certain etiquette expected of away fans when seated in enemy territory. There is often a smattering of those in the West Upper whose allegiances would be sussed in most other grounds by their suspicious silence. Yet, at Highbury, they are noisier than their regrettably reticent neighbours. However, I rejoice at the fact that we are all able to enjoy the spectacle without segregation, like civilised human beings (or perhaps it's the sadistic pleasure I savour as they suffer the inevitable). Nevertheless, while it is expected that they will react to their team scoring a goal, it is extremely impolite to be too exuberant.

I wouldn't dream of dissing the home fans in most grounds around the country, unless I had a death wish. It therefore drives me potty on the odd occasion when someone takes advantage of the fact that they are surrounded by a passive 'prawn sandwich' brigade who aren't about to 'stick one on 'em'. It wasn't just me who thought the cavorting Blues fan celebrating Crespo's strike right in front of us was somewhat OTT. She denies it now, but I could have sworn I saw Róna accidentally spitting bits of bagel at him during the break. Cudicini's gift-wrapped winner wiped the smile off his face and my sweet satisfaction was rounded off as I caught sight of him rubbing the ear which had been in the line of fire of my unremitting, most fortissimo barrage.

Sadly, even my doughtiest decibels won't have carried my encouragement to Kiev. Yet, after finally producing some of the sort of football we know them to be capable of, if we can maintain the momentum and fortune continues to smile upon us, hopefully my three-point celebrations might be audible to *Irish Examiner* readers in Cork!

13

Champions League: Tuesday, 21 October (A) Arsenal 1 Dynamo Kiev 2 Henry (80)
Premiership: Sunday, 26 October (A) Arsenal 1 Charlton Athletic 1 Henry (39)

More misery in Eastern Europe sees Arsenal with one point from the first three group matches; Vieira rushed back, aggravates thigh injury and misses next two months; a battling point in south-east London as Henry responds to Matt Holland theatrics with flawless free-kick.

With a single point to show for our opening two Champions League games, and with only one victory in our previous eleven European matches, many of us were hoping that we might kick-start our campaign in Kiev. After we'd quashed the Chelsea threat at the weekend even without our midfield maestro, perhaps the mood of optimism in the camp might be reflected in a midweek rout. Yet, as a miserable Tuesday evening progressed, most of us would have been more than happy to have sandbagged a single point from the many farcical mickles that made up this muckle of a miserable match.

We were 1–0 down at the break and I found myself looking for distractions, trying to recall the Ukrainian equivalent of the British hot dog and burger half-time fare. I couldn't remember if there had been anything on offer in the Olympiyskyi Stadium on a similarly miserable night almost five years back, when I was there in person to witness us being clinically torn apart by a Kiev side featuring Shevchenko and Rebrov.

That previous result aside, my reminiscences were nevertheless immensely preferable to listening to the TV pundits pour gloom and doom on this present-day damp squib, with talk which suggested that, even with three more group games to go, the Arsenal were down and, probably very nearly, out. I managed to lose myself in my reverie, reminding Róna of my meeting in Kiev with Vlad, the Ukrainian Gooner from the Arsenal mailing list on the Internet, who, despite being quite so geographically challenged, had supported the Gunners from afar for several years without ever having the slightest opportunity to witness them play live until that night. I was very sad that it didn't turn out to be a successful one. Imagine poor Vlad going to work the next day and having to suffer being mocked by all his mates. In Vlad's shoes, I would have doubtless spent the weeks leading up to the game pulling all their legs about the leathering the Arsenal were about to give the home team and would therefore have been forced to pull a sickie for at least a month! However, in spite of the outcome, it was a real buzz being able to give him Róna's ticket so that he could stand amongst us Gooners and join in with all the chants he'd previously only read about or heard on the occasional TV broadcast.

Better still was the night before the game when I persuaded Vlad to accompany me to watch the Arsenal training on the stadium pitch. Without any official journalistic credentials, the only thing I could find in my pockets with a photo on it (other than my passport) was an out-of-date England Supporters Club membership card. I encouraged Vlad to persuade the local constabulary that these were bona fide press credentials and, having given him my camera to hold, that he was my photographer/translator. While I doubt it was a crime for which he might endure ten years hard labour in Siberia, I guess his timidity might have been related to the fact that he didn't fancy invoking the wrath of the rozzers if our duplicitous exploits were discovered. The prize, however, was sufficient persuasion and, mercifully, we encountered two uniformed officials with niet English, who were suitably convinced by my bright yellow ID. Can you imagine the thrill for Vlad, who went from never having seen the Arsenal in the flesh to attending Arsène Wenger's press conference? Then, as the team wandered back to the coach after their session on the pitch, I mercilessly muscled him into having his picture taken with, first, Seaman's arm around his shoulders, then likewise with Lee Dixon!

I tell you, I enjoyed an interesting trip to Kiev and my old Gorbachev-style titfer has kept out the cold on many a brass monkey night on the terraces since. However, the absolute highlight of the longest outing I've ever undertaken whilst following the Gunners was without doubt the vicarious delight of watching Vlad in seventh heaven as he passed his Gooner academy initiation with distinction, complete with picture proof to show his pals and a new-found knowledge of all the (extremely limited) lyrics and tunes to assorted Gooner anthems.

The Arsenal might have returned from the Ukraine with happier memories this time, if it wasn't for our goalie gifting Kiev a second and Kolo smashing his effort against the crossbar while we were camped in Kiev's area for the final ten minutes, after Titi had nicked one back. For me, the frustrations of not even salvaging a point were summed up with the sight of Kolo beating the turf, tortured by his missed opportunity.

At least the clocks going back on Saturday night gave us an extra hour's lie in on Sunday morning and, as opposed to those occasions in spring when I've neglected to take note of the fact that they've gone forward, at least there was no chance of turning up for kick-off an hour after the match had started! I wonder how much Arsène might have appreciated an opportunity to turn his clocks back a little further. I have no doubt, with hindsight, he would've had major regrets about the club captain's costly appearance in Kiev; it was confirmed that Vieira's injury was worse than at first thought and that the original two-week estimate for his absence was wildly optimistic.

It was bright and sunny when we left Highbury en route to The Valley, but by the time we'd popped up south of the Thames on the other side of the Blackwall Tunnel it had clouded over and suddenly there was a nip of autumn in the air. Compared with the commercial behemoths that the Arsenal and their like have become, in an age where corporate prawn-sandwich eaters are the most highly prized punters, I love the convivial family atmosphere that one gets from a friendly club like Charlton. Although, I do vehemently object to the fact that Arsenal fans are constantly penalised on our travels to The Valley and most other Premiership grounds these days.

Away matches at most of the clubs visited by fans of the likes of Arsenal, United and Chelsea are categorised as expensive 'Category A' games. As a result, we are often forced to pay a premium compared to visiting supporters from some of the lesser lights like Birmingham, Southampton and Pompey. I have a vague recollection from my economics lessons as a youth of something called the Scissors Principle, which I believe governs the laws of supply and demand. Don't ask me to explain, aside from the obvious fact that the high demand for tickets to see the Arsenal means that we have to pay more than most other footie fans. For example, it costs us thirty-five quid to watch a match at The Valley when other visiting supporters pay perhaps a tenner less. It's become all the more common for clubs to categorise matches in this manner. As a result, it amounts to a considerable financial burden for us Gooners over the course of an entire season, as we get our pockets picked due to the club's increased popularity. It's yet another indiscriminate tax on our loyalty (as ever)!

As is common at many relatively modern grounds, for this costly sum we get to sit in the incredibly cramped conditions behind the goal at The Valley. By comparison, these would make a seat on your average charter flight feel like a full-length double bed. Personally, I think the way they cram folks in like sardines is quite dangerous. In the event, heaven forbid, of some emergency, the overcrowding makes these seating areas far harder to evacuate than the old standing terraces. But that's another argument altogether. What gets me is the fact that I am only 5 ft 11 in. and relatively lean compared to some of the large beer bellies which accompany regular boozers to a game. Yet I frequently find that my knees are crucified by the back of the chair of the row in front. Fans rarely remain in their seats when watching from behind the goal and it really gets my goat. It's not the standing I object to, but the incessant bobbing up and down every few seconds which drives me barmy. Although it's welcomed at The Valley because at least it restores some circulation to my legs and saves me from partial paralysis by half-time!

I often find myself wondering how the hell some of the many more well-proportioned Gooners manage to cope in such crowded circumstances. At Charlton, for example, I need to ask six people either side for their assistance if I want to manoeuvre my arms to find my cigarettes. At least they can all enjoy the same salmon without having to move an inch (whether they want to or not). Lord only knows the problems encountered by the serial nose-pickers. I pity the poor folks who have the misfortune to find themselves adjacent to me in such close confines, on such nervous occasions as Sunday's game. While I make every effort not to blow smoke up their nose, it's possible that they still end up inhaling an entire pack during the course of such an intense game.

The dangers of passive smoking are far from the only perils of this Premiership race. If the season continues in the current unpredictable fashion, we are all going to end up needing pacemakers to prevent our hearts pumping at an unhealthy rate. In fact, on Sunday, the discomfort of one particular Gooner was such that he almost departed this mortal coil on the spot. It's Charlton's 'sarf' London neighbours whose fans have a reputation for offering visiting supporters an alternative means of transport away from the ground, according to the infamous chant, 'You're going home in a London ambulance'. Sadly, it proved all too accurate for the Gooner who suffered a suspected coronary during Sunday's tense proceedings.

It was obvious something was afoot when police activity at the back of the stand had everyone standing up to see what was going on behind them instead of watching the match. Much in the same way as a crowd will gather around a man looking up at the sky in the street, with our sheep-like tendencies on the terraces, only one person has to jump to their feet for us all to follow, fearing we are missing something. Just before the final whistle, the stadium announcer confirmed a medical emergency, requesting that Gooners in the upper tier turn left on their way out because there was an ambulance blocking the usual exit. I sincerely hope he has long since recovered, but his experience was a stark reminder to any fan with a suspect ticker to take it easy during a season which should, by rights, have come with a government health warning.

Into The Valley
27 October 2003

I am often told that the Irish equivalent is a far more informative programme than Des and his panel of pundit dunces on ITV's flagship Saturday night football show. I am sure that the majority of football fans are looking forward to the eventual return of *Match of the Day* as a much-missed old friend. Although, even if God almighty was making a simultaneous appearance on Parkinson on the Beeb, doubtless I would still find myself drawn to the taciturn deliberations of Townsend, McCoist and co., leaving proof positive of a higher power to later viewing on the video.

The Arsenal's recent efforts to reduce their wage bill has ensured that we've become even more interested observers than usual. While our own game at The Valley was Sunday's pay-per-view offering, the Premiership programme the previous night provided us with an opportunity to appraise Moritz Volz marauding down Fulham's right flank against Man Utd. In the subsequent highlights of Leeds versus Liverpool, we were able to witness the wing craft of Jermaine Pennant. I wonder whether Peter Reid will pick Pennant to play against us at Elland Road this Saturday? Talk about a conflict of interest. I am sure instinct will govern Pennant's actions but it would hardly be the best career move for the youngster to create or even score a goal against the club which currently holds his contract.

If Arsène is correct about it costing us points over the course of a season to blood a youngster, it would seem sensible to let them hone their craft at the highest level, and let our competitors pay the price both in terms of their income and the cost of the odd probable error. Yet, as happy as I am that Volz and Pennant might have several opportunities to help the Arsenal's cause in their performances for their current clubs against our immediate competitors, there is no disguising the fact that their absence adds to the depressing lack of strength in depth within the Arsenal squad.

Despite the fact that fortune played a considerable part in the continuation of a catastrophic Champions League campaign in Kiev, the Arsenal's recent woeful European record ensured a week of media bewilderment over this apparent chink in Wenger's tactical armour. I in no way wish to belittle our learned leader, in fact I bow to a knowledge so great it makes many in the game appear no more qualified as management material than the very important Ma who washes the Sunday team's kit. Nevertheless, the more years I spend watching football, the more convinced I am that it is in essence a simple sport.

In my humble opinion, the Arsenal's European malaise is not a matter of a lack of confidence or naive tactical limitations. On the contrary, I believe the World and European Cup winners in the Arsenal camp approach matches against the likes of Kiev and Moscow far too certain that their class will out. As a consequence, their efforts often lack the sort of intensity which is more common in Premiership football, where certain clubs constantly compensate for the limitations in their abilities with their work rate.

It seems as though some play on autopilot and are only stirred from their reverie and begin to roll up their sleeves once they've surrendered the lead. I sat here tearing my hair out last Tuesday as I watched them lay siege to Kiev's goal for the final 20 minutes, wondering why they couldn't produce such a concerted effort at the beginning of the game before they were two goals behind.

Moreover, as was evident in our increased effort only after going a goal down at The Valley on Sunday, this problem is also prevalent in the Premiership. Perhaps we are lacking a more vocal leader, someone capable of stoking the fire in their bellies? Many of us are pleasantly surprised that we continue to retain the top spot. Since we are some way from producing Championship-winning performances, our success must be in no small part be due to the spirit fostered in a stable squad.

Although I definitely get the sense that we are suffering from a lack of competition in the squad, as some players appear far too comfortable with a first-team place that is virtually guaranteed, I certainly wouldn't advocate the chopping and changing of the Chelsea model, where there are almost three players competing for every place in the team. However, I believe there are those who might benefit if Arsène introduced a little insecurity into our squad's cozy lives. I felt a little vulnerable myself about visiting The Valley on Sunday. It was nowt to do with the outcome of the match. Few north of the river fancy foraging for the passport necessary for the trip to the less than salubrious south London, but I always look forward to playing at Charlton. In the shadow of the Millennium Dome, it's only just 'sarf' of the River Thames and such a short hop that it's almost a home game

There's no mistaking the friendly family atmosphere at The Valley, which is in complete contrast to the extremely hostile environment of their nearby neighbours at the New Den. My mate Mick, a recent émigré to Athlone, was back in London and decided to take Ró's place at the last minute. He enlightened me about a pedestrian tunnel in the vicinity which runs all the way to the Isle of Dogs. Anyone mad enough to walk through when Millwall are playing at home is apparently putting themselves in mortal danger. Whereas, thankfully, there isn't a psychopath in a surgical face mask to be seen amongst all the elderly women, kids and families supporting Charlton.

My trepidation was ticket related. The Arsenal's financial plight and the boardroom rift had resulted in a working environment which my mate in the box office no longer enjoyed. I have always collected my away tickets in person but, since his shock departure in the summer, tickets for two of the five away games have gone astray in the post with a sticker on the envelope addressed to: 'Do Not Send'! I am not sure whether it's a result of stupidity or a concerted effort to get me so pissed off that I relent and risk the post like everyone else, rather than continue bothering the 'beautiful' box office staff (12 years of schmoozing my mate to the point where I assumed we'd eventually be in clover when he became box office manager, and I have to begin brown-nosing from the bottom again!!).

Unlike Man City, at least I didn't have to fret for a couple of hundred miles without tickets in my sweaty mitts. Besides, after an extra hour in bed to dally with my dream of last season's 0–3 slaughter, embracing some of the most swashbuckling footie ever seen and in perfect footballing weather, with the sun sparkling in the bright blue sky of a typically brisk autumnal day, even my standard pessimism was a struggle. Never fear, it took just a few storm clouds and the realisation that the Arsenal continue to be totally reliant on Thierry Henry before my mood soon matched the rapidly mutable meteorology.

Thank heavens for Henry. I might be an unbeliever but it doesn't stop me going to bed every night praying for Titi's well-being. There isn't another footballer who is quite so enthralling as Henry. It is not just what he can do with a ball which makes his efforts worth the price of admission alone. Even super-skilful players like Pires and Ljungberg adopt a somewhat scuttling gait when running with a ball at their feet. Titi has this economy of movement, eating up the ground without appearing to expend any energy and with a certain grace that is football played as ballet.

There was entertainment enough that no one could have dropped off like the fan shown on the telly dozing at White Hart Lane. Yet the rather fulsome match reports result from the fact that the Arsenal have flattered to deceive all season. In my opinion, until the likes of Pires, Wiltord and Ljungberg start earning their corn by weighing in with a worthwhile contribution, the Arsenal will continue to perform like a misfiring V12 engine, unable to unleash our wicked acceleration. However, it is encouraging that we remain ahead of our domestic rivals despite the fact that we aren't (as yet!) firing on all cylinders. I will wait to see how we get on against Kiev before deciding whether it is worth booking a hotel in Milan. However, if I am hedging my bets, it's certainly not because I have given up the Gunners Champions League ghost.

14

Carling Cup: Tuesday, 28 October (H) Arsenal 1 Rotherham United 1 Aliadière (11); won on pens
Premiership: Saturday, 1 November (A) Arsenal 4 Leeds United 1 Henry (8, 33) Pires (17) Gilberto (50)

Youngsters retain Carling Cup interest via penalty shoot-out; Arsenal fines total £275,000 for Old Trafford incidents, in addition to individual player suspensions; big guns back for imperious exhibition at Elland Road.

While we are very privileged to watch some of the world's greatest artists ply their talented trade each week, it is almost inevitable that we mean little more to the club than the sixteen hundred-odd quid cost of our season tickets, making us totally interchangeable with the many thousands who've been waiting years for a chance to take our place. Moreover, a large proportion of punters at THOF turn up each week with the attitude of a theatre audience. They sit back on their cushioned seats (at least they are in the West Upper), waiting for the curtain to go up on each performance and the entertainment to begin. Actually, I suppose an analogy with a pantomime might be more accurate, as the audience invariably boos the baddie in the black and the 'he's behind you' mustachioed mischief-maker with a foreign accent and a funny costume, and they'll occasionally be encouraged to cheer if the performers throw them a bag of marshmallows.

However, fans at clubs like the Arsenal demand satisfaction for their money and the promise of some silverware at the end of every season. While the high price of our entertainment and the extremely limited availability of tickets means that, for all games other than this once-a-season Cup outing, the seats around us are largely restricted to a fairly affluent and increasingly elderly 'audience'. By contrast, the few thousand fans at lower league clubs tend to turn out to support their local team, rain or shine, knowing full well that the chances of any success during their entire lifetime might be very limited. Affordable ticket prices mean that three generations of the same family can all go and sit (or stand) together, surrounded by the same familiar faces every season.

No doubt, I have a somewhat sentimental view of life in the lower leagues but I have no intention of confirming this because I couldn't change the habits of a lifetime, even if I wanted to. Although, who knows, it might be a different story if I had a family with young children. I know of devoted Gooners who have season tickets for clubs like Barnet or Watford. The cost and the scarcity of seats at the Arsenal makes trips to Highbury an impossibility for them. Not wanting to deprive their children of the same fun-filled family outings they experienced with their fathers on a Saturday afternoon as a child, they have no choice but to go elsewhere.

Nevertheless, as much as these folks would love to initiate their offspring to the joys of the Arsenal religion, in typical 'grass is always greener' fashion, when I visit smaller clubs around the country to watch a match amidst these 'real' footie fans, I can't help but feel a little jealous. I have this romantic image of a very inclusive atmosphere, where fans are on first-name terms with everyone at the club from the turnstile operator to the bod who serves them their half-time bevvy, and have been surrounded by the same bunch of locals for donkey's years, dishing out the jibes to their journeyman striker with the dodgy knees whose sponsorship with the local butchers comes with the bonus of a nice bit of beef.

I also wonder whether such trips might serve as a lesson to some of our mollycoddled kids who've spent their careers so far amongst the splendour of the Arsenal's amazing facilities. One would hope it might be a reality check for them, illustrating the sort of massive step down they could expect if they fail to continue to work their socks off and end up being released. However, our ball had come out of the hat first in the Carling Cup third-round draw, providing a home game against Rotherham.

For the Millermen, the prize of drawing a Premiership club can provide a financial lifeline for Nationwide teams and a trip to THOF would give them a rare sniff of the big time. In comparison, Wenger would be fielding a selection of the Arsenal's brightest young sparks, offering them a tasty carrot with their first opportunity to trot out of the tunnel under the floodlights, with all the buzz of a big Highbury crowd.

The Arsenal don't include this competition amongst the seven Cup ties which are pre-paid with our season tickets and they now always put a warning up at the box office to advise those buying the reduced price tickets of the possible team changes. I assume it's a means of preventing claims for refunds from dissatisfied fans who aren't prepared to pay for anything but the first team. If I was sad to miss out on an unusual away outing, at least home matches in this competition permit an opportunity to pick up a relatively cheap seat behind the goal. You often hear the crowd at one end screaming 'shoot' when a player is an inordinate distance from goal. With the foreshortened view, it's sometimes hard to suss out what's occurring, even with my binoculars. Yet, although our seats near the halfway line at the front of the West Upper provide the optimum view of the proceedings, it makes a pleasant change to have an alternative perspective and to be able to enjoy a little more atmosphere. Sitting in the North Bank on Tuesday, we sure got plenty of bangs for our mere ten bucks. Rotherham were finally eliminated long past the bedtimes of many of the kids present, following a seemingly endless penalty shoot-out where I was beginning to wonder if physio Gary Lewin was going to get a turn.

I Can't Believe It's Not Butter
3 November 2003

Three–nil up by half-time on Saturday and, on glancing up, I noticed that the East Stand at Elland Road is named the Lurpak Stand. Quite appropriate, I thought, considering we'd swept through them like a knife through butter. Now, whether it was because the knife was hot or the butter merely tepid I am not sure, because this wasn't quite the scintillating Arsenal performance which produced the same scoreline last season. Perhaps, with their financial problems and the Viduka fiasco, we caught Leeds on a particularly bad day. Yet, on the evidence of my own eyes, the way the lambs of this Leeds defence laid down, they look very much like relegation fodder.

It is sad, really, because hearing how heartily the 30,000-strong Elland Road massive sang their hearts out, raising the roof of the Revie Stand with 'We're gonna win 5–4' and 'Let's go f***** mental', sung with more than a little irony, one could not only be forgiven for wondering which side was winning but for thinking that these passionate fans deserve a little more than this miserable side. Perhaps the most poignant reflection on this club's immediate future was how little of his customary grit and determination Peter Reid has managed to inspire in the team.

By contrast, if you were looking for evidence of the healthy spirit within the Arsenal camp, there was a wonderful moment when the entire team gathered around Gilberto in one huge huddle to celebrate the Brazilian's goal. I have a feeling that the FA might have done us a favour with all the bans resulting from the Old Trafford fiasco. We won the League by seven points after being docked two for the previous, far more serious punch-up at United in '91. I still have a vivid memory of Tony Adams holding the trophy aloft on the Town Hall balcony whilst being serenaded with the theme tune to our Championship run-in, 'You can stick your f***ing two points up your arse'.

I am hoping that similarly the FA's punishments this season might act as a focal point for the entire squad to rally round and plug the gaps as necessary. Hopefully, come the end of the season, we might be expressing our gratitude to the authorities in a similar fashion. That's assuming Thierry Henry can stay fit.

Henry dazzled again on Saturday to the point where the Leeds players all looked positively terrified by his presence. Up until now, Titi has been responsible for retaining the top spot virtually single-handed (aided by our opponents' inconsistencies). As a result, as winter draws nigh and the temperatures continue to drop, I grow increasingly fearful of the potential for pulls and strains with every breathtaking burst of Henry's incredible pace. His importance is such that I'd want to wrap him in cotton wool. Yet, when I asked Wenger if he was tempted to take Titi off at the break, he responded that he didn't think it was necessary because Henry 'didn't have to dig deep, physically'. It must have been soul destroying from a Leeds perspective to know they'd been torn apart by Henry playing only at half-throttle.

That he doesn't accept defeat graciously is probably what makes Wenger such a winner. However, in triumph, he is invariably most humble and hearing his glowing reference to the Leeds youngsters (Milner and Lennon), I find it dumbfounding that anyone can accuse the demure Frenchman of arrogance. Although, I have to admit to being a bit disappointed to hear Arsène rising to Fergie's bait on Friday. In my opinion, he should have risen above what appears to me as a puerile ploy to deflect media attention from the factious Ferdinand feud. Still, it appears that Fergie will have time aplenty to plot any subsequent stirring of his oversized wooden spoon when he is confined to another spell in the stands for his allegations that the Arsenal had done a deal with the FA.

On Saturday, there were some more encouraging signs from midfield runs by the likes of Ljungberg that our reliance on Henry might not be quite so total in future. Although, from behind the goal, it looked like he was half an hour late in arriving, even Pires popped up in the penalty area to slot one home (albeit from a fairly acute angle from which a keeper as capable as Robinson should never have been beaten). The contribution from midfield might be crucial if we are going to conquer Kiev at Highbury tonight. With our narrow playing surface, we often struggle to break European teams down, especially when Henry can't go to the bathroom without being accompanied by at least a couple of markers.

For what it's worth (well, everyone else seems to have had their tuppence worth), my theory about our European tribulations is that we tend to be too tentative compared to our domestic performances. I don't think there is a team anywhere which would be comfortable defending our counter-attacking at its best, when we break from the back and bear down on the opponent's goal in numbers before they are able to get ten men behind the ball. But, all too often in Europe, we appear to overcomplicate our play with additional sideways and backwards passes which ruin the element of surprise.

Perhaps it is a psychological effect of the number of games played in these group stages because there is less pressure for a result when there are games remaining in which sufficient points can be earned to qualify for the knockout stages. Well, we'll find out tonight, when we will hopefully witness a positive reaction to the pressure of knowing that only three wins from three can guarantee our progress.

Meanwhile, I am glad that the exertions of a north London Derby come after our European exploits. My Spurs friends are so gloomy about their prospects that they are unable to even muster the usual bluff and bluster but, as we know, form goes out of the window in such circumstances. However, in an era when some players change clubs more frequently than their underpants, you have to wonder how many of those involved actually appreciate the long-term repercussions of their efforts (or the lack thereof!) for those on the terraces.

15

Champions League: Wednesday, 5 November (H) Arsenal 1 Dynamo Kiev 0 Cole (88)

Premiership: Saturday, 8 November (H) Arsenal 2 Tottenham Hotspur 1 Pires (69) Ljungberg (79)

Ash leaves it late for a priceless header as we record the first win of our European campaign and retain a slim chance of progress; Derby day fortune as late goals from wide boys wipe the smiles off Spurs' faces.

I was a big fan of Guy Fawkes Night until we got our dog. Before Treacle became part of the family, I often used to spend a small fortune on the biggest and baddest imported fireworks from China and enjoyed setting them off on the green in the middle of Highbury Quadrant. Nasty, inconsiderate neighbour that I am, there were times when I would end up taking the piss out of party-pooping residents who came on to their balconies to holler their disapproval. I suppose it's poetic justice that I'd end up turning into one of them. In light of the trend towards temporary shops which open up just to flog fireworks and the variety of religious and social festivals, the thunderclap of noisy fireworks seems to be far more prevalent than I can recall as a kid. So, instead of one night a year, poor Treacle has to suffer these explosive salvos for months at a time. It is a problem for most pet owners but it's particularly painful for us because our dog is so sensitive to the resonant sound.

Treacle gets depressed for weeks at a time, disappearing into her shell and any nook or cranny she can find in the flat for some security. I am always terrified she is going to electrocute herself amongst the jumbled mass of cables when she tries to hide behind the TV. She doesn't have many choices in our small flat but her favourite hidey-hole is behind the sofa, and it's horrible seeing her disappear behind there almost every night for a couple of long months, trembling for hours at a time. As a result, I end up running around our flat, trying to find the right window from which to scream at the young pyromaniacs responsible for the racket who, I imagine, just like myself in the past, don't fully appreciate the psychological distress they are causing the dogs and cats, and their owners. Although, these days, if I'm firing off a volley of verbal abuse at the kids around here on the subject of sex and travel ('f*ck off!'), it's tempting to do so from behind the anonymity of the net curtains, for fear of the sort of vindictive acts of revenge whereby we might come down the next day to find the car vandalised.

Having gone through the whole gamut of homoeopathic remedies over the past couple of years in our efforts to ease poor Treacle's anxieties, we had finally resorted to a sedative from the vet. The dog was, therefore, suitably dosed up before sunset on Wednesday when the London skyline was lit up with the multicoloured explosions which I imagine might bring back bad memories for the pensioners who survived the Blitz. Watching the build-up on the box before heading out the door, there was no escaping the ominous stats for Champions League Group B. Inter and Kiev were top with six points, Moscow were third with four, and we were bottom with the single point we'd earned in Moscow.

I wasn't sure what to worry about more – a pointless trip to Milan as part of the Arsenal's ignominious exit from Europe or Treacle somehow reducing the contents of our flat to ashes, still terrified in her tranquillised state. I managed to persuade Ró that the pooch would sleep through it all and that she could accompany me without having to worry about the dog. However, I wish I had been as confident as I sounded. If we hadn't headed out the door together, I might have nipped back to pacify myself by popping a couple of Treacle's happy pills!

Perhaps there was a smell of cordite in the air, coming from all the Catherine Wheels and Roman Candles going off in back gardens, as we *walked around to the West Upper. Or was it just my heightened senses playing tricks before the battle commenced? Approaching Avenell Road, there's no mistaking the familiar Highbury odours of horseshit and the more appetising fragrance of fried onions wafting from the burger stalls. But as we approached the turnstiles on Wednesday, I could sense the mood of tension amongst 38,000 Gooners arriving for the most important game of the season so far, as the ground was enveloped in a palpable funk of trepidation. Even at the Library, most midweek matches under the floodlights usually generate a special atmosphere, with Gooners coming straight from work and downing a few inhibition-easing bevvies before the game. Unlike weekend matches, everyone turns up at the turnstiles at the same time and, despite arriving early for once, it was as if the crush of Gooners anxious to get to their seats was some sort of conspiracy to keep us from making kick-off. Apart from the odd impatient shout from latecomers at the back who arrived expecting immediate entry, we all shuffled along in silence, like a queue of school kids outside the headmaster's office, hoping that the punishment which awaited us inside wouldn't be too painful.*

What Sort of Mettle are We Really Made Of?
10 November 2003

I guess us Gooners were spoilt for good last season by the gobsmacking brilliance of so many of our performances. This Arsenal side set such an incredible standard that everything else appears so mundane by comparison. Having raised the bar of our expectations to such seemingly unobtainable heights, there are many Arsenal fans and plenty in the media who can't appreciate simple three-point pleasures and the stuttering performances which have seen us grind out a quarter of this season as the only unbeaten side in the land.

A repeat of the 4–1 thrashing of the Elland Road relegation fodder was merely a reminder of the difference between last season's completely devastating display. Similarly, our encounter with our north London neighbours was never going to live up to the tonking they suffered when they last dared to show their faces at Highbury (Titi Henry tearing them asunder virtually single-handedly with his goal-of-the-season contender). Nevertheless, there was a certain pleasure to Saturday's somewhat fluky success which was a nostalgic throwback to the 'Lucky Arsenal' of yesteryear.

By contrast, a dismal decade since their last success at Highbury has left Spurs fans so demoralised, with their expectations so stunted that, for those who continue to attend this annual meeting, it must be a loyal act of masochism equivalent to self-flagellation in religious terms. At least going a goal down within five minutes guaranteed an even more intense atmosphere on Saturday. You can imagine the Lilywhite euphoria in their corner of Highbury as Anderton rekindled all their hope for the best part of an hour, only to see it extinguished by a cruel twist of fate with Freddie Ljungberg's deflected shot. I almost felt sorry for them as we sadistically sent them packing to the sound of 'Beat the Arsenal! You're having a larf!'

It's not surprising that Wenger was left blaming fatigue for our somewhat lacklustre showing. I was left exhausted merely by all the tension of our midweek Champions League clash. I can't possibly imagine the physical cost of hammering at Dynamo's door for almost the entire 90, with the lads left pounding the length of the pitch as the game became more stretched at the death and our efforts to keep our European hopes alive were becoming increasingly desperate.

Having both suffered and celebrated, over the years, at the hands of so many unexpected turns of events before the fat lady sings, I am usually the last to give up hope in such circumstances. Yet, on Wednesday, I have to admit that, like the rest of the Highbury faithful, I succumbed to being resigned to our fate for about the last ten minutes. Usually Wenger's gung-ho efforts to snatch victory from the jaws of defeat, by throwing four strikers into the fray, would have us Gooners out of our seats, screaming our heads off in an effort to inspire one last gasp blitz before the final whistle with a passion which might obliterate any thought of the players' oxygen deficient limbs. Whereas for 88 minutes on Wednesday we were strangely silent, as though we all believed our Champions League hopes were also already exhausted. I was sitting back, slumped in my seat, almost certain that Sod's law was going to leave us with a trip to Milan which would be hardly worth taking with nothing but pride to play for.

Still, it didn't stop me superstitiously grabbing for Róna's hand every time the ball came within shooting distance of either goal. The tension became so unbearable that by the time Ashley Cole popped up with his 88th-minute header, I was gripping her hand so tightly that I nearly broke her wrist as I levitated out of my seat and punched the air in joyous relief that we would hopefully be sitting in the San Siro in two weeks' time with our qualification prospects intact. I thought it most appropriate that it was the only home-grown player on the pitch (Parlour having been subbed) whose never-say-die commitment resulted in a sprint out of defence and into the penalty area to steal the winner.

Although it would appear that Inter have stopped their Serie A rot, I have always fancied our chances to exploit their weaknesses on the wide expanses of the Milanese pitch. It is our last group gamewhich is my greatest concern, as I envisage a similar slog to last week, against a Lokomotiv side who will have undoubtedly learnt from all those who have come to Highbury and achieved their aim of defying our ability with an obdurate defence.

However, no matter how far we are destined to travel on this season's European adventure, one cannot possibly overestimate the importance of last week's result. The margins between success and failure in football are so small. We expended so much effort on Wednesday and, without that last-minute winner, I am certain that the Arsenal would have suffered such a blow to their morale that we wouldn't have managed to find the resolve for Saturday's comeback. Our premature exit from European competition might have blighted our entire domestic campaign.

Instead of which, we go into another international break with renewed faith that our Champions League fate rests in our own hands. What's more, we've somehow managed to retain our place atop the pile, whilst remaining unbeaten in encounters with all of our most earnest competitors without ever having settled into the sort of stride of which this side is most eminently capable and, of late, without the crucial driving force of our team captain, Patrick Vieira. Aside from our two further European games, the Arsenal now face a programme where we don't come up against a 'quality' team until our trip to Stamford Bridge on 21 February.

Unlike last season, we certainly won't have shot our bolt before the end of autumn. There have been some slightly encouraging signs recently, like the sight of Pires appearing in the box in time to tap home on Saturday. Hopefully, we can play our way into some kind of form when it matters, just in time to tonk the lesser lights of Leicester and Wolves, while our competitors are taking points from one another. Although I am worried that the opposite might prove true; unglamorous trips to the Midlands might not be enough to galvanise this team out of what some perceive as a tendency to go a goal down, a by-product of the fatal belief that winning is just a matter of turning up.

The quality running throughout the Premiership these days is such that in almost every opponent there is someone capable of making the most of momentary, complacent lapses. Many suggest it is the results against our immediate competitors which are most crucial but, in my humble opinion, it will be our performance in the coming period which will determine our true Championship credentials. There is no motivation required for titanic encounters against Man Utd or Chelsea. Yet with the possibility of our squad being down to the bare bones, it will be bringing home the bacon on a miserable afternoon in Bolton or Birmingham which could prove the Gunners' greatest burden.

16

Blank mid-November weekend for Euro 2004 play-offs; Down Under, Jonny Wilkinson kicks all 24 as English egg-chasers knock out the French.

No Substitute for a Spherical Ball!
17 November 2003

After spending my formative years at a school where association football was positively frowned upon and, worse still, having to endure a certain amount of egg-chasing after lessons on some Saturday afternoons when I wasn't able to skive off to Highbury, I suppose I retain a subliminal aversion to the philistine sport.

Nevertheless, I have to admit that I thoroughly enjoyed the antipodean derby on Saturday morning.

I'm no aficionado but I've never watched in its entirety a more engrossing encounter of this rough-house game. At least I didn't feel cheated out of a lie-in like I did last weekend after forsaking my bed for the Boys in Green's sorry World Cup swansong. Yet I suppose they didn't have the sort of help the English had, with the heavens opening to hinder the Gauls' passing game on Sunday.

It wasn't just Ireland's exit from the Rugby World Cup which I found myself regretting this past weekend. There were plenty 'if onlys' watching the admirable efforts of Wales and Scotland against Russia and Holland in the footie. The 1–0 result in Glasgow was remarkable from the point of view that Holland have household names playing in virtually every position, while there is nary a well-known player in the entire Scottish squad. There is a good chance that the Dutch will overcome the single-goal deficit in the Amsterdam Arena. Yet, as it stands at the moment, the atmosphere on the Algarve next summer will be somewhat more sterile if the genial orange and green armies are absent (the Portuguese are undoubtedly counting down the days to the arrival of the cantankerous English contingent!). If Ireland's non-participation is painful now, we'll be positively pulling our hair out in a few months, when there will be no escaping the blanket coverage of Portuguese jamboree.

There was wall-to-wall live sport for us addicts over the course of the weekend. If watching both forms of footie wasn't enough to send me goggle-eyed, I sat through several hours of glorious skills performed on the green baize. Perhaps this was comforting because the snooker surface was the closest thing to the perfect pitch at Highbury, since what I really miss during a Gunners-free fortnight is some proper partisan participation.

Sure, I was up for Wales and Scotland (especially as underdogs) but I wouldn't have been exactly devastated if either had suffered defeat, and I certainly wasn't going to get my knickers in a twist over an England versus Denmark friendly. In fact, with only Arsenal's Ashley Cole involved and with the mother-out-of-law over from Dublin, I wish I'd watched Rooney and co. in one of the round-the-clock replays and gone out to Sunday lunch instead.

The one game which might have got me salivating was Germany v.

France but coverage of this was nowhere to be found on my multitude of satellite channels. An evening with Thierry Henry these days is almost guaranteed first-class entertainment for us football lovers and I understand he didn't disappoint with his redoubtable contribution to all three goals against the Germans. If there's a rare dearth of disparaging remarks about my favourite nation, my diplomacy might well be related to the fact that I've just read that the latest hopes for financing Ashburton Grove rest on a group of German investors.

Come Sunday, I was so fed up with the ersatz substitute of international football that I couldn't concentrate on 90 minutes of Brazil v. Peru. Gilberto provided the Arsenal connection but recently his football has been sufficiently uninspiring that many Gooners are convinced he is more Millwall than Copacabana.

Deprived of my beloved Arsenal for ten days now, I'm getting pretty depressed. I don't want to turn on my TV and watch some Beckham lookalike duping fawning Orientals with a couple of keepie-uppies, leeching on football's seemingly boundless bandwagon. And with bombs going off in Turkey, it is neither appropriate, nor do I particularly want to see Golden Balls' albeit handsome face staring up from both front and back covers of the tabloid press. We appear to be living in a society where the media are obsessed with the periphery. All I want is my regular fix of real footie to distract me from the madness which surrounds us.

Obviously, I understand the economics of it all. The Beckhams have replaced Lady Di as the bestsellers of newsprint on this star-struck planet of ours, and scandal and salacious gossip are the stock in trade of the tabloids. Yet it frustrates the hell out of me that this fervour for fruity headlines is now the fuel which drives our 'beautiful game' in detrimental directions.

I personally doubt the FA would have raised an eyebrow over Alan Smith's innocuous bottle-throwing incident if they didn't fear the wrath of the red-tops and the rumpus resulting from the selection of a prospective felon (it didn't prevent the Yanks putting one in the White House!). Nor, might I add, would the Arsenal be facing such a severe rash of suspensions if it weren't for the entire media's maniacal reaction to the Van Nistlerooy-inspired immature posturing after our match against Man Utd.

Perhaps Smith's bad-boy karma is to blame but I can't help but feel sorry for the cruel twist of fate which befell the young lad. To get picked by Sven from a pitifully poor Leeds side is a feat in itself but, on the basis that the rash of injuries which resulted in his inclusion are unlikely to be repeated in the near future, he must have spent the weekend sitting at home thinking that the FA had blown his one and only chance to make an impression prior to Portugal 2004. I bet such career-hindering consequences weren't on the minds of those who sent Smith packing!

Meanwhile, there was some light-hearted relief on Monday with the news that none of the Irish players were harmed in the armed raid on the Portmarnock Hotel in Dublin because they were all able to hide behind Damien Duff's wallet!

One person who will be wrapped in cotton wool this week will be Jonny Wilkinson. With England finally making the final of a World Cup, the media here are trying to rekindle the spirit of '66. Yet you have to look no further than Highbury for an example of the comparative impact of the two sports. You didn't have to be a footie fan to know when England scored against Brazil in Japan because the rejoicing resounded around this entire estate. Whereas the tranquillity in Highbury Quadrant was hardly disturbed on Sunday by a single voice saluting the feats of Wilkinson (and it wasn't mine, since I didn't want to disturb the missus!).

Speaking of voices, the most bizarre aspect to events in Australia has been the sight of these big butch fellas singing along emotionally to the falsetto tones of the seemingly castrated troubadours chosen to sing their national tunes (including Ireland's cacophonous clichéd cop-out). I might have a passing interest in Saturday's match in Sydney but, in truth, it certainly won't delay my departure for Birmingham. I don't think I've ever been so desperate to see a match at St Andrews and it will be Matthew Upson's defensive failings (hopefully) that will be of far more interest to me than those of the Wallabies.

17

Premiership: Saturday, 22 November (A) Arsenal 3 Birmingham City 0 Ljungberg (4), Bergkamp (80), Pires (88)

Dennis leaves Upson eating his dust but a three-goal margin flatters workman-like Yellows

Probably the best week of football of the entire season didn't start out too well on a personal level. Poor Nell and I ended up listening to much of the first half of the match at St Andrews on the car radio after I'd dawdled as usual about departing. By the time I eventually picked him up, it wasn't much more than an hour before kick-off. Birmingham is one of our shortest hops up the motorway but I hadn't taken into account that it would take most of this time just struggling to get out of London!

Like most of the country's sport lovers, I'd spent the morning watching Jonny Wilkinson penalty kicking England to Rugby World Cup glory against the Aussies. Yet, even with extra time, the game Down Under had finished before noon, so there was no real excuse for being late. After all this time, Nell treats my tardy timekeeping with an air of resignation. I think he'd fall over in shock if I ever actually turned up early!

My record for leaving late was probably a Coventry game a few seasons back, when we were still stuck in traffic on Stroud Green Road (five mins from Highbury) with about forty-five minutes to make kick-off. On that occasion, Ian Wright was kind enough to wait for us to walk into the ground twenty mins late. He stuck the ball in the net seconds after we'd taken our seats. We weren't so lucky on Saturday when a far-too-impatient Freddie took a mere four minutes to find the net against the team with the best defensive record in the League. In some respects, Freddie's strike took the pressure off. I didn't need to put my foot down and drive like a lunatic in the pouring rain as we'd already missed the goal and at least we arrived at St Andrews in one piece. But it was approaching half-time when I finally pulled up and, having missed most of the first half, I was feeling terribly guilty. So, I let Nell out as close to our entrance as possible before looking for somewhere to leave the car,.

It seems to be a common practice for local authorities to make regulations around football grounds so complicated that you need a degree on the subject to know, for example, whether the single yellow line applies on match days. Or you have to walk half a mile in the opposite direction to find an applicable sign which might just give you a clue as to the specific regulations. To my mind, it seems like a massive scam to maximise parking-fine revenues from unsuspecting football fans whose votes the local councillors don't have to count on. It wasn't so long ago that the London Borough of Islington extended their match-day parking scheme to the Quadrant. I have to laugh (because it is supposedly better for you than crying!) at their claims that the scheme is for the benefit of local residents. Personally, we cannot apply for the necessary permit because both of our cars are registered to my ma's address. Having had two cars stolen from outside the flat since we moved in, I probably couldn't afford the premium if they were insured at our address.

As a result, we have to go through this incredible palaver of playing shuffle-car on match days, moving the two motors to a pitch outside the controlled zone before fans start arriving and you can't find a legal pitch for miles around. Judging by the way the Quadrant empties on match days, there must be many other residents in the same predicament. Consequently, away fans turn up for almost every game unable to believe their luck in finding so many empty parking spaces so close to the ground. I am often out there walking the dog, offering fans a friendly warning, as I know exactly how maddening it is to return after the match to find the cost of your expensive outing has suddenly increased by a needless fifty quid.

Yet the council must be making an absolute fortune since the Quadrant was included in the scheme. Walking home from every match, we pass car after poor, unfortunate car with a parking ticket on its windscreen. Some weeks, we see footie fans with forlorn faces who've just had to fork out a hundred quid, followed by a wait of an hour or so before their car is unclamped and they can begin their long journey home. It's definitely far more of a hindrance than a help to local residents on the couple of days I've overslept, or we've both had a brainstorm and forgotten to move the cars. Not only has it cost us a small fortune in fines but I've then had the dilemma of either moving both cars, driving miles away to find a parking space and doubtless missing most of the match whilst walking back, or taking the risk that it's a weekend when the clampers won't come out and then spending the entire match sweating over whether our woes might be added to with the couple of hundred quid cost of getting both cars released.

At least in Brum it was so close to the break that I didn't need to risk abandoning the motor and spend the remainder of the match worrying about it. The problem was that, having successfully applied for a post-match press conference pass, I didn't want the press officer to think that I simply hadn't turned up, so I had to walk all the way round the ground to find the press entrance. I then spent most of the break trying to find someone who knew what I was babbling on about. The teams were just coming out for the second half by the time I'd had some success. Yet, despite the away fans entrance being only a hundred-odd yards away as the crow flies, I had to walk all the way back around the ground again because of the way Birmingham organises the segregation of the two sets of supporters.

The Arsenal were straight out of the traps as I hurried to our entrance. Listening to the commentary on my terrace tranny, I was almost grateful to Maik Taylor when the keeper, on-loan from Fulham, made a fabulous fingertip save from Henry. I would have been absolutely gutted to have missed another goal by just a few seconds. Needless to say, I was exhausted by the time I found myself struggling along the row to my seat. Thankfully, the Arsenal were at least kicking towards us in the second half, so I had a decent view of the goalmouth action. But they were dreadfully cramped conditions in a dilapidated stadium which didn't even have a clock, let alone any screens so we might see replays of what took place at the other end of the pitch. It seems I was far from alone in my opinion, joining in with an amusing Gooner chorus of, 'Thirty-eight quid! You're having a larf'.

Still Walking (on Terra Firma!) in a Bergkamp Wonderland
24 November 2003

Sometimes it's a pity that our Monsieur Le Prof is such a pragmatist. After a vintage Dennis Bergkamp performance on Saturday, of the scintillating sort which some of the more sceptical amongst us thought they'd long since seen the last, in Wenger's shoes, I would have stuck Dennis in a cab straight from St Andrews and made certain his driver didn't spare the horses until he'd reached the San Siro, Milan. The measured opinion of our level-headed manager (for whom harebrained would be the idea of having the whole bottle of wine rather than the one glass!) is that, 'three days is too short to travel so far at his age'!

Yet, in the immortal words of The Beatles, Bergkamp will be able to sing 'When I'm 64' for another 30 years. We watched him roll these back even further in Birmingham, when Dennis dug deep and discovered the necessary speed to leave trailing in his wake mere whippersnappers who weren't long out of nappies when he was already wowing us for the Netherlands.

Perhaps it's wishful thinking on my part because I am so desperate for Bergkamp to shine in a swansong season that would befit a player of his immense stature. There's no doubt that Dennis is much more cerebral than the majority of his peers (now, there's the definition of a back-handed compliment). I am pretty sure that I've perceived, even in pre-season, a certain intensity to his performances which have alluded to an awareness of his increasingly impending sporting mortality. It's as if he's found a renewed determination to squeeze every last drop out of his illustrious career. Yet, after a couple of not-so-spectacular seasons (according to the sublime standards set by Bergkamp himself), Wenger's focus on Dennis's longevity has meant that his time on the park has been all the more fleeting. And, as someone who has always played his way into form, he has often found it a struggle to impose himself on matches. Especially when playing under the pressure of knowing his number is favourite to appear first on the subs board.

It's always at this crucial stage in the Champions League qualification process that the perennial question crops up about the disadvantages of our non-flying Dutchman. If I never again hear the miserable likes of Lawrenson pontificating on the matter, it will be too soon. None of the pundits appear to appreciate the fact that Bergkamp was 'bought as seen', his phobia well publicised in the contractual packaging which left everyone at the club in absolutely no doubt that there was never any possibility of him making like BA from the A-Team (after flogging it for more than a decade, hasn't Ally

1 & 2 The new 'Home Of Football' takes shape and the old West Upper entrance in all its art deco glory.

3 & 4 Gunners on tour in Moscow and on that magical night in Milan (Red Square, Moscow, 30 September 2003 and the San Siro, Milan, 25 November 2003).

5, 6 & 7 '71 . . . 2004: 33 years after Ray Kennedy did it, the Gunners rub the enemy's face in it once again by winning the Championship at White Hart Lane (v. Spurs, 25 April 2004).

8 Arsène might know, but none of us had a scooby how to escape enemy territory intact (outside WHL, 25 April 2004).

9 For those still stuck at WHL, these were the scenes of merriment they missed on the steps of the Marble Halls (outside THOF, 25 April 2004).

10 Fancy dress is now de rigueur for the last away game of the season (v. Fulham, Loftus Road, 9 May 2004).

11 Ticketless Gooners gather for a glimpse of Arsène's New Invincibles through the cracks in the gates (v. Leicester, 15 May 2004).

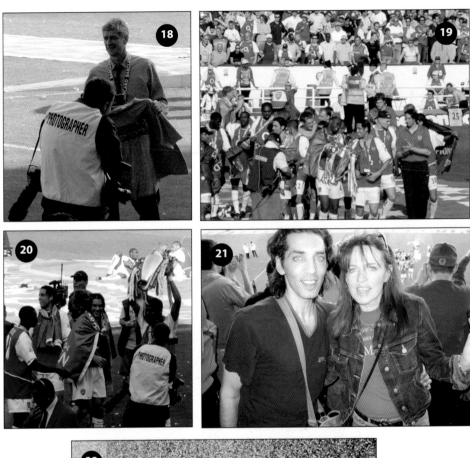

12–22 The flags were out at The Home Of Football as the Arsenal finally complete their historic achievement. Arsène enjoys the irony as he's presented with a Comical Wenger T-shirt (18), while Róna and I wallow in another wonderful afternoon to be a Gooner (21) (v. Leicester, 15 May 2004).

23–28 Glorious Gooner memories from the parade to the Town Hall, Upper Street, 16 May 2004 (no wonder it took so long when the buses were being towed by the old boy in his chair!).

29–32 Three Musketeers . . . three Staffordshires (no resemblance, but my mate Kevin (pictured centre, above) and our pooch Treacle (picture centre, below).

McCoist got a mate to tell him this crack is wearing a tad thin?).

To fully appreciate how dear most Gooners hold Dennis Bergkamp and the special place he has in our hearts, you need to bear in mind that we'd suffered several years of an indigestible domestic diet consisting of weeds like Hillier, McGoldrick and co. when the seed of this fabulous Continental flower came into our Arsenal lives. Over the years, we have become spoilt as this blossomed into the veritable cornucopia of colour that is the current Arsenal squad. Yet I still vividly recall the tingle of anticipation and incredulity at the thought of one of the world's very best players actually coming to humble ol' Highbury to ply his trade in red and white every week.

In fact, Dennis arrived during Bruce Rioch's brief reign but to most of us he represents the essence of Arsène's revolution and, in the Arsenal advent calendar, Bergkamp's appearance in an Arsenal shirt was the equivalent to the birth of Christ – the first day of the rest of our glorious Gooner lives. He can therefore do no wrong in the eyes of most and it was quite moving to see him wearing the captain's armband on Saturday. I've watched all season as, despite his best efforts, nothing seems to have quite come off and yet I've continued to claim that he has always been only a couple of confidence-inspiring strikes away from 'clicking'. The sight of Dennis curling one into the top corner was once so common that it was no longer deemed worthy of comment. Whereas, on Saturday, I couldn't recall when he last came up with a contribution to the scoresheet.

This was hard to believe, considering the way he casually lifted the ball over Taylor with such aplomb. I was actually dumbfounded that he'd conjured up the opportunity – I'd heard Frank McLintock on Sky only a few hours earlier saying that when Upson was at Highbury he was the second-fastest player behind Henry. From behind the goal, I was convinced our centre-back cast-off was going to run Dennis down, especially as the youngster didn't have the bother of the ball at his feet. I've watched the replay several times and, although Upson continues to tread water, the surprise (and the satisfaction) won't wear off.

Having rediscovered the yard of pace which we all assumed age had robbed him of and such a rich vein of form, it would seem criminal to make him miss the next match. I reckon, if he was left to his own devices, Dennis would gladly walk to Milan, if required, because he will be only too aware of how few opportunities he has left to influence the outcome on the biggest stage in club football. Playing (or, sadly, as it seems, not) against the team who sold him to the Arsenal, he'll probably be the most devastated of all of our squad should we end up making another premature exit. I can't help but wonder if one of the reasons Wenger won't let Dennis be driven to Milan is because he doesn't like the idea that his team selection might be influenced by all the trouble taken to get Bergkamp there. It must have been painful on a previous occasion when they sent him on an incredibly arduous schlep, only for him to spend an entire evening on the subs bench!

Still, whatever the outcome in Milan, I certainly don't intend to come back empty-handed. Hopefully with a carrier bag full of cheap cartons of cancerous coffin nails, I could end up showing a financial profit, albeit a decidedly unhealthy one. What's more, our entire trip to Italy is really a bonus because for 88 minutes of the contest against Kiev, I grew increasingly convinced that we wouldn't be going at all.

At least I got to see that goal, which is more than can be said for our first on Saturday. Having only arrived a few minutes after half-time, there were some puzzled looks when I left my seat a few minutes before the final whistle. Mercifully, I was standing beside the bulkhead trying to decide if the press conference was worth another trek around the stadium, or else I might have missed our third, as well as the first. Unlike the poor sod I met at the bottom of the stairs! I imagine I must have sounded just a little smug as I passed on the details of Pires's goal.

If only he'd known I'd actually travelled all that way for just 40 minutes of football. In the end, I managed to mooch in to hear the managers without anyone challenging me for a pass, so at least I got to worship at the feet of Wenger for a few minutes. Moreover, Dennis's delightful effort was truly one for the treasured memory album (who knows how many more of these he will tuck away?) and, as they say, was worth the entrance fee and the trip to Brum alone.

18

Champions League: Tuesday, 25 November (A) Arsenal 5 Inter Milan 1 Henry (25, 85), Ljungberg (49), Edu (87), Pires (89)

Premiership: Sunday, 30 November (H) Arsenal 0 Fulham 0

San Siro glory as Gunners salvage Champions League campaign in stunning style; despite a glut of chances, down-to-earth on Sunday with first goalless draw at Highbury in donkey's years.

From the concrete of the Bullring and Spaghetti Junction on Saturday to Milan's Il Duomo and the Galleria Vittorio Emanuele (beautiful glass-covered arcade beside the cathedral) on Monday. I was grateful for the flight, if only for a glimpse of the golden orb as we flew over the Alps but sadly, despite the contrast in locations, it was just as grey, damp and gloomy when we landed in Italy as it had been in Birmingham. It continued to teem down for most of the trip, although before this outing was over the weather would be irrelevant.

We flew into Bergamo, about 30 miles from Milan, a mere stone's throw by Ryanair's standards. I shouldn't grumble: if it wasn't for the cheap flight phenomenon, we wouldn't have been travelling in the first place. When the trolley appeared on the plane with refreshments, Róna announced that our chocolate bar and coffee had just cost us more than the basic price of our flights!

Noticing the Irish accent of the bloke in front, we naturally struck up a conversation. It turned out that he and his girlfriend had flown into Stansted from Germany to travel to the game. In one of those 'small world' coincidences, he'd not only been a barman in the Gunners pub around the corner, but was pals with the Irish family who lived below us in our block in the Quadrant.

I'd spent hours looking up hotels on the Internet but I couldn't bring myself to book anything. Up until Ashley Cole's last-minute smash-and-grab against Kiev, we might have decided not to bother wasting any more money on a meaningless trip to Milan. If I was going to have to write off the cost, I didn't want to end up adding to the pretty painless price of the flights. But not booking any accommodation prior didn't prove to be one of my better decisions.

We offered the other couple a lift in the hire car I was collecting at the airport, in the hope that we could tag along with them and try to get a room in their hotel. However, although I had little trouble following the signs and finding my way into Milan, none of us had the foggiest where we were going once we got there. From the 40-ft paperclip which loomed into view in the town centre, my guess was that Milan was hosting an office supplies convention. Initially, this was a friendly landmark but I soon became seriously wound up when we found ourselves lapping the sodding thing for the fourth successive time. We eventually parted company with our passengers at the central station and the pickle we were in soon became apparent. Left to our own devices, we discovered that it was trade fair month in Milan and none of the reasonably priced hotel rooms offered on the net were available for love nor money.

Róna must have run into around 20 city centre hotels, returning to the car each time with the disappointing news that they were either fully booked or taking unfair advantage of the circumstances by charging through the nose. After an early start that morning, I was getting increasingly frustrated as fatigue set in and I struggled to negotiate a route through the rush-hour traffic, in the rain, without really knowing where I was going and with loopy Italian roadhogs making it impossible to read the confusing road signs. I became so desperate to dump the car and find somewhere to put my feet up that we eventually gave up on the city centre and headed out of town, following signs for the San Siro. I was no longer concerned with sightseeing or meeting up with other Gooners the next day and would happily have settled for somewhere to lay our weary heads closer to the ground. By that stage, I was far more interested in a hotel where, if it took me the next 24 hours to recover, I could simply roll out of bed and into the stadium, and at least be guaranteed to make it to the match.

It was such a relief when Ró eventually came back to the car with some good news. I couldn't have given a monkey's by then if we were going to have stump up the same exorbitant rate as a hotel room we'd refused hours back. What's more, by the time it came to checking out, we would have experienced the giddy euphoria of one of our greatest performances ever. One couldn't really put a price on the privilege of being present for that sort of sensational footballing pleasure. Ever since the group-stage draw, I'd fancied our chances in the San Siro, believing our players were more likely to perform on such a glamorous stage (as they did last year in Rome's Stadio Olimpico) than in the less elegant surroundings in Eastern Europe. Nevertheless, to insure myself against the possibility of disappointment, I was actually out relatively early the next day on cigarette manoeuvres. Having emptied all the local tobacconists of cartons of soft-pack Camels, whatever happened on the pitch that night, I wasn't going to be coming home empty-handed.

As an addict of the evil weed, I've previously always enjoyed the fact that one isn't made to feel quite like such a pariah on the Continent. So, with carrier bags full of fags, I was flabbergasted to discover the displeasing irony that I could no longer enjoy a cigarette with my cappucino in any of the millions of coffee shops in Milan. With so many smokers, I would have thought Italy would have been one of the last countries to introduce a smoking ban. Is there no hope for us nicotine fiends?

Don't ask me how we managed it, but after we'd sought refuge from the rain in the shopping centre opposite our hotel, downed a delicious plate of pasta, taxed the plastic on some obligatory Italian duds and shot some footballing breeze with the locals, kick-off time had crept up on us. I guess I might have inherited the tardy gene from my dear old dad but I seem to have developed it into a fine art. I actually love the excitement of the game's pre-match build-up but I can't recall the last time I was early enough to see the players warming up on the pitch. It's got to the point where I can't leave for a match until we have to leg-it like lunatics. Despite being literally five minutes down the road from the San Siro, by the time we'd dumped the bags in the room and I'd sought out my Arsenal hat, scarf and assorted accoutrements, which are a superstitious necessity at every match, we were as late as ever.

It seems crazy to travel all that way, arrive a day before the game and still miss kick-off. So, having taken pot luck that the car park was within the sort of jogging distance that leaves me cursing my 40-a-day habit (between my smoking and the missus' asthma, we make a right pair), I was most relieved to hear the Champions League music blasting out as we approached the stadium. I couldn't believe it was nearly a decade since we last visited the San Siro for our 0–2 defeat to AC in the Super Cup, but the majestic stadium is just as impressive as it was then. The four terraces are connected by strange structures in each corner, containing the spiralling ramps which make it a helluva long walk to a seat in the heavens, and when these are lit up at night, like many modern stadia from a distance, the place looks like an extremely elaborate prop from Close Encounters.

When we go to these big stadia abroad, they frequently stick us as far away from the pitch as possible, where, no matter how loud we holler, we've more chance of dispersing the cumulonimbus than having any impact on proceedings. There have been times when I've even given up shouting myself hoarse because it has indeed been the equivalent of pissing in the wind. To save Ró the bother of getting out of breath on a long schlep skywards, we've got into the habit of showing stewards her inhaler in the hope one of them will be amenable enough to lead us to a lift. It is also often a great scam for getting to see a little bit more of the ground en route.

However, I felt more than a little stupid on this occasion as the steward directed us to the top of a single flight of stairs where all the Gooners were gathered behind the goal. I hate watching football from behind safety nets, which are common at grounds abroad to prevent fans throwing objects on the pitch. Yet, unlike the Nou Camp, where we needed oxygen masks to cope with the rarefied air up in the gods and where the altitude meant that the players looked like ants running around on a field the size of a postage stamp, the first result of the evening was to find ourselves in a much better pitch. You had to shield your eyes from the floodlights to see the third tier of this vast arena but the empty seats up there didn't detract from this titanic occasion. In general, European games aren't particularly well attended in Italy because the matches are not included in their season tickets. The trip to play Juve's virtual reserve side, for example, a couple of years back was pretty disappointing, the Gooner songs sounding rather hollow as they echoed around the cavernous wastes of an empty Stadio Delle Alpi in Turin. Our first visit to the San Siro was a similar anticlimax. Still, it is a measure of how far the Arsenal have come under Wenger that Henry and co. drew a 45,000 crowd this time around.

The 5–1 drubbing for the Nerazzurri was another affront to Italian pride following Chelsea's 4–0 rout of Lazio in Rome earlier that month. I don't know if the carabinieri were merely vindictive Inter fans, or whether they continue to punish us Gooners for English hoolies' crimes of the past (which is the impression one often gets from the decidedly intimidating demeanour of the police abroad) but they continued to keep us locked in the San Siro long past the end of the game in the interest of our own safety. As a rule, I never leave before the final whistle and fail to appreciate the reasoning of those who do. Only on some of our less-successful outings abroad have Róna and I ever slipped out early. The atmosphere can turn quite nasty very quickly when unhappy Gooners are locked in and have to endure the rancorous taunts of home fans who can't resist the opportunity to wind us up on their way out without fear of retribution. The vast majority of Arsenal fans are not in the least bit interested in causing trouble abroad. Often, all we've wanted to do is depart the scene of our misery as soon as possible, either to the airport or the nearest hostelry to drown our sorrows. We are all too frequently detained longer than necessary and I get terrified that tempers will flare.

On this occasion, no one cared that we were locked in as we continued our celebrations long into the night. To the contrary, we were serenading the Old Bill with, 'We're not going home'. But having run through the entire Gooner repertoire in honour of such a memorable evening, after an hour or so we were all sung out. I was rapidly becoming desperate to get back to the hotel, exhausted after scaling the peaks of the evening's emotional roller-coaster ride, and there were hundreds of Gooner day-trippers whose aircraft were waiting on the runway to take them on a long, tiring journey back to Blighty. Damp to the core on the outside and absolutely parched on the inside, these uncomfortable circumstances were making everyone a tad irate. The home fans would have long since dispersed from the surrounding environs. Instead of letting us go on our merry way, it was as if the police were determined to justify donning all their riot gear, detaining us until the happiest bunch of Gooners one could wish to meet eventually began to turn malevolent.

I always find myself embarrassed by the minority of xenophobic Gooners who start letting off steam by slagging off the police and shouting racist epithets. Worse still, I get most annoyed by all those who insist on joining in. Not only are such bigoted barrages rarely justified but I get incensed by the stupidity of the sheep who don't seem to appreciate that we are hardly going to endear ourselves to our uniformed captors. Insulting them ain't exactly the best way to achieve our objective! Mercifully, the police were impervious to this increasingly aggressive behaviour. Who knows, perhaps they were ignoring our pleas merely because they were intent on a nice little earner when their overtime bonus kicked in but it felt far more like an act of petty spitefulness. It seemed as if they detained us just long enough to miss the last of the public transport, since it was past midnight when we were finally released into the deserted Milanese streets. To my mind, this was downright stupid. Instead of us dispersing quickly, it was an invitation for trouble as some Gooners dawded outside the San Siro, standing there debating if it was worth waiting for a tram which wasn't going to come, or whether they would have to settle for a long schlep by Shank's pony.

Personally, I was hoping we might get back to the hotel in time to savour the highlights of the evening's events on the box. Yet, despite being in a hurry, by that time we were both so dry that we couldn't pass the bar on the corner opposite the stadium without stopping to slake our thirst. Being amongst the first Gooners to leave the ground after the home side had endured such abject failure, it might not have been particularly sensible to bowl into a bar in the heart of enemy territory on our tod. Apparently, other Gooners who went into the same gaff after us enjoyed a drink without any problem, but when we walked through the door, it felt distinctly like the clichéd scene from the cowboy movie – in unison, all the locals looked up from the bar to give the strangers on their turf the once over.

We might have been mistaken. With the English footie fans' bad reputation, the regulars could have just been sitting there concerned that there would be some unruly consequences when the Gooners invaded their local. But I am sure we both couldn't have imagined the bad vibes. If my paranoia meter wasn't already in the red, it went completely off the scale when we were confronted by an English geezer who welcomed us with the comment, 'I'm gonna kick your head in if you're an Arsenal fan!'

In spite of the venom in his none-too-hospitable greeting, Ró thought he might be joking. With no Gooner back-up at that moment and naturally with the safety of my missus of paramount importance (no, of course the nasty smell was nothing to do with me bricking it!), discretion definitely seemed the better part of valour, so we didn't hang around to find out. After a couple of hours' wait, we could hold on for a few more minutes and headed straight for the sanctuary of our hotel room. Refreshments from the minibar seemed preferable to the possibility of a smack in the mouth.

I couldn't wait to hit the newspaper kiosk in the morning and grab a copy of each of the three dedicated sports dailies. I am always very jealous of sports fans on the Continent. With reams of daily, in-depth footie analysis they are so well catered for. By comparison, we have to make do with a couple of columns in the broadsheets and mostly gossip-mongering amongst the utter tosh on the back pages of our trashy tabloids. My French might be fairly good but I struggle to understand a word of Italian without the aid of a dictionary. Nevertheless, there was no mistaking the eulogies in the banner headlines and I headed straight for the café in the shopping centre to pour over the praise heaped upon the Gunners. Wearing my most conspicuous Arsenal T-shirt, I was hoping I might bump into my mate from the previous day for some more friendly banter. I couldn't resist the opportunity to really put the boot in with my teasing requests for him to translate the tastiest morsels.

No matter how we've performed on foreign soil, when out on the town the following day I am always sure to wear some article of Arsenal apparel with pride. As an ambassador for the club abroad, there's always this sense that one is obliged to be polite, courteous and at least make some attempt to converse in the local lingo, in the hope of repairing several decades' worth of damaged reputations and balance the dreadful image of a small minority of boozed-up Gooner bozos who only reinforce the stereotype with their disrespectful behaviour. Although, on this occasion, I felt so swollen with pride that I would have preferred a large neon Arsenal emblem flashing above my head, instead of just having my allegiance emblazoned across my chest.

Departing from the far-too-familiar drizzle in Milan the next day, we flew back to Stansted knowing that we still needed to defeat the Russians in a couple of weeks' time to qualify for the knockout stage of the Champions League. Otherwise, there would be no more foreign jollys with which to restock my cheap cigarette stash. Still, I had a couple of carrier bags full of fags to keep me going in the near future and the sort of magical memories of a European night par excellence which will live with me for ever and a day.

'HENRY UMILIA L'INTER' (*La Gazzetta dello Sport*) Followed by Hot Dogs, More Henry and a Second Celtic Coming?
1 December 2003

The kid of a neighbour from the flat downstairs accompanied me to Highbury on Sunday in Róna's stead. If ever I become a little blasé about the privilege of our permanent pitch at Highbury, providing a rare treat of a trip to The Home Of Football for a youngster like Jamel is always the best remedy. It's extremely gratifying to witness the familiar floodlit scene with an innocent youngster's wide-eyed wonderment. I positively revel in this vicarious thrill which is guaranteed to revive many of my own goose-bump memories. It was therefore for this lad that I was most gutted on Sunday, as he missed out on the high-five festivities and euphoria which would have resulted from a goal by the Gunners.

Few would have blinked if we had drawn up at Birmingham and beaten Fulham 3–0 at home. However, obviously after such an amazing week of football, Sunday's game was always likely to be something of an anticlimax. With Chelsea about to take points from United (1–0), it was hard not to be disappointed with this scoreless draw. Poor Jamel! The Arsenal have scored in 46 League encounters at Highbury since the last time we drew a blank at home to Boro, all the way back in April 2001. So, it was bound to happen again at some point and it was just maddening that it was Jamel's misfortune to fall victim to Murphy's law.

It's hard to believe that an Arsenal side, whose reputation was previously built on their obdurate ability to bore the points off any opponent, has managed a goal in every League game at Highbury for more than two and a half years.

I was originally attracted to the Gooner faith, rather than the doctrine of 'fancy Dan' football espoused by our north London rivals, because there was something about the Gunners' irrepressible resolve which rocked my cradle. I therefore grew up on a relatively dour diet of 'boring, boring Arsenal's distinctive brand of footie, where the result was the be all and end all, and goals (plural!) were a rare bonus. To be downhearted that we were deadlocked after such a supremely dominant display was dumbfounding evidence of how far removed Wenger's entertainers are from Bertie Mee's Double winners.

Before the match, the media queried whether the Fulham manager might adopt similar tactics to those which resulted in their shock triumph at Old Trafford. However, Coleman proved he's a cute customer and that the Cottagers' fourth place in the table is no fluke. Against United, he realised that his team had to take the game to the home side if they were going to get any change out of the champions.

So, there was little surprise, as far as I was concerned, when he opted for a policy of containment on our narrow pitch.

The Sky execs might have frowned at the negative tactics which left poor Louis Saha ploughing a lonely furrow up front (such unadventurous football is hardly likely to have their punters rushing to purchase pay-per-view season tickets), yet, having left Highbury with a precious away point, Coleman's ploy certainly proved correct as far as Fulham were concerned.

Such frustrating football from the visitors is another reason I was flabbergasted to discover our amazing domestic scoring record. Sadly, we've seen far too many shut-outs at Highbury in the Champions League and I am surprised that no Premiership sides have achieved the same in the past couple of seasons. Coleman took a leaf out of Ronald Koeman's book; his Ajax team came to Highbury with similarly limited ambitions. I imagine we will be 'treated' to more of the same against Moscow next week. However, you have got to figure that if the Arsenal manufacture anywhere near as many as the 22 shots on goal (as we fired at Fulham) against the Ruskies, the law of averages should surely ensure that we stick at least one away.

Funnily enough, I had been telling anyone who would listen that I always fancied us getting some sort of result in the San Siro. Naturally, no one could have predicted the tantalising ten-minute spell when we completely annihilated the Italian side but I didn't think Inter were anywhere near as brilliant as Butch Wilkins would have had us believe after they battered us at Highbury. What's more, with our frightening pace, we are perfectly suited to playing away on the wide expanses of pitches such as the San Siro, where the home team's obligation to attack leaves them prone to our counter-attacking prowess.

I have always been frightened that Champions League qualification would come down to the wire. Lokomotiv are guaranteed to get ten men behind the ball. With so little space for us to exploit, they'll make scoring as tricky a business as possible. Should we fail (heaven forfend!), previously it would merely be seen as an ignominious but unsurprising exit – probably through the totally absurd trapdoor into the penny-ante UEFA Cup, which must seem an outrageously unfair financial fail-safe as far as the existing competitors are concerned. After inflicting the worst defeat on the Italian side in the San Siro for 42 years, the Arsenal have raised European expectations to the point where it would now be an absolute disaster if this Gunners side doesn't go on to do justice to the peerless talents of the likes of Thierry Henry and Patrick Vieira.

At Highbury, the Arsenal are usually at their best against those sides who show some ambition. If Fulham have set an example for all who follow, we are likely to spend the entire second half of the season sitting on the edge of our seats, as our opponents attempt to soak up the pressure. I'll be relying on our awaydays for some heartening relief to such Highbury stress! Still, if we had to concede top spot, I hope that it was in our favour that it was to Chelsea. If all three are still fighting it out come the run-in, you've got to fancy that it will be the first-timers who are favourites to have the collywobbles.

Meanwhile, with a fair few false dawns since the days of Brady, Stapleton and O'Leary, I am cautious about tempting fate by forecasting a far-too-tardy Celtic coming. The cultured football of Stephen Bradley continues to impress in an incredibly competitive reserve/youth-team environment, but he appears short of some second helpings if he's to gain the meat on his bones necessary to hold his own in midfield in the men's game. However, the Arsenal's FA Youth Cup challenge this season includes a teenage Irish triumvirate, with 17-year-old midfielders Patrick Cregg and Stephen O'Donnell supporting the spearhead, 15-year-old Anthony Stokes.

Admittedly, it was only against Crawley Town but this child star thumped home four goals in a third round 9–0 goalfest. Within earshot of the aeroplanes at Gatwick, those fortunate to be there on Friday night might just have seen the centre-forward's career taking off. Whatever the future might hold, Stokes has already etched himself into Arsenal folklore having arrived from Man Utd feeder club Shelbourne. Apparently, United were prepared to part with £500,000 to land this highly prized prodigy. So, it was some coup for Liam Brady to bring him to Highbury when we are led to believe that the Arsenal haven't a brass razoo.

As for Jamel, he was seduced by the smell of onions, sizzling away on the stalls around THOF. Sold out of hot dogs and bagels, there was little satisfaction to be had at Highbury on Sunday as far as grub or goals were concerned, so I bought him one on our way home by way of consolation. Yet, when I thought of the miserable scoreless draws I've seen over many years, a sausage in a bun was somewhat superfluous when Jamel had just had his fill of watching the world player of the year.

19

Carling Cup: Tuesday, 2 December (H) Arsenal 5 Wolverhampton Wanderers 1
Aliadière (24, 71), Kanu (68), Wiltord (79), Cesc (88)
Premiership: Saturday, 6 December (A) Arsenal 1 Leicester City 1 Gilberto (60)

Aliadière in the ascendancy as 'the kids are all right' in the Carling Cup, where Cesc breaks Cliff 'Boy' Bastin's record as youngest ever goalscorer; Ash left ruing red card resulting from two-footed lunge and Premiership progress hampered by late giveaway of two precious points at Leicester's new gaff; Arsène Wenger rebuffs Reyes rumours.

I am no big fan of the Spanish football coverage on Sky and, although I don't watch La Liga matches religiously, if there's nothing better on the box at the weekend, I might check out how Golden Balls is getting on at Real. In light of the transfer tittle-tattle, I found myself tuning into the Galacticos' game against Sevilla. I thought I'd check out Reyes and was fortunate to have picked the one game which really thrust the youngster into the spotlight as he almost single-handedly ran Real ragged, having a hand in three of Sevilla's four goals. If the rest of the footballing world weren't aware of the winger's ability before, they certainly were now. It occurred to me that if the Arsenal were interested prior, it was likely they'd just missed the boat because this slaughter of the Spanish giants had undoubtedly added an extra few million to Reyes' price, probably putting him beyond the reach of our club's empty pockets.

This Time Next Week . . .?
8 December 2003

Winter draws nigh and as the wind whipped around the terracing on our first ever (and hopefully not our last) visit to the Walkers Stadium on Saturday, I reached inside my pocket for some protection. Róna reckons my Wee Willie Winkie-type Arsenal titfer makes me look a right dork but what do I care? It's warm and, with my lucky Shamrock badge attached, we were one up within a few minutes!

If I had known it was going to be so effective, I would have pulled my hat down over my ears an hour earlier because it had been a dreadfully dour affair until Dennis Bergkamp illuminated a decidedly grey afternoon with his inspirational assist for Gilberto's goal. A move which started out with Pires passing the ball out to the Dutchman on the wing ended with an passionate embrace from the eccentric lady beside me, as though we'd just won the Premiership itself. I wouldn't flatter myself by thinking she was making a pass; it was far more probable that this manifestation of her euphoria was related to the whiff I caught of wacky-baccy at the break.

With hindsight, perhaps someone should have passed Ashley Cole a half-time spliff, in the hope that he would chill out a bit. No matter that Ben Thatcher is a Spurs reject, or that he roughed the Arsenal's Calvin Klein model in some first-half hanky-panky with Freddie; I cannot possibly condone the rush of blood to the head which saw Ash haring across the width of the pitch to hurl himself into a shocking, potentially career-wrecking challenge. Personally, I love a game with plenty of needle and loads of argy-bargy to inflame the passions of the all-too-often impassive punters – so long as there is no intent to cause actual harm. However, as stupid as I thought Ashley was, especially since he got himself sent off in the process and put his teammates under pressure, I find I cannot be too critical.

The red and white spirit coursing through Cole's bones that causes him to stick the boot in a little too wantonly is part and parcel of the 'never say die' commitment to the Arsenal cause which was crucial in our continued involvement in the Champions League. Saturday's rough comes with the smooth of saving one last puff of breath to sprint into the box and score his crucial winner in the dying seconds against Kiev. It might be argued that Arsène Wenger should be the pumice-stone mentor who must polish off Cole's coarsest edges. Yet I will take Ashley any day, even with the occasional rash act of youthful overexuberance, rather than someone like Sylvain Wiltord and his apparent indifference.

Perhaps I was watching the Premiership round-up on Saturday

night through rose-tinted specs in need of a wipe, or is it merely my Gooner siege mentality? I didn't think there was any less intent in the incident involving Stephen Gerrard and Solano. Football is indeed a fickle pastime with Gerrard's foul not even rating a card of any colour, a review by the video panel or the wrath of that old woman Des Lynam. It remains to be seen whether Cole's eventual suspension will prove costly (someone should have told him it's the turkey that's supposed to get stuffed over Christmas). Yet considering playing ten-a-side is not exactly an uncommon occurrence for the Arsenal, he's far from the sole culprit of Saturday's two-point clanger.

If the Gooners celebrated our goal with gay abandon, then Leicester's last-gasp equaliser was a swift kick which knocked the wind out of 3,000 guts. We only left home at 1.15 p.m. earlier that afternoon. However, a fairly short and for once traffic-free trip up the motorway meant that miraculously we only missed the first 10 minutes. Mind you, there was so little of merit during the entire 45 that we might as well have saved some fuel by sparing the horses and sauntered up for a somewhat more stimulating second half. It's certainly not what I would have wished for but at least our last-minute lapse in concentration will have hopefully contributed to keeping Leicester up, as it's one of our least-arduous awaydays. Although, if we end up a whisper away from winning the title, I have no doubt it will be this draw which will be responsible for a good deal of Gooner regret!

You might have seen Leicester's goal written up as a hopeful long punt by Impey from almost halfway, Scowcroft heading it back across the penalty area for Hignett to run in and stab home. Yet, from where I was sitting, it was a lamentably lazy, injury-time effort to compete for a header by Gilberto with Pascal Cygan having switched off seconds too early, letting the scorer get goal-side. It may all be 'ifs and buts', yet neither of these two would be to blame if our blinking keeper had hung onto the ball for a few seconds, instead of twice handing possession back by hoofing it downfield. Perhaps the German's head had failed to clear after a grievous assault from Les Ferdinand's nipple?

I can only wonder as to Wiltord's excuse. Coming on as a sub for the last half hour, the French striker's apparent lack of effort was nothing short of criminal. He could have saved this game single-handedly, if only he'd deigned to run around for a few minutes and offer the Arsenal an outlet up front. OK, so the Walkers Stadium ain't exactly the San Siro but he could easily have appeased the punters by at least feigning the slightest interest. Wiltord's apathy seemed so patent to me that, in Arsène's shoes, I would have had no qualms about admonishing him with the ultimate affront of subbing the sub. I'm sure Kanu could have held the ball up and I would have rather he had brought Aliadière back on than allow Sylvain to diss us fans in such an infuriating fashion.

By contrast, Thierry Henry's commitment is often such that his only crime can be not knowing when to conserve his energy for those areas where he is most effective. I'm told it's been three years since the Arsenal played in the Premiership without both Titi and Vieira. Let's hope Wenger hears 'Present, sir' from his star pupils when taking the register on Wednesday and awards gold stars to both by the final whistle. Going out of Europe last season put everyone on such a downer, it was as if there'd been a death in the Arsenal family. Surprised to find ourselves installed amongst the bookie's favourites after our amazing Italian escapade, expectations have now been raised to the point where the mood will be even blacker should we fail against the Muscovites.

Vanquish Vassily and co. (I assume there's at least one amongst the Russians' numbers) and, who knows, in the words of the wise one, 'This time next week we could all be millionaires' emotionally speaking, riding along on the crest of a wave of confidence which might carry us through a merry month stuffed full of modest encounters. Not to mention avoiding the cream in the knockout stages of our next Continental adventure. Mind you, if all of our opponents were females, as far as our date up at Elland Road in the third round of the FA Cup is concerned, I certainly don't fancy ours much!

20

Champions League: Wednesday, 10 December (H) Arsenal 2 Lokomotiv Moscow 0 Pires (12), Ljunberg (67)

Premiership: Sunday, 14 December (H) Arsenal 1 Blackburn Rovers 0 Bergkamp (11)

Home win gives Arsenal first place in Champions League group; seeded status lands us a satisfactory draw with Celta Vigo; Gunners go top after grinding out a single-goal victory against Rovers.

One Egg May be un Oeuf but One Goal . . .?
15 December 2003

The time when the traditional '1–0 to the Arsenal' was considered job done at Highbury is a distant memory. According to the old joke, 'one egg may be an oeuf' but these days one goal certainly isn't. With memories still fresh of Leicester's last-gasp kick in the guts the previous weekend, half-time at Highbury on Sunday found me hoping that we weren't going to end up ruing a couple of golden opportunities to establish a comfortable two-goal cushion.

It wasn't so long ago that the failure to bury a ball set up on a plate for an Arsenal player would have resulted in the entire audience getting on the culprit's back with an audible groan ringing around the ground. Instead, the consistency of the high-calibre football on offer at Highbury has seen the home crowd become a little more patient. We tend to applaud the delightful football which creates the opportunities, even when there is no end product, in the knowledge that there's no panic. Unlike London buses, there will be another one along in a minute.

However, as with Blackburn's previous, recent visits, after the break the ball continued to be attracted to Brad Friedel's big hands, like metal to a magnet. By contrast, the hands on the clockface above the Clock End wouldn't move quickly enough. They crept around, far too slowly for my liking, towards 4.45 p.m. and, the longer the score remained at 1–0, the more one sensed a tide of tension sweeping over the terraces, transmitting itself onto the playing surface. After blowing four of the last six League points and the Blues slipping up against Bolton the previous day, a victory was vital both to re-establish our superiority at the top of the table and to stamp out any thoughts that Blackburn had become a bit of a bogey team.

As we gripped our seats for the white-knuckle ride of the entire second half, Souness and his side sensed their opportunity from the increasingly nervous atmosphere and the somewhat leaden Arsenal legs after our midweek endeavours against Lokomotiv Moscow. Like the footballing equivalent of two chess grandmasters, when Souness attempted to force the issue with the substitutions of young Steven Reid and Andy Cole, Wenger responded by replacing the grace of Bergkamp with the graft of Ray Parlour. Arsène retained the energy of Edu in reserve to trump Souness's last card of an ineffectual Dino Baggio. If Baggio was a boxer, his season at Blackburn amidst the hurly-burly of the Premiership would be one fight too many. I guess at least he doesn't have to worry about any blows around the head whilst he's sitting on his backside counting all his bread!

It's at times like the last half hour on Sunday that I wish Highbury wasn't quite so deserving of the Library ridicule. When the team most needed some encouragement from the crowd to inspire one last effort to secure that second goal which would have eased our anxieties and enabled us to enjoy what was left of the match, all you could hear amidst an audience of 38,000 was the sound of the players' shouts on the pitch. The announcer had informed us at half-time that the Cork hurling team were the guests of both the sponsors. While I am sure they will have been impressed by Highbury in all its glory, I bet they are used to a good deal more noise from a much smaller crowd.

Perhaps the Gooner faithful have become too blasé but we didn't once hear a rendition of 'We are top of the League' to remind our lot what they were playing for. In an almost eerie silence, save for the lonely soldier in Blackburn's barmy army doing his best to stir things up by relentlessly banging his blasted drum (thank heavens I don't have to sit next to him!), the Arsenal sat back and invited Rovers on to them. It felt as though an equaliser was almost inevitable. When it eventually came, the biggest shock was that we finally caught a break from a referee who, in ruling it out for a foul, was perhaps acting according to his conscience, after ignoring Henry's fairly blatant penalty claim prior.

The nearer we got to the final whistle, the more evident the nerves. Players who were previously retaining possession, calmly passing the ball out of defence, were suddenly hoofing it anywhere away from the danger zone. Earlier in the season, we might have succumbed to Blackburn's brief bout of sustained pressure, but thankfully our defence now has an ever-increasing look of solidity about it. Our right flank has been virtually unbreachable whilst patrolled by the immensely powerful Kolo Touré. His marauding raids forward have been so effective that everyone has almost forgotten he was only moved from centre-back to stand in for the suspended Lauren. If Kolo lacks anything in close ball control, he more than makes up for it with his amazing pace, power and unquenchable enthusiasm. There are those, including Kolo himself, who say that his brother, Yaya, is better (from the little I've seen, there is more than a passing resemblance to Patrick Vieira and not just in looks!). Yet this incredibly versatile kid from the Ivory Coast has made such a positive impression on the Arsenal faithful this season that he has almost single-handedly silenced the West Upper whingers, who would have otherwise been bemoaning our lack of transfer activity.

Still, as the January window approaches, the speculation intensifies. Personally, I prefer to focus on all the other promising youngsters on the Arsenal's books. One of the positive aspects to the weekend's heavy workout is that Wenger won't be tempted by Treble fever to include many of last Sunday's team at West Brom on Tuesday. It looks like I might end up going to the Hawthorns on my tod. While the majority might prefer to remain at home rather than schlep up to the Midlands to watch the reserves, I am looking forward to another opportunity to rate some of our exciting prospects in the hope they might produce a performance which will compare favourably to the Cup exit of their counterparts at Man Utd.

Following on from our remarkable European comeback after a calamitous start, it was psychologically important to leapfrog United in the League this weekend. I always felt that Scholes was the missing

'X' factor attributable for Man Utd's recent mediocrity. With his return to fitness, it would have been a crucial fillip if we'd presented them with top spot as a Christmas present. We were on such a high after winning on Wednesday that we could quite easily have been consumed by the hype and humbled by both Blackburn's work rate and our own bumptious attitude.

To be honest, having booked our flights to Spain, I am relieved we can forget about Europe until February and focus on domestic matters. I spent a frantic couple of hours prior to Friday's draw trying to suss out flight prices to feasible airports for our seven possible opponents. Touristically and financially speaking, Prague would have been my preferred choice. It is supposed to be a beautiful city and the flights were peanuts. Failing that, so long as we weren't drawn against either of the German clubs, it didn't really matter to me where we ended up. I think that, on our day, we are now capable of beating anyone, and the likes of Ryanair and Easyjet don't fly within 150 miles of the 4 remaining destinations which the draw might throw up. So, all my research was in vain.

Meanwhile, I am absolutely made up that Thierry Henry is about to receive the recognition he truly deserves as currently the greatest footballer on the planet. I don't think Ronaldo has done enough in the past year to merit nomination. You could argue that Zizou is a more gifted player all round but, in my biased opinion, he's had better years and Titi has entertained more than his compatriot during this period.

Fergie was probably just stirring the pot with his 'one-man team' taunts but he missed the point. As important as Henry is to the Arsenal, the key to our ability to beat the very best is the contribution from the like of Pires and Ljungberg. Titi terrifies the life out of our opponents and it will be crucial that his teammates can conjure up some goals while Henry distracts most of the defence. My optimistic mood is founded on the fact that after a few frustratingly fallow months, both these two appear to be finding some of the form which made them Highbury heroes in the first place. Henry is brilliant and will only get better but mark my words, if we are to fulfil our European and domestic promise, it will depend on Robbie and Freddie scoring double figures.

21

Carling Cup: Tuesday, 16 December (A) Arsenal 2 West Bromwich Albion 0 Kanu (25), Aliadière (57)
Premiership: Saturday, 20 December (A) Arsenal 1 Bolton Wanderers 1 Pires (57)

Into the Carling Cup semis with a lesson in finishing for Baggies; Rio Ferdinand handed an eight-month ban by the FA for missed drugs test; outplayed at Reebok despite taking the lead.

Apart from a rare opportunity for an unusual trek to a club I haven't visited before, another attraction of the Carling Cup, as far as I am concerned, is that since Arsène started using the competition as a proving ground for the youngsters, the away games are guaranteed to sort out the Gooner wheat from the glory-hunting chaff. I adore these games because while there might be a few million watching on the box, for the 1,000-odd Gooners who bother to make the trip to support a second-string Arsenal side, it's as though we're all members of an exclusive club.

I have to admit to being a dreadfully unsociable bugger. I suppose it has something to do with the fact that we live so close to THOF and that I don't really drink, but I very rarely make it to a pub before the game (I'm invariably far too late). As a result, I may have communicated with thousands of Gooner mates on the net in recent years but I haven't met very many of them in person, and therefore only have a handful of close football pals. Nevertheless, it amazes me that Róna and I can go to an FA Cup final at the Millennium Stadium and, unless we've specifically arranged to meet up with other Gooners, there's every possibility that amidst all those thousands of Arsenal fans, the two of us can go the entire afternoon without recognising a single soul.

Whereas, at a match like the one at the Hawthorns, I was standing people-watching with my pre-match cuppa and everywhere I looked there was a familiar face. Folks with whom I might have shot some Arsenal breeze, whose names I don't know but whom I often spot at most away games. Total strangers whom I've happened to sit next to on a particularly joyous Gooner occasion, when our inhibitions have evaporated with the euphoria and we've ended up hugging each other as if we've been buddies since birth. Not forgetting the few Gooner pals that I do know personally, whom I invariably bump into at every away game and many of whom are the sorts of folk whose opinions I might respect but who seem to spout opinions from the exact opposite end of the spectrum to my own. Amongst football's most intriguing attractions is the potential for a friendly barney with your buddies which leaves you wondering whether you've actually been watching the same game!

At the Hawthorns, I spotted two Gooners I often see at away games, and who were once kind enough to pick me up when I had a brainstorm and decided to try to hitch a lift back from Ipswich. Our train home had broken down and with thousands packed in the station and only a raised-eyebrow response to my enquiries as to how many hours it might take to get the train shifted and provide a replacement, I suddenly decided to start walking with my thumb out. I was following the crowds without really knowing where I was going or having the sense to check with a local that I was heading in the right direction. When the throng began to thin out as fans reached their parked motors, I began to grow a bit concerned and finally decided to impose myself on these two Gooners. With every step, my situation was becoming increasingly bleak, but mercifully their white van was stuck on a verge which was more mud than grass, or I might still be walking back from East Anglia now. It was a stroke of luck, as I was able to ask for a lift after assisting them with a push.

These two were straight off the stereotypical footie-fan conveyor belt. With their cropped hair, they could have been particularly corpulent lookey-likeys for the Mitchell brothers from EastEnders. Tweedledum and Tweedledee might not have been paid-up members of the BNP but I doubt that we had very much in common other than our love of the Arsenal. Although they didn't refuse my request for a lift all the way back to London, I am not sure they would have offered out of the goodness of their hearts. Perhaps I'm being unfair and it's just my natural cynicism. Crammed in between these two behemoths in the front of the van, I was doing my best not to invade their personal space. I am not sure I would have been particularly chipper about a total stranger intruding on my own Gooner awayday ritual. Maybe I drooled on Tweedledum's shoulder when I fell akip? Or perhaps they were just pissed off at being unable to pick their nose and fart at will, as some might with more intimate mates? Yet, despite the fact that I could have sworn we were on the way back from a win, the atmosphere in the van was somewhat frosty.

The three of us were in such close proximity that I couldn't really turn my head to get a good look at them. That is, not without worrying about sticking my tongue in an ear (not on a first date!). It might be my emasculated memory for faces or the fact there are thousands of almost identical Gooner geezers at every game, but when I next tried to say hello to one of them at a match, I was completely blanked. I am not sure whether he did it on purpose after recognising the odd bod who didn't fit in with his perceptions of a proper Gooner (no beer gut for starters) or he just didn't have a scooby who I was. Maybe it was me, and the strange looks were due to the fact that I had the wrong feller? As time has passed, I've grown all the more unsure of myself, to the point where I can now walk past these two at away games without the faintest look of recognition passing between us and, as a result, I sometimes wonder if perhaps it was all a peculiar dream.

Meanwhile, one thing was certain at West Brom: this 1,000-strong, loyal band of hail-and-shine Gooners were going to keep themselves warm by singing their hearts out and if the home fans weren't going to create a proper Cup atmosphere, we had to do it for them. Sylvain Wiltord might not have been worthy of our efforts but the kids were a credit to the shirt. With the aid of West Brom's wastefulness, they kept us on course for the semi-final.

As we prepared for Saturday's trip to the Reebok, the massive charabanc that is the world's football media had already parked up at Bolton's stadium a day prior, waiting to unravel details of 'forgetful' Ferdinand's ban. I might have made kick-off the next day if I'd joined them! It is absolutely marvellous to be able to to circumvent the dreaded elevated car park that is the M6 motorway around Birmingham now that the long-awaited Midland Expressway, the section of toll road which bypasses Brum, has finally been opened. Nevertheless, in the event of bad weather conditions, or an accident along the remainder of the M6, it only means that one comes to a halt in the horrendous jams much more quickly. Poor Nell once again bore the brunt of my tardy travel plans. We left London in sufficient time to reach the Reebok before kick-off if the conditions had been ideal and I was able to break the speed restrictions all the way. However, the conditions were anything but and in a dreadful downpour, we found ourselves literally crawling along, later than ever.

Luckily, there was a live commentary of our match on the radio or I would have felt that bit more guilty because we wouldn't even have been able to hear what happened during most of the first half. Apart from Clichy playing for the suspended Ashley, Wenger had reverted to the same side that had beaten Blackburn the previous Sunday. As it turned out, if we were going to miss half of a game, I don't think we could have chosen a better one to miss than the Arsenal's mediocre first 45 against Bolton. They hardly managed a single shot on target. In a fashion similar to the way parents might talk about their offspring – 'your child' when they have disgraced themselves and 'our child' in most other instances – I've just noticed my tendency to do likewise and refer to the Arsenal as 'they' when they're useless and 'we' when I'm proud!

It was close to half-time when we finally pulled up at the Reebok. As we have done on previous occasions, we pulled into the train station car park just across the road from the stadium. The signs in this car park warn that it is solely for the use of passengers travelling by train. Yet, after an exhausting journey in dreadful conditions, I wasn't about to start looking elsewhere. Besides, at least I only had 45 mins to worry about a parking ticket, instead of the entire 90! Almost synchronous to me pulling up the handbrake, the rain started pouring down in stair rods. By the time we'd covered the couple of hundred yards to some cover, we were both completely drenched. Naturally, the rain returned to a slight drizzle that same second. If I was a superstitious feller, I might have wondered if the fates were conspiring against us.

If it wasn't the fates, then it must have been the box office or the postal service. Just like our matches at Man City, Charlton and Leicester, my tickets for Bolton hadn't turned up in the post and I was once again forced to collect duplicates. On most occasions when Róna doesn't accompany us, Nell and I usually flog his ticket so the two of us can sit together, but it was far too late for such shenanigans and Nell went in whilst I continued circumnavigating the Reebok in search of the ticket office. Obviously, the blinds were down with no sign of any life at the 'tickets for collection' windows and, after much frantic banging on the glass, I eventually attracted someone's attention. By the time I returned to the correct turnstile, having finally got my sweaty hands on a ticket, it was also closed. I was forced to head off to find a steward who could help.

We hadn't stopped for refreshments en route because we were so late but I'd assumed that at least we'd arrived in perfect time to beat the queues at the break. I must have been really starving to be salivating at the thought of the suet and other unidentifiable contents that make up a Pukka Pie. If I could smell Bolton's delicious half-time comestibles, however, I certainly couldn't get to them. There was some consolation in knowing I wasn't the only one to be caught out by the terrible traffic, as I picked up three more late Gooner arrivals whilst searching for an open turnstile.

It was a relief to finally find a steward who was prepared to assist and he led the four of us back the way we'd come, before banging on a gate to get one of his colleagues to let us in. Once inside, I was so busy trying to find my seat, concentrating on matching up the details on my ticket with the directions on the various signs overhead, that it took a few moments for my senses to kick in and for me to realise that there wasn't a 'gertcha' cockney accent to be heard amongst all the half-time hustle and bustle. Nor was there any sign of a single person wearing red and white. As surreptitiously as possible, I zipped up my coat to cover my Arsenal scarf – we'd been led right into the enemy's midst, amongst the home fans. The steward might have been very helpful but he obviously wasn't particularly high on the evolutionary scale.

Mercifully, at the same moment that this disturbing reality dawned on me, I felt a reassuring hand on my shoulder. Realising his mistake, the steward had come to rescue us before we could instigate a riot amidst the home fans who might have resented this mini invasion. He managed to pluck three of us four Gooners misfits out and I only hope the fourth person had the sense to remain schtum during the second half. We were finally admitted into the Gooner fold and, after this fiasco, the players were already on their way back out when I discovered that there was no access to the upper tier. I couldn't even wave to Nell but I wasn't about to miss any more of the match. So, while he spread out under cover above in the relative comfort of the two seats where I should have been, the only vacant spot I could find was right at the front of the terrace. Just as I was beginning to dry off a little from the previous soaking, I found myself sitting in the pouring rain. But, as they say, I guess I was already wet!

All I Want For Christmas . . .!
22 December 2003

I was so impressed by a comment written on one of my end-of-year school reports that it remains firmly entrenched in my mind some 30 years later. Sadly, it seems that the accelerator still eludes me, since according to my teacher I was a 12-year-old 'speedboat idling around the harbour'. I am not blowing my own trumpet, it's just that as we approach half-time in this season's proceedings (without the break!) and at a traditional time for a mid-term appraisal, it seems an entirely appropriate description of the Arsenal.

It would be a little churlish of me to complain. In the past, many of my Highbury highs were due to dour defensive displays where a rare goal was a genuine treat. Nowadays, we Gooners stand in absolute awe almost every week, as Arsène Wenger's side produces the most entertaining football it has ever been my privilege to watch. However, those matches involving the odd incisive break at breathtaking speed where the ball invariably ends up in the back of the net, are something of a tantalising tease. When you've witnessed the Arsenal blow away one of Serie A's best, tonking five past Inter as if they were a pale imitation of our poor north London neighbours, it makes me wonder why we are so Scrooge-like with such beautiful stuff.

Chelsea might possess a similar abundance of talent. Doubtless if they don't, their Russian sugar daddy will attempt to rectify any deficiencies during the transfer window. But if Ranieri can play Damien Duff anywhere but on the wing, where we all know he can do the most damage, I very much doubt their Italian manager's ability to effectively harness his huge hotchpotch of international talent. What's more, I refuse to give countenance to the belief that Abramovich can come over here and simply purchase himself a Premiership title. I continue to cling to the notion that his off-the-peg outfit won't be capable of coping with the relentless nature of a run-in which requires the levels of concentration and consistency that are imprinted on the memories of the two made-to-measure teams who have been there and bought the T-shirt.

I remain convinced that, at our best, this Arsenal side is quite capable of leaving both of our immediate competitors trailing in our domestic wake. However, events of the previous weekend were a poignant reminder of why we failed so miserably in the past and how we managed to fritter away our 12-point grip on the title. We might have enjoyed a Merry Christmas last time around but as we all know, it is not until May that the Championship presents are handed out.

It's been a while since I've studied Man Utd from an impassive point of view. I have to admit to being envious of the voracious way in which they went about the traditional stuffing of the turkey that was Tottenham. Much like ourselves, I believe that United's form has been fairly unimpressive up to this point. Undoubtedly, Paul Scholes's recent absence has been an influential factor. With his return to fitness and with Fergie certain to slosh the fuel of 'revenge for Rio' (whose enforced absence is likely to prove more of a financial embarrassment than a footballing one!) to fire up his squad's feelings of injustice, thereby fortifying the spirit of fortress Old Trafford, it feels slightly ominous that we've been leapfrogged at number one as the New Year dawns.

I've got a feeling that the Christmas spirit might not extend to United gifting it straight back to us! Despite remaining undefeated, the Arsenal have dropped six of the last twelve points with draws against Fulham, Leicester and Bolton. It would be great to find Glen Johnson, Eto'o, Reyes and Mexes in our Christmas stocking but I hope we've been good enough Gooners this past year for Santa to grant us the one unRio-related wish. I'd gladly settle for just some of the consistent levels of desire guaranteed from most of Fergie's original fledglings.

Who knows whether it is United's home-grown core, British–Irish grit or perhaps the Arsenal's air of insouciance surfacing in our foreign (French?) contingent, yet when was the last time you saw the Red Devils baton down the hatches after going a goal up against domestic opponents (apart from at the death of the odd close encounter)? Like the predatory sharks that they are, instead of hanging onto a slender lead, invariably the scent of blood only encourages them to go for the throat.

With hindsight, it is all too easy to criticise Wenger's pragmatism. Theoretically, replacing a forward with some midfield mettle (Parlour for Bergkamp) was probably a sensible move on Saturday but it sent the wrong signals to a Bolton side who needed no further encouragement, and left us marooned in the doldrums of our own half of the pitch for the last twenty minutes without the possibility of a 'Plan B' to nail to our mast and sail to a three-point prize. The Gunners may currently have the most entertaining player on the planet but he's hardly a striker happy to win the ball in the air and relieve the pressure by retaining possession with his back to the goal. Sadly, even at Highbury, it is such a common occurrence for the Arsenal not to capitalise on a one-goal advantage that, as the restart occurs, I invariably feel like a stuck record once again announcing in vain, 'I hope we don't sit back!'

Perhaps it's understandable considering our previous success at punishing teams with our breathtaking pace, where the opposition has been forced to chase the game. Nevertheless, since the demise of our dinosaur fab back five and our ability to count on a clean sheet, the Arsenal's achievements are largely dependent on outscoring the opposition. Ergo, attack is without doubt our best form of defence.

Titi Henry often grafts like a Trojan, harrying players all over the pitch, when personally I'd prefer him to save his energy for his penalty-area exploits. However, what struck me watching United on Sunday was how, even at 2–0 up, they all defended from the front. I didn't notice a Wiltord, drifting out of the remainder of the game, or a Robbie Pires, whose self-preservation sees him bottling out of the slightest bodily contact.

Hopefully, Wiltord, the Arsenal's most expensive ever signing, will be wending his way back to Paris come the transfer window and I'll forgive Le Bob anything as *lentement, lentement,* if he rediscovers the 'Va Va Voom' which vanished after his injury. However, on Saturday, battling against an icy winter wind wreaking havoc around the Reebok, the driving rain, 25,000-odd uproarious Wanderers fans and their side, high on having stuck it to the Kings Road swanks, it was the sort of game that couldn't be won with too many on the missing list.

Patrick Vieira in his pomp is worth three of most opponents, but until he's completely match fit we might continue to struggle against such committed opposition unless more are prepared to roll up their sleeves and sweat blood for the cause (although, we could end up reaping some reward from a robust Paddy come the run-in).

Que sera, sera. We Gooners can't really grumble considering the sorry state of affairs at summer's end: our squad stripped down to the bare bones; five utilitarian players replaced only by an unknown Swiss centre-back already with a long-term injury; Jerry Beowulf, a journeyman with a barmy reputation, in place of the ponytailed one as our principal shot-stopper; nearly £100 million in the hole we were using for want of a pot to piss in, due to a £400 million stadium development, undertaken at a time when the entire investment world was turning its back on a game which offered beautiful football but financial bankruptcy; and Arsène Wenger as the reluctant referee in a boardroom battle between those committed to their Ashburton grave interment and those favouring the sensible financial option but the footballing suicide of a 'soon' to be built Wembley!

If you'd have offered me the opportunity back then to turn the page into 2004 breathing down United's neck, only a point behind the League leaders, and as one of the seeded top eight and some people's favourite amongst the last sixteen in the Champions League (with perhaps a plum draw against Celta Vigo?), joining Boro, Bolton and Villa in a competition which leaves Gooners convinced 'We're gonna win the sh*t Cup!', I would have bitten your hand off before you could say Ruud van Sh*t Himself. Add to that being able to breathe a huge sigh of overdue relief about the Arsenal's ultimate future, having secured the inordinate amount of spondulicks required to build our new stadium (according to a far-too-vague announcement about a bevy of backers, who've yet to actually sign on the dotted line!) and we're laughing.

Arsène Wenger earned my immediate respect when he announced on his arrival that he recognised the importance of maintaining a balance in order to retain that special Arsenal spirit. Much of his instantaneous success back in '98 was based on a special chemistry which developed between a backbone of home-grown grit whose unquenchable commitment was the catalyst for the Continentals to give more of themselves than might have otherwise been natural.

If I've been afraid up until recently that these virtues have been eroded as our home-grown core has disappeared, then mercifully it would now appear that we've more cause for optimism than we've had for many a moon with a multicultural crop of youngsters to rival anything coming off the Carrington production line. Combining the home-grown fervour of Bradley, Bentley, Smith and Thomas with the flair of Aliadière, Fábregas, Quincy and Clichy (to name but a few!), the future is looking red, white and fairly rosy. Here's to a silverware-stuffed New Year.

22

Premiership: Friday, 26 December (H) Arsenal 3 Wolverhampton Wanderers 0 Craddock (13 own goal), Henry (20, 89)

Premiership: Monday, 29 December (A) Arsenal 1 Southampton 0 Pires (35)

FA Cup: Sunday, 4 January (A) Arsenal 4 Leeds United 1 Henry (26), Edu (33), Pires (87), Touré (90)

FA Cup fourth-round draw, Monday, 5 January: Middlesbrough (H)Saturday, 24 January

Excellent festive period with six points; another 4–1 victory at Leeds adds some FA Cup mileage to the Borothon.

Truth be known, FIFA and France Football might well have done the Arsenal a favour by placing Thierry Henry as runner-up in both world and European player of the year awards for 2003; if he'd won both, as most of us expected, he could have been left with little to prove. Whereas at Highbury on Boxing Day, Titi played like a man with fire in his boots and poor Wolves proved to be the Christmas turkey which got stuffed as a result.

I love the festive football schedule. During my childhood, my sister and I would hang our pillowcases on the bedroom door for Father Chanukah – consequently, Christmas means little more to me than a turkey dinner. My poor missus faces an annual struggle to stir some enthusiasm from her 'bah, humbug' boyfriend and I'm embarrassed to admit that she usually ends up putting up the tree and the lights on her tod. For me personally, this time of year just wouldn't be the same without the hectic football schedule. My only regret is that, having enjoyed the novelty of celebrating Christmas in Dublin with all of Ró's clan on a couple of occasions in the past, it has been impossible for me to join in their festivities for some years now because it would have involved missing so many matches. Nevertheless, when the schedules appear every summer (naturally after checking for the dates of our matches with the likes of Spurs, Chelsea and Man Utd), the thing I always look for is our how the fixtures fall over Christmas and Easter. The fact that there are a number of matches in a short space of time can often mean that the Arsenal's season will stand or fall on how they perform over the two holidays.

Players from these shores, such as Ray Parlour, are used to the hectic schedule – it is all they've ever known – however, with the increasing number of foreign players populating the Premiership, many of whom are used to having a winter break, it has almost become an annual tradition for them to express their shock at how many games they are forced to play and how little time they get to spend with their families. I doubt it was anything like spending Christmas on the beach with his family as he might have done back in Brazil, where the season ends in December, but it seems Gilberto was given Boxing Day off. Parlour partnered Vieira in midfield instead and, with Dennis shrugging off a calf injury, there were no other changes to the team which drew at the Reebok.

In recent years, we've been quite fortunate with the way the fixtures have fallen. If I am not mistaken, we Gooners haven't faced a long away trip on Boxing Day (when anyone relying on public transport is completely buggered) since we played at Hillsborough some years back. I am no fan of noon kick-offs, since they always tend to be even more devoid of atmosphere than usual. What's more, I have a theory that the players' body clocks are used to training in the morning and playing competitive matches in the afternoon or evening, and that's why midday games never seem to really get going until past half-time. Still, in my insular world, there are few greater pleasures than waking up on Boxing Day with a fridge full of tasty grub and the prospect of working off some of those Christmas calories on a walk round to THOF for the rare treat in our implacable Premiership of a match which is hardly likely to prove too taxing or too tense with the visit of the League's whipping boys.

Our domestic football is invariably played with such intensity that I believe a winter break might be beneficial, especially for those teams competing in the Champions League. However, I would be most upset if they messed with the traditional Christmas schedule (it was bad enough last season without the traditional feast of FA Cup third-round football on the first weekend of the New Year). What's more, the beautiful game has become so income-orientated that it is likely Premiership clubs would end up joining all the many Continental teams who spend their winter breaks involved in lucrative friendly tournaments.

As far as the fans are concerned, Boxing Day matches are traditionally family outings. I might be straying into chauvinistic territory, especially with the number of female fans these days, but I'm certain these matches are responsible for preventing many a family row, as many womenfolk are happy to have the men out from under their feet for some peace and quiet, and the blokes can avoid any conflict with their kith and kin for a couple of hours, whilst venting any frustrations to their heart's content on the terraces.

Anyway, with all that was going on in the rest of the world, I have to admit that I found the full-body search as we entered St Mary's somewhat disconcerting. It dawned on me for perhaps the first time that a jam-packed football stadium might just present the perfect target for maximum impact by a lunatic suicide bomber. More alarming was that, as the stewards did their best to avoid long delays, the somewhat slipshod searches of a record crowd at the stadium meant that it was plainly evident to us all what a doddle it would have been for anyone to evade detection. Travelling fans are used to the regular frisks, where stewards are primarily looking for anything which might be used as a weapon, but this was obviously intended to be something more thorough. Naturally, the Old Bill wasn't particularly forthcoming when I asked but I couldn't help but wonder if these supposedly more stringent precautions were some sort of reaction to the latest perceived threat from Osama and his pals. Then again, by rights we should be the safest of all footie supporters, if there's any truth to the rumours that Bin Laden is a Gooner.

The Dell was one of the most dilapidated, ramshackle stadiums in the Premiership with totally inadequate facilities. I always made sure I'd 'been' beforehand because if you actually managed to reach the front of the queue for the karsey before the players came back out after the break, you needed galoshes to get through the puddles of piss. However, with Upton Park having undergone recent redevelopment, there are hardly any grounds remaining in football's top divisions which offer the traditional fervent atmosphere of British footie. At most stadia on the Continent, the fans are totally detached from events on the pitch. By contrast, if you ask foreigners for their impression of British football, most will refer to the passion of the fans and our influence on the proceedings. At the old Dell, I loved the fact that you could almost reach out and touch a player taking a throw-in. Grounds like this must have been most intimidating for young *players but they were ideal for the entertainers of the football profession.*

It was brilliant to be able to have some interaction with the deities on the pitch. I always recall, during the big match-fixing scandal, Gooners prepared loads of phoney money for our visit to the Dell to throw at Bruce Grobbelaar. I couldn't help but admire the Zimbabwean keeper's sense of humour when he took off his cap and offered it to us, as if to collect up the dosh. Southampton's new ground might offer far better sightlines for all spectators but in an age where footie fans and their heroes have less and less in common, it is sad to think that we've also lost the ability to connect with them in this fashion. Moreover, many of the new stadiums are such homogenous structures that a ground like St Mary's has none of the higgledy-piggledy character of the old gaff. If it wasn't for the red seats, you could be sitting in any one of a number of relatively new grounds.

Ró's nephew arrived over from Dublin in advance of Sunday's FA Cup clash at Elland Road. As entertainment the day before, I decided to take Shane to watch the comedy of errors at White Hart Lane. Freddie Kanouté was top of the Spurs bill. Mercifully, the Ivory Coast didn't qualify for the African Nations Cup or we would have lost Kolo for up to a month. With Lauren having retired from international football, the Arsenal's only worry was how long they could hang onto Kanu before releasing him to play for Nigeria. Whereas Spurs had paid £3.5 million to West Ham for a player who'd already played for France's Under-21s. Pleat was understandably a bit miffed when Kanouté announced his Mali origins and that he was looking forward to the competition in the Tunisian sunshine.

We were up before oxygen is served on Sunday morning. For once, I had to suppress my tardy traditions to ensure Shane didn't miss an early goal on his first ever Gooner awayday. I didn't dare tell the youngster because I didn't want him to be disappointed if it didn't work out, but the press officer at Leeds has been such an accommodating gent in the past that I'd faxed him a request, advising him that Shane had been doing work experience at RTÉ Irish radio and that it would be a wonderful experience for the lad if he could attend the post-match press conference with me.

It saddens me to admit that I wouldn't dream of pestering the press office at Highbury with such a proposal. Not only would I have to arrange for an official request to be faxed from the Irish Examiner at least three days in advance but the Arsenal press office will rarely deign to admit me to the manager's post-match press conference. I can't imagine they would be the least bit interested in encouraging the career of a teenager.

You will have to forgive me but having been welcomed at clubs all over the country (including supposedly the biggest in the world) and after five years of promoting the Arsenal faith in my weekly column in an Irish daily paper, I feel a little bitter about the attitude of the Arsenal press office. Its employees have always made me feel as if I was something nasty stuck on the sole of one of their shoes.

I only revealed Shane's surprise after we'd arrived at Elland Road. It was about an hour before kick-off when I returned to where I'd left him, unable to hide a huge grin at having wangled press passes for both of us. I was overjoyed for my young companion that the Arsenal were kicking towards us in the first half. We were directly in line with the goalscorers and had a fabulous view of both strikes. I kept shoving Shane into the adjacent aisle to dance our jubilant jig, in the hope he might be spotted by his folks back in Dublin who were watching the live transmission. It might have been a bit presumptuous but as Arsenal retained possession and passed their way to half-time, we Gooners were already reflecting on the possibility of our fourth successive return to Cardiff in May. Despite the many magical memories since the final was moved to the Millennium Stadium, I for one will be delighted when the redevelopment of Wembley is eventually finished and a Cup final day out merely involves a relatively quick dash around the North Circular instead of all the aggravation of an arduous schlep to Wales. All the travelling aside, I am particularly fond of the traditional 'She wore a yellow ribbon in the merry month of May' as it's one of the more tuneful Gooner chants and it will be marvellous when we can sing the original version again without that kack 'Ca-a-ardiff' ending.

After Kolo had nabbed his first of the season, we were into the fourth round with a familiar scoreline. The moment the final whistle blew, I buried our Arsenal hats and scarves in my bag, it being de rigueur for there to be no public display of allegiances amongst media folk, and we dashed around to the press centre, swimming against the tide as we dodged the departing fans, trying to contain the delight which would be a dead giveaway to any Leeds fans looking to vent their disappointment. Once inside, I dug out a notepad and pen so that Shane didn't feel too incongruous amidst all the journos, and would have something to hide behind if he felt conspicuous. It was great for once to have a witness to what to me is a constant source of amazement, that the 'cream' of the British football press often can't manage to concoct an interesting question amongst the lot of them. I often find myself piping up at these *press conferences only to break the silence which the manager might view as his cue to depart.*

The one interesting revelation from Wenger was that he had intended resting Henry against Leeds. I was delighted for Shane's sake that Arsène was forced to change his mind because Aliadière was sent home sick. It would have been a crying shame if the youngster had been deprived of the privilege of being there in person to watch Thierry's man of the match performance. If anyone was in any doubt about this decision, I wouldn't have directed them to the fact that Titi scored one and made two goals, but that once again we saw him hesitating on the edge of one penalty area just long enough to complain to the ref Rob Styles that Leeds had stolen possession from him illegally, before haring all the way back, almost to the goalline, to gain it back again for the Gunners.

Transfer Window Open: But Don't Go Buying Any Small Argentinian Pr*cks
5 January 2004

Arsène Wenger reckons we'll have a winter break 'by next year'. Well, my regular compatriot in awayday crimes has already started this season. However, my horror at the possibility of having to trek north to Elland Road on my tod turned into joy when I discovered Shane would be coming for his away-match initiation. Naturally, he was devastated at the thought of missing his first day back at school when I suggested that since he was here already, he might as well stay and accompany me to our midweek encounter up at Everton.

I don't know about the players needing some R&R but unlike my pal Nell (who's going to suffer plenty of 'part-timer' stick for the remainder of the season!), I am determined not to miss a match. Never mind those poorly informed pundits who preferred Zidane and Nedved over Henry, Arsenal fans are in no doubt that we currently have 'the best player in the world' wearing our number 14 shirt.

Since nothing lasts forever and having suffered my fair share of seasons in the wilderness of footballing mediocrity, I wouldn't dream of taking our good Gooner fortune for granted. I want to be there in person to witness every breathtaking bit of skill with my own eyes. Moreover, while I might agree with Wenger that our European

Bernard Azulay 131

prospects could benefit from a brief break in the congested fixture calendar (I couldn't give a stuff for Sven's lamentations about his leg-weary international side), I would be mortified if the Premiership was about to close down for a couple of weeks just as the Arsenal appear to be hitting a purple patch.

The railways are always at their most unreliable on Sundays and, not wanting to tarry overnight in Scouse territory midweek, letting the train take the strain is sadly not an option. I will therefore have covered 800 miles of stamina-sapping motorway monotony come Wednesday night! Yet it will be well worth it for the vicarious thrill of being able to share Shane's wonderment. He's made the odd pilgrimage to THOF, which might be the perfect pitch to appreciate the amazing entertainment on offer, but with the stadium's unfortunate Library-like state, it's a totally different experience to this week's double-header.

Hopefully, the hair will have stood up on the back of Shane's neck on Sunday, as we gave it all we've got behind the goal, surrounded by a couple of thousand of equally raucous Gooners trying to outsing the choristers on the Elland Road Kop. Perhaps the home fans appreciated the way their team was out of the traps like greyhounds, and up and at the Arsenal in traditional bull terrier fashion (for 'dirty Leeds' – not to mention the odd, rabid Dobermann!) because even 1–2 down, their support remained steadfast. Surely, it's not just southern fans who are fickle, but you can be sure we wouldn't be singing our team's praises at Highbury if the situation was reversed. And we are quite loyal compared with the turncoats at White Hart Lane. Then again, I guess they've a whole heap more to whinge about!

As a potential Cup upset, Spurs v. Palace sounded an attractive proposition, so on Saturday I took Shane to see how the other half live. Of my two Spurs pals, one wasn't feeling 100 per cent and the other was so unenthusiastic that he didn't bother going. I think they gave me the ticket that was going begging in the hope that some Gooner luck might rub off my backside onto their seat. You could have knocked me down with a feather at the Spurs box office on Friday when they sold me an adjacent seat, one of the best in the house, for only a fiver (as an Under-16 concession)! I was flabbergasted.

Many people pay twice that much to park their car on a match day at White Hart Lane! Luckily, we found a free parking pitch and it felt positively weird for us two Gooners to be walking to the ground for the FA Cup third round while the two Spurs fans stopped at home. It took me back to my childhood, long before the advent of 'all ticket' matches, when you could pay at the turnstile on the day. (It must have been a nightmare for the clubs to be denied all that cash, which was once used to slip their star players 'shoe' money). With the Arsenal and Spurs playing at home on alternate weeks, I am embarrassed to admit that the old man would often take me to watch the Lilywhite enemy on a Saturday. But then, with the likes of Greaves, 'ten years before his time' Peters, Gilzean, Mullery, Kinnear, Jennings et al., I guess that I can at least talk with some authority when I say that I watched the last decent side to play at White Hart Lane!

I thought Ray Winstone was a West Ham fan but perhaps he was there as Freddie Kanouté's minder. Fortunately for Freddie, he banged one in early doors; I've no doubt the Spurs faithful would have been right on his back if he'd missed. I can appreciate Lilywhite ire but the Franco-Malian was always one of the more mercenary foreigners even at West Ham. Kanouté faces an awkward choice: collecting his £30k a week from Spurs whilst he spends a month in the warmth of the Tunisian sun involved in an international tournament or battling relegation at White Hart Lane, enduring the worst of a British winter? My Spurs mate says they won't have him back if he goes but I can't honestly see them giving the cold shoulder to the classiest player in their squad and their best, perhaps only, source of goals!

Most Gooners would say 'we woz robbed' but it felt like great value to see a live game for the same price I would pay to watch a match on pay-per-view. Although, considering Palace put up such a paltry fight, I would have been somewhat put out if it had cost us the Highbury equivalent of over a hundred quid. I suppose it only goes to prove that you get what you pay for these days!

I would have been even more indignant if our German keeper's cock-up had cost us our amazing FA Cup record. Leeds' Aussie striker left Lehmann looking like the proverbial spare penis. Not dissimilar, I imagine, to the one which was reported in the *Star* as going missing from a museum in Argentina, where it was previously the property of drug-cheat Maradona. I find myself maddened by the media when they write about the century-old record for consecutive FA Cup wins. They fail to mention the fact that if it wasn't for Henchoz's literal handiwork (with a little help from the cat-burgling boy Owen), we would have already achieved three in a row.

If we are going to continue with our undefeated run, we will have to guard against the potential for complacency as we get intimate with Boro, playing 4 games against them in only 18 days (mercifully, involving only one 500-mile round-trip schlep to Teesside). God help the opponent who has the misfortune to encounter us on the day when we string together an entire performance of precision artistry. Avid Arsenal watchers will confirm that we are producing brief bursts of beautiful football, while our influential captain remains some distance short of the dominating displays of which we know him to be capable. However, while we continue to win plaudits for the stylish sweeping moves which decorate our games, in comparison to some of the dour recent endeavours of the Red Devils, it is difficult to imagine a helping hand from a Premiership side able to overcome United's indefatigable desire to succeed.

23

Premiership: Wednesday, 7 January (A) Arsenal 1 Everton 1 Kanu (29)
Premiership: Saturday, 10 January, (H) Arsenal 4 Middlesbrough 1 Henry (38 pen), Queudrue (45 own goal), Pires (57), Ljungberg (68)

Gunners fail to ignite on a gloomy night at Goodison; back with a bang against Boro as Danny Mills becomes Gooners' enemy No. 1.

Two Wrongs Might Not Make a Right, but They Make Durkin an Honorary Gooner
12 January 2004

It was a great relief to see Man Utd finally drop a couple of points on Sunday so that their single-point advantage of earlier in the week was restored (albeit with the Arsenal a few more goals to the good). It was a result which has left me feeling a lot more optimistic than I was when I got into the car on Wednesday night, after our fairly apathetic efforts against Everton.

In times past, a point on the road was seen as not such a bad result. Yet, because we've let wins against the supposedly weaker likes of Bolton, Leicester and Everton slip through our fingers after going a goal up, each of these three games has registered the disappointment level of a defeat, rather than a draw away from home. I suppose it might have something to do with United's current relentless three-point procurement regime, in spite of the fact that our immediate competition appear to remain some way short of playing on song.

I was most disappointed for young Shane to be returning to Dublin after such a dismal performance but then not every day can be Christmas. I was just grateful that at least one of his first two awaydays proved to be a great day out. Wednesday night wouldn't have been so bad if we'd succumbed to a superb performance by the Toffees. We were merely outgrafted and outfought by an Everton side who always seem to save their hungriest performances of the season for our visit to Goodison.

David Moyes proved what a canny tactician he is, as many would have thought his starting line-up was suicide. It was Shane who first piped up in surprise, 'Are they playing with three strikers?' I incorrectly predicted that perhaps Rooney would be playing out on the left. Yet Everton had no need of any midfield spectators. They would have spent much of the evening watching the ball sailing over their heads and onto that of big Duncan Ferguson. In the knowledge that they wouldn't be able to outplay the mighty Arsenal, Moyes had struck on the perfect 'route one' ploy.

Poor Pascal Cygan will be relieved that he doesn't come up against the likes of the aggressive Scottish centre-forward every week. Our bald centre-back had a miserable night with Ferguson constantly making a monkey out of him. I assume from the fact that he wasn't on the bench, Keown must have picked up a niggle. In most Gooners' opinions, it was a no-brainer that our own 'Mr Angry' would have been much better suited to such a combative contest. It was some initiation for Cygan; perhaps the first time he's had to play against the epitome of a British number 9 (albeit in a number 10 shirt), who've gone out of fashion since the beautiful game became less of a sport and more a part of the entertainment business. I've always been a fan of big Dunc and think it is a great pity that a striker of his calibre has been prevented from having the sort of impact on the game which might have been possible without all the peripheral injuries and incidents associated with his troublesome career.

Perhaps the biggest indictment of our indifferent performance was the fact that we created so few chances. It might be frustrating but the Arsenal's far more common problem of failing to find the net from a succession of strikes on goal is a whole lot more acceptable than a rare 90 minutes when we could only conjure up a couple of promising attacks. I suppose it didn't help that an already impotent-looking Arsenal were deprived of Kolo Touré so early on. It was ironic that Kolo ended up limping off after badly bruising his foot in a typically full-blooded challenge on Kilbane, of the sort which were flying in from Everton all evening but were decidedly lacking from our lot. There is invariably a guaranteed vim and verve to Kolo's presence on the pitch, which is positively infectious, and without him the remainder looked decidedly flat.

When Everton scored their almost inevitable equaliser in times past, the Arsenal's away contingent have been so accustomed to our 'never say die' spirit being a deciding factor that we would have been up and out of our seats, turning up the volume to urge our team on, convinced that we could nick a last-minute winner. I can't tell you when but it seems like so long since we last snatched a victory at the death, from the jaws of a draw, that after Radzinski's goal on Wednesday, it felt as if it was all over. Even with ten left on the clock, it seemed as if we were resigned to our fate.

My mood went from bad to worse with the news that United were beating Bolton. I was cursing the failure of Sam Allardyce's side to come up with as concerted an effort as they had against us at the Reebok. That was until I saw the highlights on the box and realised that Bolton had really done us proud but, once again, the Red 'sold their souls to the' Devils had been bloody lucky. In view of Bolton's tradition for taking big teams down a peg or two, I'd earmarked this particular match day as one of the few with the potential for the Arsenal to gain ground on our rivals. It certainly wasn't supposed to be the other way around.

Our undefeated run has been quite remarkable but I walked away from Goodison thinking that unless United were to suffer the enforced absence of one of their crucial components – Scholes, Keane, Van Nistelrooy or Howard (who would have imagined we'd have four Yank keepers in first-class footie?) – the Arsenal might actually have to win every single game to maintain a grip on our prospects of pinching the title from United by beating them at Highbury in March.

I thought the Toons looked in terrific form when conquering Southampton in the FA Cup. Dyer has been sparkling as a makeshift striker during their injury crisis and there is something of the Vieira in the long-legged Jenas. On returning to the car, I was desperate to establish whether they were at home against United at the weekend because, if so, I would have quite fancied their chances. My optimism waned distinctly when I discovered otherwise.

I rarely bother with my phone's WAP feature (perhaps it's just me, but this wonder of modern technology would make Stephenson's locomotive look positively rocket-like) and, as a consequence, we were probably halfway back from Liverpool before I'd managed to suss out United's fixtures to the end of February on my mobile. It wasn't just the slow speed which made for depressing reading; their awkward encounter with the Toons apart, I couldn't seriously envisage United dropping a single point in any of these games.

My fatalist mood improved dramatically watching Saturday's fabulous display. If other teams attempt Everton's tactics, it could amount to a far-less-entertaining end to the season. In essence, the Arsenal weren't that different to the team which played midweek but where the Blues had been successful in stifling us, Boro, as they had before, proved the perfect foil for encouraging the very best we have to offer. I was just sad that Shane wasn't still with us to share an Arsenal display of such artistry. It might be a little churlish of me to complain after a 4–1 drubbing (when only against Wolves in the previous seven League games had we scored more than a single goal!) but if I have one minor criticism, it is that we could have managed an even more considerable improvement in our goal difference.

As I said to Róna en route home, I would be absolutely inconsolable if the title run-in is so tight that we end up conceding the Championship on account of one sloppy goal gifted to Boro. Our Library-like crowd bears some of the blame. After our fourth goal and a humble rendition of 'We are top of the League', a hush fell over the ground which made me wonder how many of us really gave a hoot. We should have been celebrating the fact that we'd leapfrogged United for the day and continued to breathe down their necks. With a little encouragement, we could have gone on to establish a record seven- or eight-goal blitz. Instead of which, Highbury regulars have become so blasé about our frequent exhibitions of brilliance that they've begun to take it far too much for granted. We can hardly blame the lads for switching off in the silence which prevailed until the final whistle. It wouldn't have been such a shock if we'd conceded a second; this would've given the result a completely different perspective.

On a more positive note, since his return from injury, all our games have been against the sort of opponents where an in-form Vieira could have single-handedly grabbed the match by the scruff of the neck. Evidence of his lack of match fitness has been seen in his failure to impose his imperious dominance on the outcome, whereas, on Saturday, we saw further signs of our captain returning to something like his peerless best. I wonder how many Boro suckers-for-punishment responded in the affirmative to our enquiries, 'Are you coming back for more?'

I was determined not to let United spoil my good mood (as they are often in the habit of doing in televised games) with a last-gasp kick in Gooner guts after an afternoon of unrequited hope. So, having sat down to watch with absolutely no expectations, I was treated to an entertaining afternoon in which the Toons showed future visitors to Old Trafford the advantages of taking the game to United. I suppose that since it was '93 when an opponent last scored a spot-kick at Old Trafford, it was always unlikely that it would be Shearer who would break this particular duck. He wasn't even given the opportunity!

I grew up with the maxim that two wrongs don't make a right, and I can't help but wonder if the officials had a TV in their dressing-room, where the ref would have seen his first-half ricket highlighted at the break. I'm sure it's not done consciously but I have lost count of the number of times I've witnessed dodgy second-half decisions from a ref who's apparently trying to balance out a blatant error before the break. I was so certain that this would be the case that I made a bet with my mate who was watching the match with me. Durkin 'the Gherkin' has been the target of several tirades of Gooner abuse down the years. His public enemy status is just a little below Graham Poll since he hasn't yet had an abusive chant composed in his honour. Although, at least he cannot be accused of being intimidated at Old Trafford, as others of his profession often are in Fergie's presence.

He certainly went up in my estimation for coming out and admitting the error of his ways on live TV, in front of the watching millions. However, I don't know who he's kidding, other than himself, about the disallowed goal! Paul certainly won't have to put his hand in his pocket in Gooner pubs for the next couple of months, or at least until the next time he errs when on duty at our gaff.

24

Premiership: Sunday, 18 January (A) Arsenal 2 Aston Villa 0 Henry (29, 53 pen)

Thierry takes the piss and the points at Villa Park; Spunky saves everyone from more embarrassment as his gammy shoulder provides a good excuse to hang up his gloves.

Some Months Still Before Bums Start Squeaking ... and I Start Bragging
19 January 2004

For adherents to the Gooner faith around the globe, it amounted to a near-perfect weekend. Not many are in Kevin Costner's privileged position, with a helicopter waiting to whisk him to and from a match in the Midlands involving his favourite 'soccer' team. According to Kevin, he was first attracted to English football as a result of 'the emotion that was in the stadium that day'. If this was at an Arsenal home game, I shall be writing to him to enquire exactly when and where? Could it have been hiding under our seats at our Highbury Library, since I've sadly witnessed little or no evidence of such emotion amongst Gooners at home games these past couple of seasons.

It's a different story away from home but perhaps someone should explain to Kevin that, while his whirlybird might have been very convenient, it's hardly the best way to participate in an Arsenal awayday. I'm sure he'll know all about suffering for his art, yet to truly appreciate the entire 'beautiful game' experience, courtesy of an afternoon at Villa Park, one must endure at least a modicum of 1 mph torture in the ever-present traffic on the excuse for a motorway which is the M6.

I'm not sure whether it's because they've been struggling to sell seats for some of the more dour displays at Villa Park, but I don't recall us ever being given half of the lower tier of the Doug Ellis Stand along the side, as well as all of the lower tier behind the goal. The Arsenal dominated the opening exchanges, producing our best spell of football in the opening half hour. Nevertheless, in the knowledge that Villa were bound to exert some pressure during the course of the 90, I was growing increasingly concerned that we might have nothing to show for our endeavours.

That was until the quick-witted Titi Henry conjured up a goal from a free-kick, where he demonstrated a speed of thought which was on a par with his amazing pace. There followed a strange few seconds of silent stupefaction, as we stood there expecting the ref to request a retake. Then as the players ran towards us, dancing their jigs of joy, it eventually sunk in that the goal would stand. Amidst the eruption of euphoric celebrations on our two terraces, the tantalising pleasure of taking top spot from our 'friends' from the north was all the sweeter for those who had been exasperated earlier, crawling up the M6 slip road, contemplating the madness of leaving the comfort of cosy beds on a freezing cold Sunday when we could have been curled up at home watching the live transmission on TV.

However, our outing was all the more tortuous. Although I made light of it to Nell and Mick, my two passengers, there was an added tension because of the outside possibility that we might break down on the way to Birmingham. It might be a semi-permanent state for many Gooners and a particularly tired old joke, but sadly a 'piston broke' on my poor old Jag on our previous sortie to Leeds. With my AA card close at hand just in case, mercifully five of my six cylinders carried us to Brum and back. With trips to Vigo and hopefully further European forays still to stump up for, a new engine comes pretty low down on my priorities.

I am just hoping that, as far as the broken cylinder is concerned, there's more of an Edu-like dependence to the operation of my old engine than the essential Henry, and that the remaining five continue to function with the fortitude and team spirit necessary to carry us on the remaining trips to Wolves, Blackburn, Portsmouth and Newcastle. Thank heavens our date in the Northeast is our last long journey and if the motor survives all 1,500 miles, it will deserve its own medal!

If the precarious state of the car was no cause for pleasure, it is the continued unpredictable quality of the game which remains its defining beauty. It may be an increasingly rare feat in an age when clubs are separated by £100 million worth of players and ever more points, yet the fascination of both neutral and partisan alike will endure so long as the Premiership continues to throw up shocks like Saturday's triumph of bottom over top (good over evil, according to some!). Ever since I sat in the car on the way back from Everton, fretting over Man Utd's fixtures and my conviction that they could survive until the end of February without sacrificing a single point, they have taken one from six! All credit for once to the red-top rabble from the *Mirror*, whose back-page spread on Sunday featured the hangdog face of Ferdinand sitting behind Fergie on the bench, under the banner 'Glum and Glummer'. At odds of 7–1, they certainly weren't alone in perhaps wishing they'd put some wonga on Wolves to beat United!

Our weekend was rounded off nicely listening to the radio commentary on our way back, as Birmingham brought Ranieri's mercenary millionaires down a peg or two by battling out a bore draw at the Bridge. I felt most pleased for all those geographically challenged Gooners in far-flung locations like Singapore and Malaysia, whose minority status means their lives are often made a misery by Man Utd's glory-hunting millions. I imagined them all with a spring in their stride on Monday morning, eager to get to work to make the most of a day when they could give all their mates some right royal stick.

I could be accused of nit-picking but personally I would have preferred for Henry to have achieved his hat-trick with an uncontroversial goal from open play. It would have been good to score one goal which David O'Leary couldn't gripe about. For a firm favourite who couldn't put a foot wrong during his long career within the Marble Halls, the softly spoken Dubliner couldn't have fallen further from Gooner grace since his departure. 'Booby' Robson's 'sore loser' snipe was writ large across the back pages when we were beaten by his Toons. Indeed, I'd be concerned if I supported a team who didn't lose their heads a little in disgust over a defeat which turned on some dodgy decisions. Arsène was also up in arms when we were on the wrong end of Ian Harte's equally opportunist strike, which has since resulted in one of ours religiously standing in front of the ball to prevent a repeat performance. However, with O'Leary having had no qualms about profiting from such a 'dirty trick' performed by a disciple at his previous club, his diatribe sounded decidedly hypocritical.

Mind you, just as a dog tends to reflect characteristics similar to its owner's (although I'm sure I don't appear quite so terrifying, nor am I nearly so soppy as our Treacle!), it's not surprising the Villa manager has become such a curmudgeon; as we informed their fans on Sunday, 'All you ever do is moan!' I could appreciate their ire. I'm pretty sure Kanu played for our penalty having already lost control of the ball. Yet, in our 'swings and roundabouts' sport, there have been plenty of occasions in the past (and doubtless many more in the future) when we've had good cause to complain '2–0 to the referee'. Of the 10,000 more who turned up on Sunday than their previous home game, I presume many (as we teased) had 'Only come to see the Arsenal'. I despair over the disappearance of such sporting traditions as applauding the opposition. When Henry's mouth was accidentally bloodied, he was accused of time wasting and the Villains were subsequently on his back all afternoon when, in truth, they should have been worshipping the ground such a gargantuan talent walks on.

Henry has certainly earned his two-week break until the end of our mini-marathon with Boro. I only hope familiarity with the Teessiders doesn't breed too much contempt in Wenger's team selection. You can't overestimate the importance of maintaining the sort of winning feeling which sees any side we put out strutting onto the pitch full of self-belief and our opponents quaking in their boots. No matter how rosy our prospects are at present, the eternal pessimist in me can't help pointing out that there are no prizes awarded in January. As Man Utd have just demonstrated, the margins between success and failure are so slim that we Gooners must guard against giving it too much of 'the big 'un' because even the very best are always only a couple of defeats away from disaster!

25

Carling Cup: Tuesday, 20 January (H) Arsenal 0 Middlesbrough 1
FA Cup: Saturday, 24 January (H) Arsenal 4 Middlesbrough 1 Bergkamp (19),
    Ljungberg (28, 68), Bentley (90)
FA Cup fifth-round draw, Monday, 26 January: Chelsea (H)Sunday, 15 February

Domestic defeat in Carling Cup doesn't really count; progress in the proper tournament to the tune of 'We always win 4–1' provides opportunity to dispose of Chelsea for fourth successive season.

Some football fan me. I blame premature Alzheimer's because instead of being glued to the box on Monday, or wandering round with a radio earpiece in my ear, as I would normally on the day of a Cup draw, I was totally oblivious, playing footie with Treacle in Clissold Park (she thinks she's Lehmann and is twice as loopy – at least Jens hasn't eaten any balls, yet!). I had to hear the news of our home draw against Chelsea from my ma, when she phoned to find out if I was happy that the Arsenal were involved in the tie of the fifth round. At a time when the FA might be concerned about the competition's stature and their ability to attract big sponsorship, if I didn't know better I would have said it was a mite fishy that the draw threw up the prospect of both a Mancunian and the most glamorous London Derby.

The Root of All Evil
26 January 2004

I took a few seconds on Saturday to scan the corner of the Clock End containing the limited number of extremely long-suffering Boro fans. I suppose I was looking for the faces of true dedication of the sort that had driven these doolally masochists to schlep to THOF three times in two weeks, travelling 1,500 miles. Mercifully, our Middlesbrough marathon includes only one outing to Teesside. With the imminent arctic snap and the guarantee that Arsène will be sticking to his guns with his Carling Cup selection policy, we Gooners won't exactly be flocking north in droves this week. I haven't been able to find anyone fool enough to want to brave the brass monkey climate and accompany me to Boro. That's assuming the match doesn't end up being postponed due to bad weather.

Considering that Boro's barmy brigade could have coughed up around £250 in train fares on their hat-trick travels to Highbury, they brought quite a healthy contingent. By comparison, I will be surprised if we take more than a couple of hundred to the Cellnet. There might be much debate about the finer, first-eleven details amongst the hardy souls who endure the second-longest trek in the Premiership but at least we won't have any false pretensions about our prospects for another Cardiff final. On our way home, after handing out another four-goal hiding to the hapless Boro, my lugubrious lunch-time mood now seemed laughable. We might have only lost the first leg of the Worthless Cup semi but I was worried about the demise of our unbeaten domestic streak. One defeat could be deemed careless but in this age of tabloid hyperbole, two bad results and the media would be rubbing their hands together. They'd be wailing about the wheels coming off in an Arsenal crisis.

Perhaps I should shoulder some of the blame for getting beaten by Boro. With the Carling Cup not included in our season tickets, I'd taken the opportunity of an alternative perspective by purchasing front-row seats just to one side of the goal. It was a revelation for Róna – as it is only if you are up so close and personal that you can literally reach out and touch the players that you begin to fully appreciate the ferocity of the beautiful game. Ró couldn't believe there could be any pleasure for the players in making contact with the sort of wayward cruise missiles that we spent much of the evening trying to avoid. Ever since I'd bought our tickets, I'd been looking forward to the rare chance of some euphoric interaction with one of the goalscorers and perhaps getting our ugly phizogs in the frame for all the folks watching back in Dublin. Sadly, the nearest I came was when Edu very kindly put out my fag with a grass cutter a couple of yards wide of the goal!

Come Saturday, I was most concerned about Wenger keeping fresh legs for the end of the season, in case the net result was premature capitulation and there were no games left in which to use them. I needn't have worried. Dennis Bergkamp's return to fitness was most encouraging. Along with every Gooner present, Dennis will have derived immense pleasure from one of his trademark chips, executed exquisitely by home-grown prodigy David Bentley, with his 'weaker' left foot (as good an argument as you can get for the positive influence of foreign players). It's about time he began to fulfil so much promise and if the proof in Bentley's pudding wasn't perfect enough, hopefully the other three strikes might put a sock in the mouths of all the doom-mongers (including myself), who've previously touted Titi Henry as totally indispensable.

Mercifully for those of us travelling, the semi remains finely balanced, with only one goal separating the two sides. But our midfield will be bolstered by our captain's talismanic presence on Teesside because of his suspension against City next Sunday. After progressing in the more prestigious tournament on Saturday, a suitably satisfied Wenger humorously suggested that the team for the Worthless Cup on Wednesday might be decided by a show of hands in the dressing-room. Personally, I am pleased that our manager has made public his intentions to stick by some of the kids and resist the temptation to resort to old war horses, who might not find this assault on the last hurdle quite so nerve-racking. For me and the youngsters themselves, it would be extremely disappointing if Arsène didn't continue to show faith in those who have got us thus far and at whose feet the Arsenal's future is beginning to look very bright.

While we know full well that Henry and his white charger have been given a well-deserved night off this week, I wonder how the Boro fans felt when they arrived at Highbury at the weekend to discover that despite Don King's best efforts on the Beeb, Steve McClaren had decided to downgrade this tournament. It's perfectly understandable, with Boro being a goal to the good in the lesser competition and so close to the final which could earn his club a crucial load of filthy lucre from European qualification. Yet I very much doubt their fans were feeling quite so pragmatic, having spent a small fortune to support a side deprived of the diminutive Brazilian who'd almost single-footedly defeated us with a dazzling display earlier in the week.

If Boro end up beating Bolton in the final, McClaren's decision to bench his best in favour of fresh legs midweek might eventually be appreciated as a bit of a masterstroke. Such logic, mind you, will have few admirers if we manage to administer a knockout punch on Wednesday and bring their season to a swift conclusion. Moreover, it seemed to defeat the object as McClaren's heart held sway over his head when throwing his three subs into the fray at 3–1 down on Saturday. They had no need of stable doors since Boro's FA Cup hopes had long since bolted. Following the announcement of the subs – 'Nemeth, Juninho and Maccarone' listed on Boro's menu – with 15 to go, most of the Highbury faithful were deliberating over what was for dessert! Call me greedy, but this Gooner gourmet is heading north for a fourth helping, hopefully with another four-goal garnish!

You'll have to forgive me if I take a moment to wallow in Fergie's misery, as it makes a pleasant change for our 'friends from the north' to be the target of a media witch hunt. After seething with indignation for so many years that he was the sole scapegoat brought to 'the bung' book, I imagine the contretemps with the Coolmore mafia which has led to the investigation into United's transfer dealings must have brought a wry smile to George Graham's face. Unlikely as it is, there would be much merriment in these here parts if, like Graham, Fergie ended up entirely expunged from the Old Trafford record books, his name removed from all the plaques on the walls as if Sir Red Nose never existed. Now, that would be an amusing turn-up!

26

Carling Cup: Wednesday, 28 January (A) Middlesbrough (postponed)
Premiership: Sunday, 1 February (H) Arsenal 2 Manchester City 1 Tarnat (39 own
    goal), Henry (83)

*Jose Antonio Reyes is signed for a reputed £17 million and makes his
debut in Highbury deluge; Titi thunderbolt wins the plaudits against City
but goalmouth spat between Ash and Le Sulk grabs the headlines.*

*It's an occupational hazard that the deadline for my Irish Examiner
column is on a Monday but it doesn't appear in print until Wednesday. It's
usually midweek matches which catch me out but the transfer of Jose
Antonio was one of my worst examples. I was picturing Green Gooners
with my column resting on their cereal box on Wednesday morning
wondering why on earth I was wittering on about boring old Boro when
the club had just completed their most expensive ever signing and the
third most costly in the country.*

*Mercifully, ref Dermot Gallagher had the good sense to make his
decision to postpone our midweek match before I'd departed for
Middlesbrough. It would have been a gutter to discover the game was off
when I was halfway there on the train. With our unpredictable climate, I
guess it was a difficult call to make. I seem to remember there was a long
spell of mid-morning sunshine that might have melted the major worry
(the icy approaches to the Riverside Stadium). I had mixed feelings about
putting the trip off until next week. Naturally, I was grateful not to be
heading to the Northeast in such arctic conditions but I'd gone to a
ridiculous amount of trouble to wangle a free first-class train ticket and it
would be devastating if I discovered it wasn't transferable.*

*Live Sky games at THOF on a Sunday can be a real pain in the backside
(literally!), especially if the earlier pay-per-view presentation is any bottle.
Two last-minute goals ensured Blackburn's encounter at the Bridge was
finely balanced and so I was left legging it around to Highbury five*

minutes before kick-off. Not only was I annoyed to arrive at my seat to discover that I'd missed out on a songsheet and some operatic efforts to stoke up the Library's lifeless atmosphere on what had been deemed 'Fans' Day', but I was upset to have missed the 'guard of honour' for Spunky, as our suspended captain presented Safehands with a token expression of our gratitude for his 13 years of loyal service.

At least I discovered why I'd heard the sound of 'Jerusalem' wafting through our living-room window earlier on. Words had been written for this stirring anthem but sadly what was being hailed in the programme as our new Highbury hymn promptly sunk without trace. 'Good old Arsenal' may be outdated and its 'Rule Britannia' tune might annoy the hell out of my missus but, to my mind, its nostalgic associations mean that it will forever remain as the 'real' Arsenal anthem. Traditionally, those chants which catch on have come from the terraces, rather than by design of some committee. Most often they are the result of someone's boozy musings spontaneously combusting into life amongst the minions. In general, with football fans' intractable tendencies, it is futile to try to force anything new upon these 'dyed in the wool' devotees.

Whatever faults David Dein might have, there can be no disputing his devotion to the Arsenal. Compared to the suits at some clubs, Dein is first and foremost an Arsenal man. I've seen him up at London Colney on a miserable wet and windy morning in his wellies, casting an eye over the next generation of potential Gunners in the company of our manager. When we beat Borussia Dortmund at The Home Of Football last year, Dein and Wenger were together in the restaurant after the game. Our German keeper's old team might not have been much cop but you couldn't help but be impressed by their fans' forceful vocal efforts. David Dein enquired, 'What can we do to encourage that much noise from our lot?'

Unfortunately, Fans' Day proved to be a bit of a washout, although I did get to hear the dulcet tones of Tony Henry. The opera singer battled bravely against the elements in his ineffectual efforts to bring Highbury to life, getting drenched on the pitch in the process, during a torrential half-time downpour.

We were all desperate to discover exactly what had persuaded Wenger to break the bank and, when Jose eventually came on with 20 minutes to go, our curiosity was immediately satisfied with his first touch. As he bamboozled Barton with a Cruyff turn, 30,000 Gooners thanked our lucky stars. Nevertheless, it was the opera singer's namesake who *proved there is only one Henry truly capable of raising the supine Highbury faithful to their feet.*

No Question Whether Gunner Jose has the 'Cahones'!
2 February 2004

Who would have thunk it! A few months back, before this season started, all the press reports were revelling in their portrayal of the Arsenal's parlous predicament. Apparently, with a plot but no pot to piss in, plans for a state-of-the-art new stadium were up in the air, the entire project suspended pending sufficient financial backing, as all the men in suits ran scared of such a substantial investment in our unpredictable sport.

Our squad was supposedly more than a little on the lean side, with the Gunners able to afford only a relatively unknown German keeper who'd spent his career shrouded by Oliver Kahn's considerable shadow, and a seemingly somewhat injury-prone young Swiss centre-back. If I hadn't seen Philippe Senderos with my own eyes, as he produced an unspectacular 45 minutes of reserve-team football in between his inordinate amount of time on the treatment table, I'd probably be concurring with all the other Gooners who've been questioning his actual existence.

With the Gunners' armoury bolstered by such unimpressive buckshot (compared to the motley assortment of intercontinental ballistic missiles bought by some of our competitors) and with a boardroom row brewing over Ashburton Grove, which saw the directors divided into two distinct camps with completely different visions for the club's future, there was hardly cause for a mood of optimism amongst most Gooners.

Even including those whose loyalty is totally blinkered, I can't believe there will have been too many of us who could have dared predict that this was a healthy basis for perhaps the most successful season ever seen at Highbury. After enduring a 0–3 drubbing against Inter as our disastrous opening gambit in the Champions League, I don't think the wildest dreams of gloomy Gooners will have imagined we would be passing the halfway point not only sitting pretty atop the pile as the team to be shot at after equalling George Graham's longest undefeated domestic run (1990–91) in the Arsenal's history but still in with a decent shout for all four competitions.

Personally, I tend to agree with Kevin Keegan's assertions that we are unlikely to last the entire thirty-eight games without at least one off-day where defeat is on the cards. At this point in time, I would be over the metaphorical moon if we could make it through another six League games without losing. It would be the icing on the cake if we could break Liverpool's longest-ever unbeaten run against our main rivals at Highbury, on a day when Man Utd's defeat might just about clinch the Premiership title; (it would be delightful but I tend to believe this particular debate is destined to go right down to the wire!).

Watching Keegan on the touchline on Saturday, his worried expression can't have inspired much confidence. Yet for a manager with a reputation for tactical naivety, I couldn't fault his 4-5-1 formation. With so many bodies in midfield, City managed to stifle most of our slick passing manoeuvres. Until Henry's 'Exocet' match-winner (which was worth the price of admission alone), many of us were wondering whether his team might poop our party with their feisty efforts.

I recall Robert Pires sitting out his first match on the bench up at Sunderland, stating afterwards that he was shocked because football in this country was sometimes like a 'street fight'; there was no such timidity from Jose Reyes. He appeared anxious to be involved all afternoon, spending much of the match warming up on the touchline. As far as I am concerned, Dennis Bergkamp will retain a special place in my heart forever, as it was his arrival at the Arsenal which signalled the start of something very special. Hopefully, Dennis will still be involved, even if only on the fringe, as perhaps the greatest era in the Arsenal's already hallowed history appears to be reaching a climax.

I hope it was a physical problem and not just his injured pride which saw Dennis disappear straight down the tunnel on Sunday. As our new number 9 was introduced in his stead, there was a certain sense of 'the king is dead, long live the king!' The young Spaniard will be no stranger to a bit of argy-bargy as his obvious adroitness has made him the number one target for his country's hatchet men and the most-fouled-against player in La Liga. His Spanish card-count alone makes him eminently eligible as a candidate for inclusion in Arsène's unruly crew. It didn't take long for the tricky forward to make himself at home with a 'handbags' incident that suggested our diminutive *toreador* was determined to send a message to all the Premiership's burly defensive *bandoleros*.

However, I have to admit that if it had been me coming from Seville's clement climate to suffer Sunday's 'cats and dogs' conditions, I'd have taken one look at the players mowing each other down in all the mud and surface water, amidst the hurly-burly of one of our higher-octane encounters and wondered what on earth had possessed me to forsake the comparatively sedate comforts of my Spanish home! And if that was his appetiser, what will he make of Tuesday's main course on Teesside and a date with the devil incarnate, Danny Mills? Hopefully, Vieira's obduracy and Reyes' inspiration will help to overcome the one-goal disadvantage. I won't exactly be devastated if our exit from the Worthless Cup saves us from the considerable cost of yet another schlep to Cardiff. I will be more disappointed if Reyes should end up on the losing side on his full debut.

Ever since the sudden news of his arrival, I've been walking around with a stupefied smile on my face. After Monday's barrage of fairly small-beer business brought the transfer window to a close, it seems incredible that on top of all the troubles at Old Trafford and the Mancunian stand-off, we have for once trumped them and everyone else in the transfer stakes. Most Gooners are wondering where the money is coming from. Abramovich might be able to blow £17 million without blinking (e.g. the £16 million Makalele hasn't made an immediate impact, so he simply spends another £10 million on Scott Parker) but the Arsenal have put all their eggs in a basket banking on Reyes' brilliance.

After having his fingers burnt somewhat with Wiltord, I don't imagine Wenger was in a hurry to act in haste again and repent at leisure. I recall that when Keegan signed McManaman, I wanted to ask him if there was any danger in signing a player who he hadn't seen play in a competitive game for three months. In contrast, Wenger had Reyes watched 40 times before he decided to act on his estimable instincts. I wonder about the cost of Arsène's caution. Mallorca's Samuel Eto'o, Reyes and Auxerre defender Mexes were mooted as our main targets after our trouncing from Inter, which was how I came to witness the Spanish starlet flagging his fabulous skills to every scout in Europe save the deaf, dumb and blind as he almost single-handedly vanquished Madrid's Galacticos. I am not suggesting they deduct the difference out of Wenger's wages but, relatively speaking, I imagine we probably could have picked Reyes up for peanuts prior to this performance.

Alan Shearer eat your heart out. Never mind Gazza's nut-grabbing exploits, apparently prior to Reyes' feet doing so much talking against Madrid, his greatest claim to fame was having his gonads bitten by a celebrating teammate in front of an audience of millions. I might be a little miffed that his arrival appears to have resulted in the departure of another young, home-grown talent – Jerome Thomas is going to Charlton because he's no longer prepared to wait a turn which might never come at Highbury – yet here's hoping that we've witnessed the start of a career in which Jose Reyes becomes renowned for breaking the balls of all future opponents and burying a few unattached ones in the back of the net!

27

Carling Cup: Tuesday, 3 February (A) Arsenal 1 Middlesbrough 2 Edu (77)
Premiership: Saturday, 7 February (A) Arsenal 3 Wolverhampton Wanderers 1
   Bergkamp (9), Henry (58), Touré (63)

Reyes' full debut ends with a goal in the wrong net and Carling Cup elimination after Keown's early bath; Dennis breaks Schmeichel's Premiership appearance record for overseas players at Molineux, where we prevail with a five-minute passing masterclass.

The trains are so unreliable these days that I often won't risk letting them take the strain on awaydays but I wasn't going to drive to Liverpool on my tod earlier in the season.

Naturally, with it being a midday kick-off at Anfield, I struggled to make the early departure from Euston that morning. I'm in the habit of buying a ticket on board – both because I am invariably late for the train and because there might be a possibility of getting away without paying. Unless Nell and I play hide and seek silly buggers, using the mobiles to keep the other informed when the conductor has passed, it's usually necessary to buy a ticket on the outbound journey. On the way back, the trains are often so full of rowdy fans (whose rowdiness usually increases in direct proportion to the number of empty tinnies stacked on their table) that you rarely see hide nor hair of any staff.

So, when no one asked me for a ticket en route, I automatically assumed I was going to get away without paying. By the time I was on my way home, delighted to be departing Merseyside with all three points, I was on the blower to everyone, smugly informing them what a cheap outing they'd missed. In fact, I think it was during one of these calls that, to my horror, a conductor appeared checking tickets. It was unheard of but I guess it was either Sod's law or something to do with the fact that it was still early afternoon and the train was nowhere near as full as usual. I hadn't prepared myself for this unfortunate eventuality but, having long since convinced myself that this was my lucky day, I was very reluctant to cough up. As I stalled for time, searching my jacket in the overhead rack, looking through all my pockets for an imaginary ticket, I must have had a bit of a brainstorm. I definitely hadn't thought it through properly when I announced to the conductor that I must have lost my ticket.

For a while there, I thought the fates might be smiling down upon me when he disappeared, but reality bit when he came back about half an hour later clutching a pad on which he'd issued an unpaid penalty notice for the extortionate full fare of £92! Realising that I'd just bought myself a whole heap of unwanted hassle, I immediately regretted that I hadn't just paid the man a relatively reasonable 50-odd quid, but it was too late by then. The following day, I sent the penalty notice off with a letter explaining that my wallet with my ticket had been lost or stolen in Liverpool (not such a far-fetched tale considering the infamous Scouse stereotype) and that I would gladly provide proof of purchase when my credit-card statement arrived. If necessary, I thought I could concoct something with Photoshop (the forger's friend) on the computer. The response I received advised me that as I hadn't furnished them with any evidence, unless I paid up immediately I could expect the bailiffs banging on my door any day now, demanding some huge multiple of the original fine.

Our next awayday of any distance was to Leeds and, not wanting to take the same risk again, I booked a train ticket on the net. I then played with the HTML code of the email confirmation to change the details to match my journey to Liverpool. Having printed this out, I phoned Walton Lane, the nick nearest to Anfield and reported my missing wallet. There was a clue as to how the Old Bill in Liverpool are quite accustomed to claims from incorrigible Scouse scallys, since the kind lady on the other end of the phone didn't flinch for one moment when I explained that it was a month back when my wallet went for a burton. She promptly provided me with the all-important crime report number. Armed with this and my printout, I proceeded to write six letters of complaint, starting with Richard Branson and then working my way through virtually every other person in authority in the Virgin Group. In my letters, I detailed how dreadful my experience was, laying it on with a trowel, explaining that apart from the trauma of discovering the loss of my wallet and all its contents, I'd suffered the humiliation of being made to feel like a fare-dodger in full view of an entire carriage load of punters.

When I eventually received a reply, I opened the envelope with some trepidation, as it wouldn't have been too difficult for them to discover the fake reference number I'd used with my moody booking. However, not only did I find a letter of an apology but there was also a voucher for a free first-class return anywhere on Virgin trains. The funniest thing was that I eventually received a reply to one of the other letters which said that the matter was being dealt with and that I'd receive a response shortly. We were joking that perhaps I would receive another voucher!

I had to wait for a journey that wasn't on a Sunday (when you just can't trust the trains) and when I didn't have any company because we couldn't both sit in first class. No one would be rushing to join me for a Carling Cup game in Boro and, as one of the longest trips of the season, I'd be getting great value from my voucher. However, Virgin don't go direct to the Northeast, so having sent in my application, it was a bit of a nightmare arranging the trip and tickets over the phone with a convoluted route via Birmingham. I felt terrible when the match was postponed because, having booked it all at the last minute, the folks at Virgin had gone to loads of trouble organising my travel arrangements only for me to have to phone them and ask if I could cancel and repeat the whole process in six days' time.

At least all this aggravation meant that there was no way I was going to blow out the trip, as I would have been sorely tempted to stop at home and watch the match on the box with all the other sensible Gooners. However, I doubt I would've had the front to phone Virign and ask them to change my booking again (they probably would have told me where to go!) and, besides, the prospect of being there for Jose's debut made it a far more attractive proposition. If my obsessive approach to the whole train-ticket saga wasn't confirmation of an unsound mind, then the fact that I set out on virtually an all-day journey to the Northeast instead of nipping up there in three hours on a direct train proved I must be completely potty. Being unable to get back that night, I justified the cost of an overnight stay on the basis that the journey was free (as was my Liverpool trip) and, after zig-zagging my way north, I eventually checked into a B&B just as the sun was setting over Boro's Transporter Bridge. It was only a ten-minute walk to the Riverside but believe it or not, having taken off my shoes and put up my feet, there was a moment when, after discovering Sky Sports on the TV in the room, I considered watching the match in comfort.

Yet in my warped mind, watching a virtual reserves side playing away in the Northeast, a goal down from the first leg, made this one of those 'must go' games which just couldn't be missed. It's easy to go and 'support' such an incredible Arsenal team at Chelsea or Charlton but come May, when hopefully the prizes are being handed out, the experience will have a whole lot more meaning for those of us who paid their dues on some disenchanting evening on Teesside. Moreover, I simply couldn't pass on this perfect opportunity to be able to look down my nose in future and sneer at all the other 'part-timer' Gooners who hadn't earned their stripes.

There were more Gooners than I expected on the windswept terraces of the Cellnet that night and, judging by the different dialects, not all of them were there merely for snob value. It's only at games such as this that one is reminded that supporting Arsenal is not an exclusively southern activity and it always makes for an amusing surprise to hear our songs sung in funny northern accents. Martin Keown's sending off just before the break hardly sent his star into the ascendancy in Arsène's book and no more than 60 seconds after the ball had skewed off Jose's foot into his own net, my mobile was buzzing with a smart alec 'waste of money' text message from a Spurs mate. In truth, this semi battle and the Worthless war were over long before that and considering how blasé we would *have been about a Carling Cup final compared with the furore of the home fans, few of us could begrudge Boro their first sniff of some silverware in 128 years. Besides, as far as my little adventure was concerned, being there was only half the fun. If travel broadens the mind then my tortuous trip must qualify me for membership of Mensa.*

FA Cup Bazookas Far Better Viewing than Jordan's
9 February 2004

I can't help but wonder if Razor Ruddock's *I'm A Celebrity* . . . sojourn in the jungle would have lasted a little longer if it hadn't been for that cosmic Cup tie between Spurs and City. Poor Razor's peeved face was a picture as he found himself prematurely ejected. Perhaps it will have been a palliative thought that the vast majority of his potential voters were otherwise preoccupied.

With my missus sunning herself in Tenerife, obviously my only interest in this salacious tosh has been to keep her informed of the celebrity comings and goings. So, when Robbie Keane's stunning strike put Spurs two up after twenty minutes, I soon lost interest in a rare walkover at White Hart Lane and hopped channels in order that I might give Ró her nightly update. Who could have imagined there would be more boobs to be seen in the exciting extravaganza unfolding on Sky? Ten in fact, in shirts the colour of the flag they should have raised at half-time, with Tottenham's tits making Jordan's bazookas look positively petite. I imagine they were as dumbfounded as the 'dead cert' punters who, at 3–0, bet over two-hundred grand on the Lilywhites (more like lily livered!) at the break with odds of 1–100 on. Even more amazing on an incredible evening all round was the mad muggins who put ten grand on Spurs to win at 1–25 on when it was 3–1, and still had faith to throw away a further eight grand at 4–11 on after City scored a second!

I am just relieved that I didn't become sufficiently engrossed to forget the footie, flicking back just after the break to find ten-man City had just scored. It wasn't the scoreline which caught my eye but the commitment from the City boys which absolutely captivated me. What with the African Nations Cup in addition to our usual fix, us addicts have been knee deep in TV's wall-to-wall coverage in recent weeks. Considering the endless hours of relatively uneventful football in comparison to this sensational seven-goal thriller, I would have been absolutely gutted not to have seen the second half, with City scoring the winner seconds before the whistle. It wasn't the thought of missing out on the malicious pleasure of our enemy's misery. If truth be known, compared to the bilious grudge borne by most Gooners, I might even have a soft spot for Spurs after so many years.

Ever since the element of serious competition between the two clubs evaporated, there's been little satisfaction in the *schadenfreude* from watching my Spurs mates suffer. Or perhaps there's more pleasure in the sadistic knowledge that my sympathy is probably far more painful than any piss taking? Nevertheless, the completely frazzled expressions on the faces of White Hart Lane's not-so-faithful shown on our screens after the final whistle almost had me feeling sorry for them. No matter how long our Highbury high continues, we'll never forget football's cruel capacity to tear out your heart and terminate all hope for yet another season, with one disastrous, belief-defying dig of fate's fickle finger.

Yet, damned as they are to a life devoid of any success, the quality of my Spurs mates' mercy is, to say the least, a little strained! I'm sure you can imagine how they danced the previous day when their nemesis, the new £17 million debutant, delivered Boro into the Carling Cup final by scoring in the wrong net. The way they wallowed in our reserves' minor mishap, one might have thought it was the Arsenal's season that was over. As a result, my compassion after their Cup calamity didn't quite stretch to remaining completely silent!

My closest mate was furthest away from this fiasco, up a mountain in the Alps. As grateful as he might have been for the timing of his skiing trip, I queried whether he felt the slightest pang at not having been present to witness this FA Cup classic in person, perhaps the most infamous game seen at the Lane for this and many a season. His response came in the form of a picture message of him lazing in a sun-lounger, surrounded by the snow and azure sky of a chocolate-box alpine backdrop. To all intents and purposes, it looked as if he had indeed 'got away from it all'.

However, amongst the ever-diminishing amount of grey matter which makes up the memory of someone who sometimes struggles to recall the scorers' names even before we've walked out of the West Upper, there remains an indelible image of Ronnie Radford tonking one in for Hereford against the Toons 30 years ago. Much like this and that wonder goal against us by Giggs (which grates all the more because I've never rated the Welshman's rampant run around a leg-weary defence of dinosaurs approaching extinction), there's no hiding place from such momentous occasions. The victims are destined to be haunted until doomsday by endless TV replays.

Whereas for the neutral, the past week or so has been a positive festival full of all the ingredients which gave someone cause to name football the beautiful game. Much has been made of the Man City faithful and their twelfth-man part in propelling their side through to the prospect of a mouthwatering Mancunian Derby in the sixth round – for the most part by the misanthropic media pundits who've made such fun of poor Kevin Keegan's failings that they can't entertain the idea that it might have been partly due to his 'I wud love it!' inspiration!

You won't find a greater advocate for the potential of fan power. I constantly bemoan the fact that audience participation is largely limited these days to a reactive, rather than pro-active crowd, although there are only certain moments during most matches when vocal support can influence the outcome. If winning games was simply a matter of 'singing one's hearts out for the lads', Wolves would have won Saturday's game before it started. As we approached Molineux a few moments after the whistle, I broke into a trot because of the noise level, thinking that we must be missing some noteworthy action. Despite having the most to sing about, the Library-like quality of Highbury has left me quite unaccustomed to the sort of volume possible from fans who are prepared to participate in their afternoon's entertainment.

I'm amazed that some papers made Vieira man of the match because, personally, I think it was the sort of muscular midfield-battle first half which, in his pomp, Patrick would have presided over imperiously. Whereas with the Wolves fans haranguing several debatable free-kicks out of the official and their team's hell-for-leather attitude, there were some seriously worrying moments. Mercifully, come the second half, Wolves ran out of steam as the Arsenal simultaneously slipped into overdrive.

I'm often teasing Tottenham fans for the way they live off the vicarious scraps from the Arsenal's increasingly rare mistakes. However, I'm embarrassed to admit that there we were at Molineux, more interested in news from Goodison than the supremely professional efforts in the game going on in front of our noses. I'd long since given up on the Toffees doing us any favours, but one learns to recognise the rumbling murmur of the terrace telegraph and, on tuning in my tranny, I joined the cacophony of incredulity on hearing that Everton had equalised.

We've grown to expect United to win with the last kick of the ball. Róna's convinced it must have been a condition in the Red Devils' deal with the one with the three-pronged fork. Still, they succeded in scraping some of the gloss off the Gunners' afternoon in the Midlands by inadvertent means. Apparently, Sky were the culprits. Within an instant of an incorrect caption appearing on screen, showing the Toffees as having taken a 4–3 lead, such welcome news swept the length of our terrace like wildfire. So much did I want to believe, that I even questioned the evidence of the live commentary blasting in my earhole.

I dread to think I've started taking our success for granted and joined all the other ingrate Gooners for whom three points away from home and plenty of football to admire is not quite enough. Nothing is more certain to guarantee the swift kick in the guts of yet another against-all-odds upset than the fateful forgetfulness that it does indeed remain 'a funny old game'!

28

Premiership: Tuesday, 10 February (H) Arsenal 2 Southampton 0 Henry (31, 90)

FA Cup: Sunday, 15 February (H) Arsenal 2 Chelsea 1 Reyes (56, 61)

FA Cup quarter-final draw, Monday, 16 February: Portsmouth (A) Saturday, 6 March

Titi's ton-up takes us five points clear at the top; Reyes reminds Ranieri it's all about quality not quantity.

Strangely enough, I thought Southampton did quite well to stifle us as we ground out a flattering two-goal triumph, but it appeared as if it was the straw which sent their manager packing three months earlier than Strachan had planned. It was a result which appeared that much more significant the following night as Boro's 2–3 triumph (over Utd) secured us some welcome breathing space at the Premiership summit.

Few will recall our German keeper's gaffe and that we could have gone in at the break 0–2 down on Saturday. Our route into the quarter-finals will always be remembered for Reyes' sensational left-foot screamer, which raised the roof at THOF with all the air it sucked out of Chelsea. Looking through my binoculars at the directors' box opposite, I spied the drawn face of Roman Abramovich. He certainly looked deflated. If I didn't know better, I might have thought he was digging in his pockets for some receipts, perhaps hoping he could claim refunds on his collection of wrong 'uns!

Money Can't Buy Blues Love
16 February 2004

Dennis's arrival might have pre-dated Arsène Wenger but this was the volley of cannon fire from the Marble Halls which first signalled the Arsenal's serious appetite for a highly prized seat at European football's top table. However, if I was over the proverbial moon at the sight of Dennis playing in a red-and-white shirt, then Titi Henry's absolutely astounding accomplishments have me avoiding all the other space junk currently orbiting around Mars. Titi's electrifying pace might have been immediately apparent but I don't think any of us could possibly have imagined (apart from Le Prof, perhaps?) that this fleet-footed Frenchman would go on to stake such a cogent claim to a laurel crown at the very summit of an illustrious list of the Arsenal's greatest-ever strikers.

His debut goal at St Mary's was a memorable occasion, mainly because I found myself featured in the following week's match-day programme. We were clearly visible in a picture of the cavorting 'Va Va Voom', standing in the front row, saluting the first of his many sensational strikes. The fact that this was the one and only time I've seen myself in the background of one of these pictures, in all the years I've been following the Arsenal, suggests that it is not exactly an every-day occurrence. Accordingly, my adjacent pal Nell has a framed print proudly displayed in his living room which has me gnashing my teeth every time I go round to his gaff. You see, I had no cause to create such a precious keepsake of Titi and me glorifying his first goal because unfortunately Nell's outstretched hand completely obscured my ugly mush. Our friendship might have survived this source of such great resentment but I've never let him forget it.

It was somehow fitting that Henry also scored his 100th (and 101st) goal against the Saints at Highbury last week. In between times, I have completely exhausted the vast array of superlatives listed in my well-thumbed thesaurus, in my humble efforts to try to do justice to the description of the prodigious entertainment we Gooners have since been so privileged to witness. Yet, in truth, even the most evocative words are woefully inadequate when trying to describe the pure athletic grace and effortless ability to turn football into a higher art form which so frequently leaves even the most sardonic amongst 40,000 spectators totally dumbstruck.

Thierry's ever-burgeoning reputation as perhaps the best player on the planet has resulted in several performances this season where he has struggled to escape defenders' undivided attentions and make an impact. Nevertheless, even at his quietest, or perhaps especially at his quietest, he manages to pull miracles out of the bag with such regularity that 'What on earth would we do without him?' has become a Gooner mantra in recent months. So, it was with a heavy heart that I headed to Highbury on Sunday, having heard only a few hours earlier about the bruised foot which ruled him out of our FA Cup clash with the free-spending Russian's Blues side.

Many might contend that the Arsenal's success so far this season wouldn't have been possible if it wasn't for the fact that Henry has been an almost permanent fixture in the side. Hopefully, some confidence will have been gained from the tonking we gave Boro in the previous round without his talismanic presence. Yet without Kanu, Wiltord, Aliadière and Ljungberg at the weekend, our problems were compounded by the absence of virtually every other established goalscorer in our squad, bar Dennis Bergkamp!

After four successive seasons as the nemesis of the Kings Road massive in this competition, any concerns I had that the law of averages might prevail were confirmed by the news of Henry's injury. There were whispers that perhaps it was a ruse by Wenger, in order that he wouldn't have to release Henry for the midweek international friendly. Yet he needn't have risked our FA Cup ambitions to achieve this objective. Henry could have merely followed the lead of Van Nistelrooy and Harry Kewell, who very conveniently limped off a few minutes before the final whistle.

Any genuine footie fan who feigns indifference about the FA Cup is either trying to kid others, or console themselves as a result of their exit. For the majority, both knockout competitions remain their last real hope of any glory. So, while I will gladly give up an expensive day out in Cardiff for the Carling Cup final as a token of my gratitude to the folks on Teesside for the midweek favour at Old Trafford, our continued good prospects in the Premiership and the Champions League wouldn't make me any less gutted to go out of the FA Cup.

Moreover, my black mood before Sunday's game was magnified by the significance of the result in a wider context. Some were suggesting that all the pressure was on Ranieiri's ragbag bunch of mercenaries and that the charming Italian's tenuous tenure at the club might hinge on the outcome of our two encounters. This was evident in a first half where there was little in the Gunners' efforts to alleviate the gloom. They hadn't quite matched Chelsea's hunger and having been needlessly booked just before the break, Vieira was still haranguing

Durkin as they departed, no doubt trying to offload his guilt on the tubby gherkin.

I opined that Patrick's second-half performance would be pivotal: either he would dominate the midfield and, in so doing, diminish the threat of Lampard and Parker; or a paranoid persecution binge would result in yet another early bath. Obviously, all the plaudits were piled upon our young Spanish prodigy. Johnny Jensen is the only player I can recall who has scored quite such a spectacular debut goal at Highbury. Hopefully, Reyes' name will appear on the scoresheet in future somewhat more frequently than the Dane's! Yet, up until Jose let fly with his left foot, he was having an abject afternoon which suggested he was weeks, if not months, away from adjusting to the pace of the Premiership.

I wouldn't know the words in Spanish but if I'd screamed at Reyes to 'pull his finger out', it might have reminded the Spaniard of a reason for leaving Seville. According to *The Times*, his defensive teammate there was guilty of sticking his finger in an opponents rectum in a cup game. If that is what he got up to in public, heaven only knows what fun he must have been as a man-marker in training!

Those Blues fans who parked their cars around the Quadrant must have wondered whom they'd wronged in a former life. If getting beaten (again!) by the Arsenal wasn't bad enough, several returned to their cars to find them clamped. I'll have to remember to be more careful than these poor sods when looking for parking down the Fulham Palace Road next weekend. I will be a helluva lot more optimistic. Hopefully, Henry will be back and I won't be heading there wondering about the consequences of Chelsea finally cancelling their Arsenal hoodoo.

If there is one enduring image from Sunday's game, it was the sight of our lot gathering for a group hug after the final whistle. It was confirmation that the Arsenal spirit is alive and well, and willing to take on all comers. It was an open demonstration of the sort of affection that even Abramovich's millions cannot buy.

We're off to Spain next Tuesday to resume our Champions League conquest. It is some coincidence that Antic, David Pleat's close pal and the person tipped to take over the managerial reins at Tottenham (amongst a casting call of thousands!), is currently attempting to rescue Celta Vigo from relegation. I've been looking forward to the trip for weeks and was very relieved when our match tickets finally turned up in the post the other day. After travelling to four or five away games this season with the worry of not having tickets in my grubby little hands and having the problem of picking up duplicates making me even tardier than usual, I certainly didn't fancy flying to Spain without them. I will be worried enough on the night without having to fret over finding tickets in a foreign language. At this stage in the most illustrious club tournament in the world, there should be no easy games. However, with Celta in turmoil having just sacked their manager and struggling just to stay in La Liga, if we can't stroll into the last eight by sweeping them aside (or at least achieve a draw away from home) then in all honesty we won't deserve our seat at Europe's top table.

29

Premiership: Saturday, 21 February (A) Arsenal 2 Chelsea 1 Vieira (15), Edu (21)

Nine years and counting since we last tasted defeat at the Bridge: 'Win the league? You're having a larf!'

The Arsenal's Whole is Far Greater than the Sum of Chelsea's Individual Parts
23 February 2004

I wonder what fans of Wolves or Man City would have made of the bloke beside me at Stamford Bridge if I'd taken a tape recorder with me on Saturday. These poor, long-suffering souls sing their hearts out week after week, playing their part in trying to pull their team back from the brink of relegation, with the retention of their precious Premiership status being their only possible reward. I am sure it would have sickened them to have heard a 'supporter' of supposedly the best team in the land slagging his side off for the entire second half, despite the fact that we were winning, away from home, in a London Derby against one of our closest rivals, accomplishing in the process one giant stride towards a Premiership prize that is just one of three remaining pots which the Gunners are still playing for. With our other main rivals blowing two more points in what should have been a 'home banker', you would have thought we would have been dancing in the aisles.

Don't get me wrong, I screamed myself hoarse during a second half in which I bellowed my head off, begging our boys to push out. There might not have been an agreement in the dressing-room at half-time but one sensed a tacit undertaking to hang onto what they had, without exerting any more energy than was absolutely necessary. I can hardly recall us venturing into enemy territory after the break and, with memories still fairly fresh of our disastrous inability to retain such a slender advantage, the tension became unbearable as the clock ticked down.

In the context of what transpired last season and the dissolute manner in which we disposed of a supposedly unassailable lead, our edginess was understandable. After all, it wasn't so long ago that this side shared something of Man City's attributes, in that our only form of defence was attack. I've always been a firm believer of the simple credo that you can't concede a goal if you keep the ball at the other end of the pitch, and I confined my exhortations to offering just such encouragement.

Whereas the constant complaining of the adjacent ingrate Gooner was getting on my 'thrupenny bits' to such an extent that I ended up trying to block out his brainless barracking by boosting the volume of my terrace tranny. Even possibly the most gifted Gunners side ever doesn't make us exempt from this sort of sour-mouthed moaner. Every regular match-goer will recognise the type. I often wonder what mayhem or even murder might ensue if they weren't able to vent a week's worth of frustration, road rage, office squabbles or the absence of domestic bliss, by taking it all out on their favourite football team.

Considering most of us would have gladly settled for a draw at the start of the day and that we would in all probability be soaking up the pressure in the second period, we would have liked to 'git while the gitting was good', 2–1 up at half-time! Yet, after the break, if our hearts were missing a beat every time we repelled another wave of the Blue tide, it must have been absolutely heartbreaking for the home fans. It was as though the Arsenal invited the Blues to 'give it their best shot' and quite patently from Saturday's evidence, their best is just not good enough. It seems our team were a whole heap more confident in their King Canute impersonation than we were.

Apart from consolidating our grip on the Championship by extending the gap to seven points, our defensive resolve was probably the most positive aspect to Saturday's triumph. For the second week running, we renewed some much-needed faith in our ability to shore up most of the holes at the back and bring home the bacon in a manner which is almost reminiscent of the 'boring, boring Gunners' of a bygone era. It's ironic when you think that the same pundits who are somewhat prematurely putting their hands up to offer to dust the silverware in Arsène's trophy cabinet were writing Wenger's team off back in August because of his apparent failure to bolster our balsa wood back line.

Our defensive unit has developed the sort of telepathic understanding which is a result of the repetitive actions of the same four or five players, week in, week out. We've not become watertight by any means but there is a certain assuredness to most everything our defence does, a direct result of the confidence surging through the squad with this remarkable unbeaten run. 'Dream on,' was my response some weeks back when it was first remarked upon that Leeds and Liverpool's all-time record stood to fall on the day United are due at Highbury, if we could continue our unbeaten streak until then. The closer we get to this opportunity of making the Mancunians' visit so memorable (for more than one reason), the more expectant I become of the law of averages losing patience and wreaking its wrath in response to such presumptuousness.

I keep studying the fixture list, with my incredulity stretched ever further, as each more likely pitfall passes without the expected failure. Those Gooners looking beyond Charlton next Saturday in the Premiership have pinpointed Blackburn away as probably our biggest hurdle in our quest for more statistical superlatives. Meanwhile, some thought the team might have also lost their 'one game at a time' focus last weekend. Yet there was little sign of them thinking ahead to Spain's warmer climes in the way they squeezed the life out of this match, with the sort of controlled display which was a perfect definition of the 30-point difference between the Arsenal and the amusing 'anything can happen in the last half hour' exploits of our north London neighbours.

With Clichy slipping seamlessly in for Cole, Chelsea attempted to probe for a weakness down this flank but the game Gaul proved a more than capable replacement. With confidence running so high, the cogs of the Gunners' slickly greased engine all seemed to become interchangeable (although no one has yet to fathom why we've got Gilberto on the right flank). Mr Abramovich might have learnt from his £120 million lesson that the Arsenal's whole is far greater than the sum of Chelsea's individual parts.

Despite Vigo's dire domestic season, I don't expect the Spaniards to be quite the pushover suggested by some pundits. As I write, Vieira is doubtful and there was a time when his absence would have left me wondering whether it was worth even bothering to travel to the airport. It is a sign of such scintillating times that I am more worried about the freshness of the seafood in the second-biggest fishing port on the planet than whether our players are in the pink.

If there is a weak link in our Championship chain, some Gooners will point to Lehmann. The gobby goalie would be giving lip to the bricks in his efforts to have a barney in an empty room. With such an apparent advantage in height and weight, I wonder why he doesn't dominate his domain by matching his mouth with his muscle, and claiming a few more crosses? Our opponents prevent him coming for corners by putting a man right under his nose but the likes of Schmeichel would have barrelled right through such lightweight obstruction. Much like Robbie Savage, he's the sort of antagonistic larrikin that other fans love to hate. However, with the German's goat definitely there to be got, many think it inevitable that the loudmouth's lairiness will eventually prove costly. My old man would have thought that we've no right to complain. He was fond of saying, 'If you pay peanuts, you get monkeys!'

Hopefully, we might be able to afford his monkey business because, astonishingly, aside from a few sublime instances (like Bergkamp caressing the ball with the outside of his foot to create our captain's first goal of the season, or the effortless 40-pass period of possession), the Arsenal have so far managed to leave all in their wake without having hit top gear. It is perhaps a reflection of our opponents' inconsistency but heaven help them all if we should hit overdrive!

30

Champions League: Tuesday, 24 February (A) Arsenal 3 Celta Vigo 2 Edu (18, 58), Pires (80)

Announcement to stock exchange confirms that funding for Ashburton Grove is finally secured; Edu, Edu, he certainly did it for me in Spain!

Supposedly, the finance for our new stadium had been sorted since the start of the year but the project got the official green light when the details of the £260 million loan (borrowed from a consortium of banks, to be repaid over 14 years) for the £360 million project were revealed. I'd missed the news of 'a historic day' (according to the club chairman) because we were already in Spain but I didn't need an announcement to tell me what I'd seen with my own eyes. The arrival of giant cranes, hoardings, and the general comings and goings on and around the site had multiplied tenfold in recent weeks compared to the relative stagnation of the past few months.

The clincher as far as I was concerned came as we headed for Heathrow on Monday. I noticed for the first time that there was something missing from the corrugated wall of the huge green shed which was a builders' merchants on Drayton Park. This company was one of the most vocal protesters about the compulsory purchase orders and, every time I drove down Highbury Hill, their building would loom into view, along with a prominently displayed 'We Are Not For Sale' sign which had been there ever since the new stadium was first mooted. That day, the sign was conspicuous by its absence and with this company having done everything in their power to obstruct the project at every turn, I knew this must be a significant moment in the genesis of Ashburton Grove. At the same time, I was both happy that the project was now moving on apace and sad to hear the certain toll of the death-knell for my beloved old Highbury home.

Vigo, Vidi, Vici (*The Gooner,* Issue 143)
27 February 2004

The sound of the 'Vieira' song wafting through the window of our hotel room signalled that the four planeloads of travel club and flight options Gooners had landed in Vigo (top left of Spain on the map, just above Portugal). They were already busy lubricating their lungs, quaffing *cervezas* at the seafront bars and cafés. According to reports in the Spanish press, in the best traditions of the British footie fan abroad, there was no dawdling in the 2,500 Gooners' earnest endeavours to drink the city dry. I doubt they've witnessed such an invasion of Brits since Drake's boats sailed into the harbour for a sixteenth-century dust-up. Mercifully, our welcome was a lot warmer on this occasion and happily the only thing that was sunk were the Spaniards' Champions League hopes.

I might have a limited grasp of the Spanish language but my 'one size fits all' sentence of '*Español es un país encantador*' (Spain is an enchanting country) has served me well over the years, especially when compared to my gormless, '*Wenn der Wecker lautet, dann steht man auf*' (when the alarm clock rings, you get up) knowledge of German. It was probably the perfect sort of schmooze to have secured us one of the few, highly prized rooms with a wonderful seaview (and a jacuzzi to boot!) from the hotel's obliging reservations staff who, by a strange coincidence, happened to be named Reyes. Yet, standing there looking out over the picturesque yacht club on a crisp, sunny day, with a clear blue sky and the white-horsed waves washing over the oyster beds in the distance, the distinctive plink-plonk of the wind strumming the boats' riggings as an accompaniment to this Arsenal medley, it seemed more than an appropriate description of this city.

I imagine the enchantment is doubled during the summer when warmer climes would enable one to lounge on any of the unspoilt beaches which litter the coastline. Still, it was a definite step up from the dowdy London we'd left behind a day before. Don't get me wrong, Vigo isn't some idyllic Spanish backwater. It's a bustling fishing port with shipyards, canneries, refineries and Citroën, the sponsors of the city's team, keeping its 300,000 residents in employment. However, with its seafront setting and a delightful mix of old and new, portrayed in the pictures I'd dug out on the net, I had been eagerly anticipating the resumption of Champions League hostilities since confirming our reservations within minutes of Celta being drawn out of the hat.

With such a hectic fixture schedule, this was probably the closest I'd come to a winter break without missing a match. Considering our current all-conquering form, I wouldn't dream of depriving myself of a single awesome Arsenal moment. The consensus of opinion about the draw was that we'd pulled a decidedly juicy plum from a potentially bitter bowl of fruit. Yet many of us were mortified by the constant media references to our encounter with Celta as a foregone conclusion. Our remarkable result in Milan might have made the rest of the world sit up and take notice; although, in private, most would admit that we needed to prove the annihilation of Inter wasn't a one-off. Repeat performances were required if we were at long last to lay to rest our infuriating habitual failure to live up to expectations on our unimpressive intercontinental travels.

Besides, not only had we never yet won on Spanish soil but the Galicians had spent the past couple of months giving this encounter with the Gunners the big build-up because their domestic aspirations were limited to clinging on to their La Liga status. All their hopes for the remainder of the season rested on the outcome and while Raddy Antic might have been employed to rescue them from relegation, the prospect of pitting his wits against Wenger on football's most prestigious stage must have been an influential factor in him undertaking such a tall task. Who knows, perhaps his pal Pleat dangled the carrot that a defeat for the Gunners might guarantee him a highly lucrative contract at the Lane?

As other matches in the last 16 of the Champions League proved, there are absolutely no pushovers left at this stage. Myself, I tend to follow Arsène's pragmatic example. I was pleased with Vigo because it would provide an opportunity for me to lose my virginity at another European venue, but if we are ever going to get this Champions League monkey off our backs and a European crown on our heads, we are going to have to conquer the cream at some point. Personally, I'm desperate to play Real and experience the Bernabéu first-hand.

Confidence might be an unlikely bedfellow for such a pessimistic bugger but even I cannot fail to recognise the fact that on its day, this side is quite capable of triumphing over any of the teams on Europe's top table. Sadly, Spunky's departure hasn't as yet resulted in us being any more hygienic in the clean sheets department but our panoply of goalscoring possibilities means that we no longer need fear anyone. What's more, you can be damn sure that we now come very close to topping the list of our Continental competition's least-favoured opponents.

For a relative pittance, Arsène has elevated this Arsenal side onto another plane entirely and I imagine as a direct consequence, I was nowhere near as nervous as usual as the appointed hour drew nigh in Spain. In the past, the outcome of 90 minutes of football has been the be all and end all of our European expeditions. No matter how much we'd enjoyed ourselves abroad, defeat would put a downer on the entire experience. But nothing was going to put the mockers on this memorable evening. I think I was fretting far more about a room with a view in Vigo than any discernible concern for our victory.

We were lucky last year when our visit to Spain fell slap bang in the middle of the spectacular *Las Fallas* festivities. Fortune smiled upon us again on our return. As if to highlight the importance of the occasion for the locals, fate had scheduled this fixture to coincide with the climax of their carnival celebrations. It was nothing like the visual feast we'd witnessed in Valencia and by comparison to its equivalent in Rio it was quite low key, but it didn't stop the Brazilians entering into the spirit of things on the pitch with their fantasy football contribution.

The carnival appears to be aimed mainly at the kids who seemed to spend all four days of our visit kitted out in various fancy-dress costumes. The big, round black ears of a miniature Mickey Mouse caught our eyes as we hurried through the early evening traffic in our taxi en route to the Balaidos Stadium. According to the somewhat biased local media, instead of this cute kid with the large doleful eyes and a forlorn-looking face, the Mickey Mouse outfit might have been better suited to the Swedish ref, who would refuse their team two 'blatant' penalty appeals before the night was out.

Our encounters abroad are a constant source of annoyance to anorak programme collectors like myself. On this occasion, in addition to a freebie pamphlet full of advertising, posing as a programme (which will no doubt be available to compulsive collectors for an extortionate price from the stalls around THOF),

Celta had gone to the trouble of printing a bilingual newspaper in which they expressed the quaint sentiment that 'we are united in football because it is our passion'. In their efforts to ensure that the union with our drunken hordes didn't last any longer than absolutely necessary, they'd reproduced a colour-coded map showing the location of the coaches for each individual flight number.

I doubt it would have dawned on them that many Gooners had started drinking soon after dawn, pausing only to pay homage to their heroes with the occasional chorus. As a result, come the eventual 8.45 KO time, there were many Gooners who wouldn't have found the stadium if it wasn't for the fulgent glow of the floodlights. Colour-coded coaches! They were having a 'larf', expecting sozzled Gooners to know their flight numbers when many couldn't remember their own names.

It seems crazy to miss kick-off after travelling all that way but contrary to the standard advice about arriving early, we never seem to learn from our unfortunate experiences as we invariably maintain our tardy traditions. The inevitable and usually unnecessary increase in an obvious police presence is always a reliable indication that one is approaching the away fans' designated entrance. I always feel that this quantity of foreign coppers, kitted out in their intimidating riot gear, only serves to raise the temperature and once they've donned their helmets and batons, they always appear downright determined to create the sort of explosive climate which might enable them to venomously vent their frustrations on any British footie fan within their vicinity.

With twenty minutes still to go, I have no doubt that the few hundred Gooners in front of us in the queue could have all made their way to their seats quite peacefully before KO, but as has been the case at almost every foreign ground I have ever visited, lamentably the Old Bill seemed intent on limiting the numbers entering the stadium, thereby creating the inevitable logjam which is always the source of understandable aggravation. Sure, it is many Gooners' own faults for lingering over one last drink, but inebriated tempers were always going to become frayed as we stood there trying to fathom a single feasible reason why the queue hadn't moved.

I always fear for the missus's safety in such circumstances, as the match began and the pressure from the back of the queue increased.

I can't help but conclude that such mishandling by the miscreant plod was a purposeful effort to spark the sort of problem which might have given them an excuse to start swinging their batons. The most maddening response came from those Gooners who sunk to a racist barrage, because their insults were hardly likely to gain us quicker entrance into the ground.

Mercifully, we eventually made it to the front. I hustled Róna through the threatening cordon of riot police, past a Gooner with a blood-spattered forehead who was intent on continuing his argument, before we got caught up in any retaliation. We managed to survive this chicken run and make it to some seats with my ego and Ró's breast both slightly bruised by this completely senseless confrontation.

I suppose by now we should be more than used to being treated like animals on such outings. Obviously, Gooner crowds include the inevitable number of xenophobic Neanderthals who deserve nothing more and whose reprehensible behaviour abroad often leaves me embarrassed, even ashamed, to be identified as part of the same tribe, yet by and large we Gooners have managed to foster a friendly reputation across Europe in recent years as a result of so many relatively trouble-free trips. Remarkably, despite being high on success, huge Spanish-style spirit measures and anything else the hospitable locals had to offer, the papers the following day carried reports of only one single, regrettable incident involving a Gooner. Still, it seems our reputation counts for nothing and, after our traumatic entrance, we were only just beginning to focus on events on the pitch, just in time for the tale of two Edus.

Considering that we'd been starved of Champions League football during the past couple of months and that it was an occasion of such significance for the locals, I was surprised to see so many empty seats. Perhaps this was related to the live coverage on Spain's principal free-to-air channel, while Bayern v. Real was being transmitted on pay TV. However, watching the highlights package later that night, I was shocked to see that the same was true at virtually all the other games. It must be a sore point for UEFA suits, who might struggle to sell the sight of rows of empty seats to the cash cow sponsors. When you consider how many seats we sold to mere group games at Wembley a few years back, you have to wonder where the problem lies.

Even with the aid of my binoculars, I got little more than a glimpse from our end of the ground of the goalmouth kerfuffle which led to Edu prodding home for our first. But there was no mistaking the torrent of claret pouring from the Celta goalie's conk. Home fans were incensed, thinking he'd been knobbled by Edu's knee but, as far-fetched as it sounds, we saw on the replay later that it was a case of the keeper's face making contact with our innocent midfielder's leg (honest, yer honour).

Most of us were still on a euphoric high when their Edu rose majestically to head home from Silvinho's free-kick. Though it was annoying to concede from a set-piece and you could criticise Paddy because he was beaten to the ball in the air, I prefer to compliment an incredibly well-taken header. It is ironic when you think of all the passport shenanigans which saw Silvinho being shipped out somewhat abruptly (some say to avoid a scandal), while Edu was sent home to bide his time until his dodgy paperwork had been sorted.

Having conjured up a crucial away goal, the trivial matter of an equaliser wasn't going to impinge on our enjoyment. Up until then, the Spaniards seemed to have swallowed a little too much of the Arsenal hype and were guilty of showing us far too much respect. However, their goal was a signal for the floodgates to open, as if it suddenly dawned on them that we weren't completely infallible.

Antic appeared to have directed his side to devote their attentions to the relatively inexperienced Clichy. The poor young Gael had a torrid evening, regularly being turned inside and out, although I wonder whether Pires should perhaps share some of the blame for not being a better big brother. If Robbie had displayed a little more defensive responsibility, he might have saved Gael from some of his embarrassment. Nevertheless, you won't catch me complaining because nothing is a more certain confirmation of the fighting spirit currently coursing through our squad than the sight of Pires actually attempting a tackle.

I wasn't sure if I'd dreamt up an unlikely image of Dartagnan throwing caution to the wind, actually attempting to gain possession the previous weekend. We've grown quite accustomed to Pires's self-preserving instincts. These usually result in decidedly wussy-looking, half-hearted challenges. Yet there he was again in Vigo, manfully making his presence felt with the rare sight of him making physical contact.

The Serb's side nearly caught us cold as they came out after the break. Again, their Edu breezed past Clichy but when Mostovoi's header came bouncing harmlessly back off the crossbar, it was another one of those moments when you can't help but wonder if the writing is on the wall and this is perhaps to be our season.

The best of the Edu show was yet to come in the second half, which meant that thankfully it took place right in front of Gooners' eyes. We rushed back to the hotel afterwards, mainly because I wanted to watch a replay of this goal to confirm exactly what had transpired. Considering, up until now, as Edu himself has happily admitted, his right foot's only role had been for standing on, the spectacular arc of his shot was indeed something special. But I don't think the TV pictures really did justice to the belief-defying prelude.

As I replay the goal in my mind's eye, it seemed to take place in slow motion with me becoming increasingly dumbfounded as Edu's twinkletoes tricked their way around first one, then two and, astonishingly, a third Celta player. If it was Titi or Dennis on the ball, I would have been convinced they'd tried to do too much but this was the affable bleedin' Edu, working the ball with the sort of incredible dexterity that would have made Johann Cruyff himself look positively mediocre. The Celta defence were left looking about as mobile as the lumbering multistorey container ships we'd seen plodding into port each day.

The fact that Edu capped this pièce de resistance with such a consummate finish was simply stupefying. Amongst all the whooping and a-hollering, Gooners were turning to one another with looks on our faces as if we'd just witnessed the Second Coming. A ten-minute chorus of 'Edu, Edu' ensued (surely Gooner songsmiths can concoct something slightly more lyrical?) and although it was annoying to concede a second equaliser from another sloppily defended set-piece, I think fatigue more than anything was responsible for this lapse in concentration.

Besides, it might have left our strikers inconvenienced by having to go down the other end and get another goal but at least we were treated to yet another fine team move, which culminated with Pires passing the ball into the net for the winner. At the time, I thought Titi had over-gilded the lily and should have gone for it himself but TV replays proved me wrong because his teammate was much better placed.

Our leg-weary defending apart, the only other disappointment on the night was our Spanish starlet's failure to impress. The assumption that Jose might find a little more time and space than he has so far in frenetic domestic encounters might prove true in other European matches but the press had given Reyes such a write-up on his first return to Spain that Celta weren't about to let him embarrass them easily, and paid him particularly close attention. He seemed to be surrounded on the rare occasions he received possession. I suppose the positive aspect is the implication that he was creating space for others.

As I have said, I'm usually the most merciless teaser of those part-time Gooners who depart before the final whistle, as I've never understood the mentality of those who are able to leave such an unpredictable sport before the last ball has been kicked. Nevertheless, after the absolute tedium of an outrageous two-hour lock-in after the match in Milan, where deliriously happy Gooners were eventually in danger of turning nasty in their frustration, and after our aggravation gaining entry earlier, I really didn't fancy the possibility of a repeat performance. I think I've only ever left early previously when I've been the passenger in someone else's car and the driver has made the debatable decision. With a few minutes to go in Vigo, it suddenly struck me that the game was virtually done and dusted and if we moved quickly, we would beat the police barricade and could be back in our hotel room in time to catch the post-match reflections on the box.

Every time we go abroad with the Arsenal, I make the decision to take my tickets from the club, preferring to sing and shout with all the Gooners instead of the relatively civilised experience of obtaining seats amongst the locals. As we circumnavigated the Balaidos Stadium, I was sorely tempted to nip in one of the open gates to find a vantage point from which we could watch the dying moments. After each subsequent negative experience of being treated like an animal with the rest of the Arsenal fans, I increasingly find myself questioning the sanity of my decision, especially when risking the missus's safety.

I wonder if it wouldn't be better if there was no police presence at all? Or perhaps, more realistically, why they can't learn something from the far-more-sensible crowd techniques of the British bobbies? I suppose the need to keep the visiting supporters sequestered is often dependent on what transpires during the game. On this occasion, the Galicians didn't go home as elated as us Gooners but they were still clinging to their Champions League prospects, albeit by a thread. Celta certainly hadn't let their fans down, after giving such a good account of themselves. What's more, they still had their carnival to celebrate and naturally they were joined by many of those who didn't have a flight to catch.

Segregation certainly wasn't necessary later that night, as fans of both teams were united by the universal language of football on a square near the seafront. Perhaps it's a sign of old age but I find I get so emotionally involved in our matches that I was far too pooped to participate in this particular knees-up. Instead, I celebrated watching the highlights on the box with my feet up in a relaxing jacuzzi. We didn't really have to be there to feel part of the festivities, as the sea breeze carried the sound of both sets of supporters, serenading one another well into the wee hours.

31

Premiership: Saturday, 28 February (H) Arsenal 2 Charlton Athletic 1 Pires (2), Henry (4)

Historic day for me: actually present to witness two goals in the first five minutes, which are just enough to see off Addicks.

Springtime for Gooners in Germany?
1 March 2004

The song says, 'And now you gotta believe us,' and as Charlton's Johansson very nearly pooped Saturday's party with his injury-time bicycle kick, when the ball hit the post and bounced harmlessly away, I turned to Róna and said, 'We're gonna win the League.'

If my fate-tempting utterance should result in the end of our unbeaten run and the rapid disposal of our nine-point cushion, you know exactly who to blame. Yet with the competition apparently falling over themselves to throw away any prospect of pegging us back, it would appear that, as far as the Premiership is concerned, the only thing the Arsenal have to fear is complacency.

Charlton's brave second-half challenge and their last-gasp blitzkrieg left us Gooners holding our breath, with our hearts in our mouths. But following our consummate first-half effort, it would have been an absolute travesty if we'd failed to take all three points. It was a fabulous 45 minutes of flowing footie which was more reminiscent of some of our runaway victories early last season than some of our stuttering successes so far this term.

There was a time when, on the weekend after a midweek sortie to foreign shores, Arsenal fans would be expressing their concerns about how we might cope with the possibility of a Champions League hangover. However, it would seem that fatigue is not such a significant factor when you are as stocious with success as we currently are. Where Fergie appeared to underestimate the Cottagers by benching Horseface and Giggs, Arsène included all our big guns as the Gunners flew out of the traps, intent on finishing the job before five minutes had elapsed.

I was just grateful that I'd promised to deliver some pictures to the editor of the Gooner fanzine to add some flavour to my Vigo match report. Otherwise, I would have still been indoors until a few minutes before KO, instead of shooting the breeze with Kev at the Arsenal bookstall opposite the North Bank.

If it wasn't for Kev coaxing me, I would have undoubtedly ended up with my West Upper neighbours teasing me as to why I'd bothered turning up because I'd already missed all the excitement. Ironically, when I emailed Kev to express my gratitude, I discovered that he'd actually been deprived of this delectable five-minute feast of football by hunger pangs and a curative fishcake from the Highbury chipper. At least he couldn't want for a more sympathetic ear for his tale of woe. As the pot who has missed countless early goals, I was hardly in a position to poke fun at Kev's coal-coloured kettle.

Unfortunately, the third goal, which might have enabled us to put our feet up and relax for the remainder of the afternoon, never materialised. As a result, we spent the entire second half on the edge of our seats, teetering on an exhausting emotional tightrope. On the pitch, a heady mix of nerves and leg-weary laziness left us uncustomarily hoofing the ball away from danger during the last few minutes. I received a phone call from Cork from a Gooner who was getting intermittent radio reports. Desperate to pass on news of Fulham's equaliser at Loftus Road, he wanted reassurance from the 'frontline' that we weren't really clinging on.

In their admirable, albeit somewhat futile efforts to improve the Highbury Library's reputation, following on from the washout that was Fans' Day, I discovered in the programme at half-time that Saturday's game was supposed to be 'Flag Day' (despite the fact that the biggest of these has long since been banned from the stadium for health and safety reasons). Perhaps we'd blinked and missed it because even with my binoculars, I couldn't see a single flag during the break. Nevertheless, there was indeed a discernible difference in the atmosphere this weekend which had little to do with the admirable efforts of the 'Arsenal Atmosphere Group'.

In the past, the tangible tension which would have resulted on the terraces as we failed to kill off an opponent would have transmitted itself onto the pitch and produced an even more nervy, error-filled ending. Whereas on Saturday one suddenly sensed that we've become so high on the scent of success that the stands are now filled with a bloodthirsty pack of hounds prepared to bark their heads off in pursuit of our prey. I don't recall hearing the West Upper whingers leading the singing. Yet there we were last weekend, finally fulfilling our 12th-man responsibilities, 'singing our hearts out for the lads', summoning up the sort of atmosphere to inspire one last surge of adrenalin on the pitch.

It was brilliant to hear that we Gooners weren't going to sit back in silence and watch our side blow *our* title a second successive time. However, any concerns I had that we might be helplessly watching a slow-motion replay of the Arsenal's Premiership bandwagon careering into an anticlimactic crash again, in vainglorious technicolour, were allayed when fate's forcefield sent first Stuart and then Johansson packing with a flea in their ear.

Superstitious Gooners, such as myself, have witnessed several similarly propitious signs this season which might suggest perhaps, just perhaps, that the time has come to add the one missing honour to the illustrious list in the front of our match-day programmes. It might not weigh so heavily on Wenger's shoulders as it does on Ferguson's, whose first taste has left him with an insatiable appetite. Yet you can be sure he is more than aware that his relative shoestring Cinderellas won't truly have fulfilled their destiny until they've claimed this crown and with it their rightful place amongst football's European royalty. Even at senselessly short odds of 10–1 for what amounts to a near miracle, you won't hear the 'T' word passing my lips. But when Celta hit the woodwork at 1–1 in Spain, somewhat prematurely I found myself wool-gathering about whether Gelsenkirchen might be warm in May.

32

FA Cup: Saturday, 6 March (A) Arsenal 5 Portsmouth 1 Henry (25, 50), Ljungberg (43, 57), Touré (45)

FA Cup semi-final draw: Monday, 8 March, Manchester United, Villa Park, Saturday, 3 April

Standing ovation for Henry from staunch south coast fans as the Arsenal in all their pomp storm into semis.

Arsène diplomatically left Pires in London but he wasn't missed. From the scintillating opening salvo to us taking the piss out of Teddy when he got so excited about his consolation goal at the death, this was a dream day out. A welcome distraction of wonderful football from the media's focus on the scurrilous La Manga scandal surrounding Leicester's sunshine break.

Monday's draw throws up a semi with Man Utd. When Villa Park is selected as the venue instead of the Millennium, it seems like the perfect opportunity to settle a five-year-old score.

A Jolly Green Gooner Jamboree
8 March 2004

Smothering with a debilitating cold, it would have been far more sensible to stop at home, snugly ensconced in the warm, watching the events unfold at Fratton Park on the box, in the company of Motty, Lineker and co. I could even have savoured the coverage of the sensational Six Nations match. Yet after my appetite had been whetted by the hors d'oeuvres from Old Trafford, the increasingly rapid beat of the red-and-white heart, which belongs to Henry and the lads, finally ruled my befuddled head. So, as the Boys in Green kicked off at Twickenham, I began my mad dash to the south coast. As Nell is my Gooner equivalent of Holmes's Dr Watson, it was logical to meet at Baker Street. By the time we'd crossed the river and scythed through the south London traffic, 75 minutes remained for us to race along the A3 and reach Pompey before the ref's whistle.

It was amusing to hear the sore loser on the radio this morning moaning about how many of his colleagues have suddenly started shouting about their Irish ancestry. I felt like phoning in to inform him that this is exactly how the Irish feel every time the English media lays claim to anyone from the Emerald Isle who excels in their sport. I consider myself an adopted Irishman but I could have been born in Timbuktoo and I would have still been up for the Irish on Saturday. The smug gloating over here ever since the success Down Under of those philistines who play with their funny-shaped balls has really got my goat. As far as I am concerned, considering the number of participating countries and the fact that, in this part of the country, this particular code of 'rugger' is limited principally to privileged kids at private schools, they have little more right to their world champions label than the Yank baseball teams.

Moreover, my brother-out-of-law was over for Saturday's historic humbling of the jingoistic home team. I guess it was with Con in mind that Nell was forced to endure my 'Come on Ireland' ear-bashing for the entire journey. Even through the gloom of the early-evening mizzle, I could still make out the wonderful wooded scenery of some of Hampshire's most picturesque countryside. Yet with England having just eaten three points out of the nine-point lead, I was hardly the most appreciative observer as the radio reception became hostage to the hilly terrain. There was a five-minute period when we almost missed the Pompey turn off, as I waited frantically to hear that the home side hadn't scored. Mercifully, Irish eyes remained bloomin' exultant.

We were also pretty chuffed to have squeezed into a parking pitch and strolled to the ground with time enough to bolt down a salmonella burger before the game started. In estate agent parlance, Pompey's decrepit old ground would be deemed to have 'plenty of character', in contrast to the somewhat soulless concrete structures which have sprung up all over the country ever since the corporate juggernaut set its sights on the jugular of the very culture of 'club' football.

I am usually delighted on the rare occasions our games are shown live on terrestrial TV because it means my ma gets to enjoy the contest in a somewhat more exciting environment than the customary teletext updates (sod my trepidation about the three-trophy 'T' word: perhaps the most portentous sign of a truly sensational season will be the possibility that Mum might at long last succumb to desecrating the walls of her precious castle with an unsightly satellite dish). However, having taken a raincheck on our regular Friday night dinner because I wasn't feeling up to it, it didn't sit too well that I was then able to schlep all the way to the south coast. I could envisage the frown on her face seeing the pictures of us Gooners standing on an uncovered terrace in the teeming rain.

Honest, Ma, I still adore your chicken soup and if I didn't need it prior, a shot of Jewish penicillin was probably just what the doctor would have ordered after such a soaking! Although, I would have to be at death's door to deprive myself of the sort of footballing feast that this Arsenal side are currently serving up. Still, I might not have been quite so desperate if this wasn't my first-ever Fratton Park parade. With the weather intruding on our pleasures, there was an instant, as I wiped the rain from my specs, when I questioned my sanity.

Yet within seconds of the start, a sensationally slick passing move resulted in a stunning shot from Reyes rebounding off the crossbar. Standing behind Hislop (in the Intercash Stand, which would be more aptly named 'Outacash'), almost directly in Reyes' line of fire, there wasn't a more perfect pitch from which to appreciate the Arsenal's first-half party. Any doubt about what I was doing there disappeared with what was a hair's breadth away from being yet another 'goal of the month' contender.

Instead of an audible expression of anguish at such a fabulous failure to find the net, we are now in a position merely to purr in awesome admiration of such a tantalising example of technique. There is now an innate sense amongst us Gooners that not just another one but another half a dozen 'will be along in a minute'. Even the elements offered their seal of approval as the rain ceased completely (who knows, perhaps the miracle-working Wenger had a word?). It might have been a full 25 minutes before Henry finally made his mark but it seemed almost inevitable right from those magical opening moments. As with Wenger's class of '98 and our early-season exploits last term, the confidence coursing through this side is the catalyst in a chemical reaction which has liberated all eleven from any technical limitations and taken this team onto another level.

Don't get me wrong, despite Harry Redknapp's world-beating eulogy, I refuse to be drawn with all the tabloid sheep into the media bandwagon's 'best ever' debate. At least not until we've actually got some trophies to throw on the table. Avid Arsenal watchers cannot fail to accept the obvious chinks in our armour, especially those who delighted in a decade of perhaps the most dour, defensive unit on the planet: as was said about Dennis Wise, our bargain-basement keeper could start a row in an empty room – he appears to attempt to intimidate the opposition rather than dominate his box; as a converted midfielder, Lauren is still learning his defensive duties; Edu's impressive efforts might at long last have demanded Gilberto's displacement as captain Paddy's partner in the middle but such is Arsène's somewhat unfathomable faith in the Brazilian World Cup winner, that he's found him a home out on the wing, where I very much doubt he's played before. You'll have to forgive those of us who know not what he does but Gilberto's so bleedin' indispensable to Arsène that, legitimate or otherwise, he must be someone's son! I believe Wenger sees him as a similarly vital cog in the Arsenal's engine as Makelele was for Madrid.

Nevertheless, while I remain convinced that we might pay a hefty price for Lehmann's antics at some point, any such weaknesses are not nearly so likely to be exposed when their conviction has unleashed a level of composure which has them all performing with the chutzpah of eleven Pelés. The first half of the season saw the flowering of Kolo Touré but recent performances have seen Edu positively blossom. Some of the media pundits mistakenly waxed lyrical about the disguise on the Brazilian's lay-off to Ljungberg for our second. In truth, Edu has hit such a rich vein of form that he's rightly been going for goal any time he gets within range, with his bludgeon of a left foot. He was in the process of doing likewise on Saturday when he looked up and, seeing Freddie more suitably placed, selflessly put it on a plate for our Swedish sex god.

It was the sort of move which sums up the clarity of thought in the heat of battle which has me confident that we can take on all comers. I'm hoping that we've already done the hard work against the Spaniards and that both the battle and the war were won in Vigo. I'm desperate to draw their illustrious compatriots sooner rather than later, not just to rubber stamp our spiralling reputation but because I'm dying to have our day in the Bernabéu. I'd feel a little cheated if we end up meeting Madrid in Germany. Will you listen to me, getting way ahead of myself when we've not yet secured a quarter-final berth? I hope the Gunners aren't guilty of such dangerous daydreaming and are still bursting with the vital 'one game at a time' blinkered focus because Blackburn on Saturday has loomed large for some time as our most likely banana skin.

Newcastle, Liverpool and United all present potential stumbling blocks to our record-breaking bonanza but I worry that after our midweek exertions, the less-glamorous surroundings of a half-empty Ewood Park are the most likely surroundings for complacency to raise its ugly head. It's been a bit of a Gooner graveyard in recent seasons and you can be certain Souness will have his troops primed to take the utmost advantage if there is any suggestion that our success is simply a matter of just turning up.

Meanwhile, the neutrals might have preferred it if the FA Cup draw had kept the country's two footballing titans apart until the final, but along with many of my fellow Gooners, I couldn't possibly be happier with our forthcoming clash in the semis. There is a certain synchronicity about this encounter which makes it an absolutely tantalising prospect. It will be almost five years to the day that our season came to a horrific conclusion in a replay at Villa Park of the very same fixture, as Man Utd kick-started their assault on a Treble. It feels like more than a quirk of fate that we should be thrown together again, at long last finding ourselves with an opportunity to erase one of our worst nightmares of recent seasons. Hopefully, this time, the shoes will be on the exact opposite feet, as it should prove our opportunity to snuff out United's season and any last scent of silverware, while our success could be a similar springboard in surmounting club football's highest crest.

According to my strong belief in the law of averages, that first defeat should be drawing ever closer for us. Should it come, I will be ducking for cover to avoid drowning in a tidal wave of tabloid tales of 'The Wheels are coming off Wenger's Treble wagon' (when not a single Highbury soul would dare let the dreaded 'T' word enter our heads, let alone fall fatefully from our mouths). However, I have every faith in the lessons learnt at the school of hard knocks and have no fear of us blowing our nine-point lead in last season's profligate manner.

33

Champions League: Wednesday, 10 March (H) Arsenal 2 Celta Vigo 0 Henry (14, 34)

Draw for Champions League quarter- and semi-finals, Thursday, 12 March: Arsenal v. Chelsea play winners of Real Madrid v. Monaco

Premiership: Saturday, 13 March (A) Arsenal 2 Blackburn Rovers 0 Henry (56), Pires (87)

Collina takes charge at Highbury as Gunners ease into the Champions League quarter-finals; strictly business breaking down unambitious Blackburn.

Three seems to be the magic word as Arsène picks up another manager of the month award, Dennis and Edu share player of the month and Titi receives an award for being the first player to notch 20 Premiership goals. Man Utd exit the Champions League to Porto, as the Arsenal and Chelsea go through to a meeting in the quarters which is greeted with mixed feelings (the Bridge or the Bernabéu? Difficult choice). A tasty trip to Madrid or Monaco awaits the victors in the semis. We are indeed wary as the Ides of March leave us facing two meetings with both Chelsea and United over two weeks at the end of the month and Easter, which will decide our season.

A Henry free-kick special and his George Best impersonation of nicking the ball from Friedel for a goal, which was sadly disallowed, light up a long day out at Ewood Park. It's probably fortunate that Fergie had a pacemaker fitted a couple of days earlier, as Wrighty's stepson ensures United aren't even top in their own town, with City winning 4–1 in the Mancunian Derby.

One Goal is Un-Oeuf
15 March 2004

I was up with the lark last Friday. By the time all eight balls were in the hat for the Champions League draw, I'd written six pages of notes after trawling the Internet for the previous three hours, seeking out all the permutations of cheap flights to any of six destinations on either of the two possible dates.

These flight-finding missions have become an integral part of my Champions League experience. The further we progress in the competition, the more I cane my poor credit card. I end up working myself into an impatient lather, waiting for the moment when I can let my fingers loose on the keyboard to collar a bargain, before going on to brag to all my Gooner mates who haven't been so quick off the mark.

I'd already started making bookings to Madrid, Milan and Monaco, so I could hit the appropriate 'confirm' button the second the UEFA suit announced our opponents. Obviously, my feelings were more than a little mixed when I discovered all my considerable efforts were in vain. Apart from saving a small fortune, I suppose I should be happy because we seem to have the Indian eye over Ranieri's side. It is also brilliant that Dennis Bergkamp might at long last have an opportunity to exert his considerable influence over our Champions League progress.

It's been a while since Dennis wasn't a virtual automatic exclusion for away legs and, while the trip to Stamford Bridge will cause Wenger no such dilemmas, I can't help wonder whether he'll continue to rule him out of the away leg, if we should progress to a titanic encounter in the Bernabéu? With the undoubted inevitablility of Dennis's professional mortality, it would be dreadful if he was denied the opportunity of such a spectacularly suitable swansong.

And if you think I am getting ahead of myself with such fate-tempting thoughts, wait until I tell you that this 'dyed in the wool' pessimist wasn't prepared to let all his hard work go to waste, and in an uncharacteristically foolish and wanton act of faith (considering the capricious nature of our sport), I went ahead and booked our flights to Madrid. For someone who is too superstitious to speculate a red-and-white cent on the outcome of an Arsenal match, it is strange behaviour for me to gamble not only on us beating Chelsea but also on Madrid beating Monaco. Students of the form book might see it as a fairly safe bet. Personally, I'm hoping that if (heaven forfend) the worse should come to the worst, I might be able to flog our flights to Chelsea fans. Or, if necessary, I could cough up an amendment fee for a flight to Nice.

Should the Arsenal stumble at Stamford Bridge and come up short once again in our expectations of a European semi, I guess my brinkmanship will be as much to blame as my Gooner mate, who has suggested on his website that we should apply for tickets to the final in Germany to avoid any disappointment as a result of a ridiculously meagre ticket allocation. Yet, in truth, even a killjoy like myself couldn't fail to be affected by the air of optimism currently enveloping the club. A precious season ticket at Highbury this season is like having an adjacent pitch to St Peter himself, while the faces of the rest of the Premiership are pressed up against the gates to our Elysian Field, enviously peeking through.

There was a sense in our performances against Pompey, Charlton and Celta Vigo that this side has slipped into overdrive. While we've salivated over instances of sublime footie all season long, we're now witnessing entire performances played with the sort of swaggering rhythm which really makes us worthy of all the plaudits pumping out from the sycophantic media.

I am invariably left hurrying home, not sparing the horses, because I'm so high on the thought of savouring such fantasy football frame by frame in super slo-mo replay, again and again. Moments like Dennis's inch-perfect pass to put the first goal on a plate for Titi against Celta and our deity's delicious free-kick on Saturday, aimed for the sizeable breach in the wall vacated by Sol Campbell, with the astonishingly precise arc into the very top corner of the goalmouth which was possibly the only point beyond the mammoth reach of man-mountain Friedel. I firmly believed that we'd knocked much of the stuffing out of Celta in Spain and didn't expect too stiff a contest. Raddy Antic's side had just suffered a 1–5 defeat at home to relegation rivals and with Henry bagging a brace within half an hour, I got the distinct sense that the Spaniards came out in the second half with damage limitation as the extent of their ambitions.

Supremely dominant displays such as this are having a knock-on effect in the Premiership. The Arsenal are now deserving of such respect from our domestic opponents that on Saturday, Souness set his Blackburn side's stall out with two banks of four which hardly emerged from their own half. They sat back and challenged us to break them down. It must have been very frustrating fare for the home fans, watching the Arsenal play keep-ball for long periods of the game, waiting for the inevitable injection of pace which might pick Rovers' heavily guarded lock.

Still, their manager would have been hailed as a hero if he'd succeeded in salvaging a precious point. He'd have you believe that they might have achieved this ambition if it wasn't for the 'poxy decision' which resulted in Henry's goal. My respect for Souness is such that I will put his bitterness down to the heat of his disappointment in the immediate aftermath of the battle. On reflection, he should realise that Henry might have reproduced the same fabulous feat a few minutes earlier when the ref ignored a far more obvious offence in exactly the same spot.

However, if I was a Rovers fan, I'm not sure I'd agree with Souness's tactics. I believe it was a distinct lack of respect which led to our defeat last season, as Rovers took the game to an admittedly less-resolute Arsenal. Duff and Dunn might have made a crucial difference but they certainly didn't triumph by merely preventing us from scoring. Just as United appear caught in the downward spiral of dwindling confidence and disastrous results, the Arsenal appear to be gathering momentum on an upward curve, where victory appears guaranteed even with the relatively mediocre performance witnessed at Ewood Park.

Last season, one goal was never enough and, instead of confirming the outcome with a second in the closing stages, you can be sure we would have been sweating in expectation of an impending equaliser. When I asked Wenger about the difference between now and then, he pointed to a 'defensive solidity' which enables us to rest assured in the knowledge that, 'We will score at some stage'. However, it is not just the Arsenal's innate belief but the snowball of lavish praise which has produced a complete lack thereof in opponents like Rovers.

I'd be lying if I said I didn't luxuriate in Man Utd's last-minute misery as they exited Europe. How could any ABU (Anything But United) not enjoy the rare sight of the Red Devils being for once on the receiving end of such a gut-wrenching defeat (seconds after the commentator fatefully told us that their toes were in the quarter-finals). And their Derby day despondency was a source of even more merriment. Red Mancunians will become even more of a rarity in a city where their Blue counterparts won't let them live this one down for at least a decade. No football lover can resist an opportunity to tune in to watch this Arsenal side perform. Yet I grow increasingly weary of Gooner enquiries of, 'Are you watching Manchester?'

It might not be as many miles as the trek to the Northeast, but the 500-mile round-trip drive to Blackburn is without doubt one of the most arduous outings in the Arsenal calendar. Perhaps, as a consequence, Saturday's crowd included a larger proportion of northern Gooners, who have suffered more than most during a decade in the Mancunian shadow. Personally, I know they are watching and I could care even less. The song suggests that United continue to maintain some significance, when the maladroit Mancunian star is spinning so far out of orbit as serious competition that they now belong with the White Hart Lane bunglers, out there on the fringe of the Gunners' glorious firmament.

Forgive me for gloating but as the glory-hunting Moaner millions head for the hills, I'm off round to Highbury to secure our seats for a lip-smacking semi and hopefully another ecstatic European night at Stamford Bridge. After leading United to the land of milk and honey subsequent to so many lean decades in a silverware-starved desert, if anyone could continue to dodge the bullets from the insatiable fans one might have thought it would be Fergie.

Meanwhile, we've the small matter of achieving a result against Sam Allardyce's battle-weary troops before we can equal the undefeated record. But if the ranting and raving in the press and on the radio are a premature requiem for Sir Alex, then it would appear that it only remains for the Mancunian funeral to pass the legitimate 'Home Of Football' in order that we might nail down the lid of the coffin.

34

Premiership: Saturday, 20 March (H) Arsenal 2 Bolton Wanderers 1 Pires (16), Bergkamp (24)

High winds hold up kick-off at Highbury – after a magical first 30 minutes, a nervy second half leaves us all hanging on.

Does the Fat Lady Like a Cigar?
22 March 2004

Supporting a football club is rather like a middle name: it might fall into disuse now and again because it's a source of embarrassment, but there's never really any question of changing it. Basically, you're stuck with it for life. Considering the sort of sensational football this Gunners side are capable of at the moment, I certainly wouldn't want to be supporting anyone else. Still, I often declare my jealousy of others, such as the fabulous Pompey fans. Hail or shine, they turn up week in, week out, season in, season out, knowing full well that their chances of winning anything are extremely faint. Yet they continue to express their loyalty by singing their hearts out for the entire duration of every 90 minutes.

I suppose it has something to do with different expectation levels but I often have cause to comment that if we were getting beaten anywhere near as badly, far from supporting our lot in such a staunch fashion, the Highbury crowd would be getting on the players' backs and booing them off the pitch. It might seem somewhat churlish of me to be having a moan at this point in such a majestic season – after all, we've just carved out yet another notch on the cannon barrel of this record-breaking run by equalling the undefeated feats of those illustrious Leeds and Liverpool sides of yesteryear. What's more, even if we fail (heaven forbid!) to secure a single point in the final nine Premiership fixtures, we couldn't finish below fourth and have thus guaranteed our crucial Champions League place – but there was hardly a murmur of approval from the Gooner 'audience' making their way out of Highbury on Saturday. Admittedly, the West Upper heart of the Highbury Library isn't exactly renowned for its exuberant support (with the exclusion of yours truly). However, I refer to our 'audience' because the hangdog expressions on the faces of the majority of the frigid fans exiting the North Bank gave them the appearance of a not-so-nattily dressed West End theatre audience heading home after having watched a particularly dodgy play, not daring to open their gobs because they're not sure if they've been ripped off for thirty-odd quid, or if the deep symbolism of the plot was way over their heads.

On Saturday, we heard one solitary fan attempting to savour the moment by trying to start a chorus of, 'Who the f*ck are Man Utd?' I am usually so spent after 90 minutes of shouting my head off that I rarely join in with the post-match rejoicing that is more commonly heard away from home; however, I offered this lonely enthusiastic Gooner my vocal encouragement, in the vain hope that our introverted fans were just waiting for someone to start them off. But it was like preaching to the unconvertible and, as we passed my singing partner, I hollered out, 'You've got a hard audience there, mate!'

Róna reckons it's a London thang (but then recent experiences on the capital's raging roads have made her particularly cynical about the actual existence of the cheerful cheeky cockney chappy). But it's not like we haven't heard similar complaints about the complacent crowds at Old Trafford and Anfield. Perhaps there are plenty at Highbury who have become far too blasé to bother acknowledging anything less than the sort of success which will result in our lot running around the pitch with a plethora of silver pots?

Personally, I believe the principal problem is the fact that football has become such an expensive hobby that our stadia are increasingly populated by the 'prawn sandwich' brigade. A few moments scanning the passionless, miserable mugs scuttling along Avenell Road confirms the meagre amount of uninhibited youngsters attending home matches these days. My Arsenal experience might never be the same again when we eventually leave my 'Home Of Football' for the last time. Yet I am praying that the powers that be won't just pander to the well-heeled with a plentiful supply of pound notes, or concentrate solely on milking the corporate cash-cow for all it's worth when they open the gates to a 60,000-seater Ashburton Grove. I fervently hope that a blinkered focus on making a fast buck doesn't result in a failure to take advantage of a fabulous opportunity to foster the long-term lifeblood of the club, with considerably more concessions for kids. Currently, you are more likely to get an audience with the Pope than a half-price seat in Highbury's extremely humble family enclosure.

Unlike those publicly listed clubs who have to pander to shareholders' demands for dividends, hopefully the Arsenal's private status might permit a less-greedy pricing structure from Gooner guv'nors who purport to have the club's interests at heart. Additionally, a policy of attracting lifelong punters in their teens is not the purest form of philanthropic altruism. What I will never understand is that 3,000 relatively affluent Gooners (these days, you can't follow the Arsenal around this country and the Continent without having a few quid) are only too happy to sing their hearts out on their travels and are all too often nowhere to be heard at Highbury.

After 30 years of watching the Arsenal, I get so wound up that I sometimes want to shake Gooners out of their silent stupor by screaming, 'Do you have any idea quite how privileged we are?' After cutting my Gooner teeth on the tedious triumphs of the infamous flat back four, I fully appreciate the Wenger-inspired miracle of a side which includes both an indomitable spirit and astonishing skills in equal measures. In the last 20 minutes on Saturday, I am not sure whether it was the media-hyped millstone of the undefeated record weighing heavy around our necks or, more likely, our loss of momentum, but fatigue became a factor in our struggle to retain our grip on the game after Allardyce had obviously bawled out Bolton for showing us far too much respect. Perhaps it was the positively tangible air of tremulous tension transmitted from the terraces to the pitch?

Whatever the cause, it was all too apparent that we could have done our bit to drag the Arsenal along another few anxiety-ridden miles on the road to Damascus, with a rare reprise of our 12th-man role. I am often tempted to try to orchestrate some singing myself. From my vantage point, front and centre of the West Upper, there are times when I feel like turning around and screaming at the sedate audience sitting on their hands, 'How much do you really want it?' But then, I could be waving my willie around amongst the redundant residents and the only rise I would get would be a few raised eyebrows (at least I wouldn't require a baton!). I couldn't understand how 30,000 Gooners could resist an opportunity to have a direct influence on proceedings. How much more satisfying would Saturday's match have been if we'd been responsible for an atmosphere which might have inspired an adrenalin rush which obscured the effects of the lactic acid in the players' legs, for one last push, flying to the final whistle in typically fine style, instead of a terrifying scramble?

After the gung-ho tone of last week's epitaph to Fergie (in their 4–1 Derby day fiasco) and Bolton's poignant reminder of our perfunctory imperfections, perhaps I should offer Gooners a timely reminder that back in '91, Chelsea proved to be the single solitary blemish in an otherwise unbeaten League campaign. Moreover, Spurs fans might cling to the memory but history won't recall that we were perhaps only a Gazza free-kick away from reaching the FA Cup final and the possibility of another memorable Double. It doesn't matter how close you come, without the silverware to show for your efforts, there's still no cigar!

35

Champions League: Wednesday, 24 March (A) Arsenal 1 Chelsea 1 Pires (59)

Premiership: Sunday, 28 March (H) Arsenal 1 Manchester United 1 Henry (50)

Keeper's costly cock-up gifts Blues a goal; Gunners come straight back to silence the Bridge and claim a moral victory; undefeated for 30 games this season, the Gunners make history but Man Utd's late equaliser puts the mockers on our merriment.

The intense media coverage in the build-up to the all-London Champions League clash ensures a night of knotted stomachs and chewed fingernails. An away goal in a frantic Cup tie gives us the advantage on the night. Nevertheless, an air of anxiety appears to encroach on the Arsenal's supreme confidence.

Honours are even in Sunday's 'Clash of the Premiership Titans'. We might have come away with the Arsenal's name inscribed in the record books but I can't escape the abiding feeling that we'd missed an opportunity to stamp the sort of superiority which might have extinguished all of United's FA Cup aspirations.

Over Land and Sea (if Only We Can Get Past Drayton Park!)
29 March 2004

I was tearing what's left of my hair out last Wednesday evening, even before we'd arrived at Stamford Bridge. Departing Highbury late as ever, I fully expected to have to battle my way through London's tortuous rush-hour traffic, but I didn't expect to come to a complete standstill after only a few seconds of having started the car.

I will be pleased if thousands more Gooner aficionados are able to get tickets when our ambitious new stadium finally comes to fruition. Yet, if this sentimental old fool had mixed feelings about our increasingly impending departure from the famous Marble Halls beforehand, it seems I now have good cause to curse the ambitious Ashburton Grove project every time I leave home. In fact, I might be destined to denounce the ongoing disruption resulting from the building works possibly twice daily for the next couple of years.

Apparently, the club have issued an edict amongst their staff that it is forthwith to be referred to as the 'new stadium' instead of Ashburton Grove, in order that their new baby doesn't get lumbered with a moniker which might hinder its eventual sponsorship potential. As this prime piece of London real estate has lain fallow for so long, it is interesting to witness the wholesale changes as the stadium and the vast assortment of ancillary buildings rapidly begin to take shape. However, it would seem that in the local council's infinite wisdom, the powers that be have decided to close off a couple of roads in the vicinity. The resulting gridlock around the Grove was an absolute nightmare last Wednesday and is likely to remain so for the foreseeable future. This is our main route from home to virtually everywhere. The irony wasn't lost on me that the concrete on the foundations has hardly had time to harden and already our new stadium was 'nausing' up my chances of making it to a match. Not any match mind, only a Champions League quarter-final. I hope it's not an omen!

After taking nearly an hour to make it across just one set of traffic lights at Holloway Road, mercifully we sailed through the early-evening gloom and were searching for a precious legal parking space in SW3 as the players took to the Stamford Bridge pitch. I was already sufficiently stressed out about being even tardier than usual as a result of the impasse at Drayton Park, not to mention fretting about the most crucial football match of the season so far and the key to our first-ever Champions League semi-final. But we were so late that I was forced to abandon the car in a bay which wasn't legal until 8 p.m., with the additional trauma of knowing we might return to find a fifty quid parking fine on the windscreen if it was detected by a traffic warden in the next twenty minutes.

It was a calculated risk. Considering the negligible cost of travelling to our quarter-final match compared to any of the other potential opponents, I would have happily forked up for the fine rather than waste any more time driving round and round in search of an alternative pitch. It would have been a paltry price to pay for qualification to the semis. Moreover, what's a mere fifty-quid flutter for someone who has already presumptuously spunked up for flights to Madrid? Last season, we would have left the Bridge without an away goal and would have been guaranteed to find a ticket on the windscreen on our return to the car but the way fortune has been favouring us Gooners this term, it was no surprise to find ourselves going home having got away with both.

Ranieiri is indeed an endearing gentleman, and I think it's downright ridiculous to expect a coach who created the best team spirit seen at the Bridge for decades without spending a red cent last season to instantly conjure up the rabbit of a squad with a winning mentality out of thin air, merely by throwing the Russian's millions into the Blues' hat. Nevertheless, I really don't rate the Italian's managerial credentials. Perhaps he's a great coach but as a club's *capo* he's far too nice a feller. Judging from his animated antics on the touchline (I haven't the foggiest what sort of affliction St Vitus's dance is but Claudio appears to be suffering from it!), his fruitless efforts to get his players to follow his instructions would suggest that while there might be a whole lot of love between them, there's far too little respect.

As we hurried along the Kings Road to our entrance, it was the first time I'd heard Chelsea's new *Kalinka* theme tune, and it is indeed a catchy little number. I was picturing their players dancing out of the tunnel squatting and kicking in choreographed Cossack style! In light of the pressure applied by Chelsea in one of the best performances I've seen from the Pensioners, the result might be perceived as more than acceptable. One would think that the fact the Blues now have to score at Highbury will play perfectly into the Gunners' counter-attacking strengths.

Yet no matter how crucial that all-important away goal is, I wish in some respects that we still required more. Experience has taught me to be most wary of awkward encounters where a 0–0 draw will suffice. It can result in players resting on their laurels, merely attempting to maintain the status quo and, if matters should go awry, it can prove impossible to build up the necessary momentum.

Moreover, there have been certain indications in both of our mammoth encounters this week which might give one cause to question whether these are the cumulative effects of fatigue, or perhaps the first sign of complacency raising its disconcerting head. Players like Vieira have set such supreme standards that I suppose with our relentless fixture schedule, the occasional rare indiscretion is inevitable. With his pacific 'smile, man' pre-match exchange in the tunnel with United's frigid under-führer, our captain certainly didn't display the demeanour of a player primed to go on the 'B of the bang'.

Paddy's overall performance against Man Utd might have been sufficiently peerless to deserve the man of the match award from some quarters, yet there was the odd, rare lapse which could lead one to wonder whether he's been wallowing a little too much in the wall-to-wall media hype. He'd have to be a saint not to succumb to a little too much self-belief!

I noted when he allowed Djemba-Djemba to get goalside of him in midfield that he managed to recover possession by means of the extension of one of his extraordinarily long legs. Paddy might have been good enough to get away with it in this instance but I would be a lot happier if he retained a tight rein on the opposition for the entire 90, without slacking off for a second. Against the likes of Milan's Kaka (should we come up against perhaps the only player to have scaled the same heights as Henry this term), he might not be afforded the opportunity to redeem himself.

Meanwhile, I am hoping that the momentary loss of concentration in some, is more than made up for by those Gunners who have positively come into their own in the last few games. Pires and Edu appear to be relishing every magical moment on what we hope will prove to be a 14-game road to Gooner glory. In the space of a few weeks, the Brazilian has gone from being a 'jack of all, master of none' replacement in Arsène's mind, to the most composed player on the pitch. In some cases even taking on the 'main man' mantle of our imperious captain.

As for Le Bob, I am bound to *manger* on a few of my own bons mots because he's taken plenty of stick from me for his previous penchant for levitating three foot in the air in avoidance of the odd lunge that promises even the slightest possibility of any pain. I've also cursed his horizontal hanky-panky, conspicuously attempting to con the ref when he might have remained vertical and conjured up a valuable effort.

It can't just be a consequence of Frank Lampard (by the by, 'Lean Lamps' would be far more appropriate than 'Fat Frankie' because he's long since lost all that baby fat) yanking his Gallic chain because Pires is playing like a man possessed, courageously getting stuck in where once he would have just jockeyed his opponent, tearing around the pitch like a Trojan with an uncharacteristic work ethic that might give credulity to the tales of alien invasion. That Dartagnan dared damage his coiffure with his crucial, headed goal – as they say, 'nuff said.

Young Gael Clichy might have been guilty of allowing the cross which led to United's late goal on Sunday but he would have been the man of the match choice of most canny Gooners. According to the media, the Arsenal's only purchases last summer were Lehmann and the promising (albeit, sadly, injury-prone) Swiss defender, Senderos. Plucked from the relative anonymity of France's fairly mediocre equivalent of our Second Division, the £250k transfer of Clichy almost went unnoticed. It's the perfect example of Wenger's amazing talents and his unflinching ability to create such influential oak trees out of unknown, tiny acorns.

Wenger was criticised by many for gift-wrapping United's equaliser with negative substitutions but in truth we'd already shut-up shop, sitting back and inviting United to give it their best shot. Arsène was merely hoping that fresh legs might help our cause by relieving some of the pressure. Whether it's fatigue, too much self-belief or the fact that the ball has been running for us so frequently recently, but we appear to have developed delusions of invincibility. We should have known better against a wounded animal of United's calibre.

Such sucker punches from a side who might be down but who never know when they're out are not so common these days but Man Utd remain the archetypal last-minute merchants. I only hope we bring the lessons learned from such a fatal mistake to the momentous semi on Saturday. It was sad that Sunday afternoon fell so flat after we'd just attained the truly incredible undefeated achievement. However, if there's a silver lining, it could be that we won't be arriving at Villa Park quite so cocksure, perhaps riding for a fall, but will instead be sufficiently focused to stuff United for an entire 90 as opposed to the 75 minutes of last weekend's warm-up!

Sid and Nancy, I mean Sven and Nancy (sorry, but I have this image of Sven as Sid Vicious, in his leather pants with a safety-pin through his nose, standing on the stairs in the 'My Way' video sticking two fingers up to the British media!) slipped out of Highbury with ten to go and missed the climax completely. I can only assume it was at Nancy's behest that they both went off prematurely because it was such a captivating conclusion that even the Arsenal's regular part-timers were lingering for the final whistle. Sven would have been no more mistaken about the result than the fallacious stories in the following morning's papers about his future. Then again, in truth, who apart from the tabloid scandalmongers actually gives a monkey's about the comings and goings of the national team manager (and his missus), as long as his side succeeds on match days?

36

FA Cup: Saturday, 3 April, Villa Park, Arsenal 0 Manchester United 1

Red Devils delighted to rain on our Treble dreams; a positively spineless showing from our supporters is reflected in a below-par performance on the pitch.

We should have known it wasn't going to be our day when the woodwork and some defiant last-ditch defending prevented the Gunners from taking an early lead. The fact that Gary Lewin was hit by a coin was evidence of the United fans' fervour as they roared their team's efforts to reduce this game from a contest of skill to a bruising battle. If we were going to end up out of the Cup with a collection of bookings, I only wish one of them was a result of kicking Ronaldo, their step-over show pony, into the stands. Spoilt Gooners were left blaming anyone else but themselves, as Arsène's decision to try to rest Titi came under fire. Although, his critics failed to mention the fact that United's main man was also absent (it was Grand National day, so perhaps he was otherwise occupied at Aintree). Somehow, the consolation of being able to focus on our two other assaults on silverware came as little solace. After the sparkling footie during his last trip, Ró's nephew was back over from Dublin. I don't think he'd ever seen the Arsenal lose before!

The Silence of the Lambs
5 April 2004

Everyone recognised that the four games in the past fortnight were a make or break point in the Arsenal's amazing season. You'll already know whether we were broken by the Blues on Tuesday night, or have bounced back after the gut-wrenching disappointment of Saturday's defeat to make it into the semi-final of the Champions League for the first time in the Arsenal's illustrious history.

I have to admit, in all honesty, that having schlepped to Cardiff for the past three successive seasons, I am not unduly distressed about missing out on another expensive outing this May. Especially as it would have proved a none-too-glamorous encounter. Millwall have made admirable efforts to achieve respectability, attempting to eradicate the recidivist hooligan element that revelled in the sort of savage acts which reinforced their 'no one likes us' disrepute.

Nevertheless, if the infamous surgical masks have vanished from the terraces, it doesn't mean that the violent right-wing Neanderthals who wore them have simply stopped supporting the south London side. A rare derby against the Arsenal might have proved an irresistible invitation. All their worst psychos might have come crawling out of the woodwork, wanting to settle ancient scores and prove, off the pitch, what might have been a poignant mismatch on it, their adrenalin pumping at the prospect of giving the Premiership-softened, bourgeois Gooners a good bashing.

Their encounter with the Mancunians might prove just as attractive and I pray that come May, the Welsh constabulary are suitably prepared. It won't be an advantageous advert for Britain's beautiful game if they can't contain this particular passion play within the Millennium Stadium and it spills over into the streets of Cardiff.

Hopefully, we might have bigger fish to fry four days after the FA Cup final. And if we've negotiated Beechers Brook and The Chair in Chelsea and Madrid, the last thing we'd want is a mêlée with Millwall as a warm-up for our greatest-ever challenge in Gelsenkirchen. Not that any disdain I might have felt for this domestic competition meant that I was any less devastated by Saturday's debacle against the Red Devils.

The Arsenal fans' only success of the day was that most were sitting comfortably in their seats at kick-off. An accident at Spaghetti Junction saw United fans still breathlessly bowling into Villa Park just before Scholes scored (fortunately for them!). Mayhem on the M6 has been responsible for us Gooners missing more than our fair share of semi-final footie. I will never forget hobbling to the Holte End on crutches, grateful for the TV on our coach, which meant that, unlike many, we at least saw the only goal of the game against Wolves in '98. We were caught in the clutches of the motorway morass, frustratingly within sight of Villa Park's floodlights, whilst being entertained by the Gooners who were daft enough to dive off an eight-foot embankment after abandoning their cars and their unlucky driver. Consequently, in the hope of avoiding the worst of the hold-ups, most Arsenal fans had left at the crack of dawn.

I thought I'd been clever plotting up at a hotel one junction past Villa, but it meant we were caught up in a bottleneck of United fans on our way back. We ended up missing the frantic first few minutes, as the Arsenal began a bad day at the office with their failure to bury the first of five great chances. Worst of all was the longest-ever trudge back to the car afterwards. Or at least it certainly seemed that way when surrounded by celebrating United fans. Naturally, they were cock-a-hoop; but not about having made it to the final and the likelihood of an FA Cup consolation prize (when only hours earlier they might have expected to end the season empty-handed). No, the congratulatory chorus grinding a hole in Gooner heads suggested that they were far more concerned with putting the kibosh on the possibility of the Arsenal repeating (and belittling) United's own Treble feats. It was strange that they were so focused on this possibility, before most of our fans had dared be so presumptuous to even entertain talk of the fateful 'T' word.

Personally, I wasn't grieving because the Gunners had frittered away a rare Treble chance, or for our failure to break yet another record with a fourth consecutive FA Cup final. Along with Dennis and any other Arsenal players involved in the 240 minutes of football which culminated in Giggs running round Villa Park showing off his hirsute charms five years back, I badly wanted to beat United on Saturday to exorcise the ghosts of '99. Some of these were laid to rest in last season's fifth-round Cup tie at Old Trafford, with the Welsh wing-wizard's passable Jonny Wilkinson impersonation in front of an open goal, when it was harder to miss than to score. It's funny, after going on to win 2–0, I don't recall ingrate Gooners giving Arsène any stick that day for leaving Henry on the bench.

Yet, such was the synchronicity on Saturday with the '99 semi, which turned out to be the springboard for United's Treble, that I never dreamed our downfall might be due to a lack of desire on the day. If I was disappointed because our players were devoid of the sort of fire so obviously burning in United bellies, I was downright flabbergasted by our fans' feeble efforts. It was as if the Arsenal had brought an 18,000-strong army of the Library's most silent lambs, who simply sat back and accepted their fate.

After United took the lead, I kept staring through my binoculars at the other end of the ground in the hope that I just couldn't hear the Gooners in the Holte End. When our team most needed a lift from the terraces, the Arsenal's 'audience' remained completely becalmed. All I saw was a sea of inertia! Perhaps they were all similarly blasé about the prospect of proceeding to a fourth Cardiff final. Yet so voracious was my appetite for this particular victory that I was not only blue in the face but completely hoarse long before half-time. Sadly, it seemed that United and the vast majority of their fans were that much hungrier than the Gunners (certainly in the first half) and our impotent army. We usually make more noise with only a couple of thousand! Perhaps the early start left our lot exhausted. But I couldn't fathom getting up before the cock crows to travel all the way to Birmingham, only to be a silent bystander, allowing events to transpire without bothering to at least try to influence matters.

It's all too easy to criticise with the benefit of hindsight, but Le Prof's Henry ploy has paid dividends in the past. I might be a great believer in always starting with your best available team and I couldn't for the life of me comprehend what possessed a pragmatist like Wenger to throw Aliadière in at the deep end, only to sink like a stone. However, Arsène is a manager who's worked absolute miracles with relatively meagre resources. He would have to be guilty of several seasons' worth of misdemeanours before Gooners would be entitled to gripe about the man who is single-handedly responsible for the greatest entertainment we are ever likely to witness at our Highbury Home Of Football.

We ended up listening to music on the drive home because I just couldn't bear the sound of the same sad saps who couldn't be bothered to raise their voices in support of our team berating our manager on the radio phone-ins. It was the height of hypocrisy. If I wasn't sufficiently embarrassed by their woeful vocal effort at Villa Park, their whinging left me ashamed to be included amongst the same tribe.

Fatigue and a little too much confidence could have been the recipe for a defeat which was frankly long overdue. Our midfield was guilty of not tracking their opposite numbers, possibly leaving them to a back line which has so rarely been breached. But I shouldn't really single anyone out, on a day when no one shined overall. Although, at one point in the second half, Paddy seemed to be trying to rescue the situation almost single-handedly. Our reticent captain's 'lead by example' efforts to rally the troops were admirable but if we were lacking something, perhaps it was the sort of inspirational captain who could have turned and roused our fans from their torpor with a single clenched-fist gesture.

If anything, Saturday's demise was even more frustrating than the defeat five years ago. Personally, I have never rated Giggs's ability to run the exhausted dinosaurs of our defence ragged quite so highly. Yet, as I recall, the Welshman's 'wonder goal' was the only thing to separate two evenly matched teams. Whereas we missed an opportunity at the weekend to reinforce the marked superiority of the current Arsenal squad. We favoured United with a fillip for the future, which Fergie will undoubtedly use to rebuild their badly bruised confidence, when we should have left them facing any forthcoming encounters with the same sort of inferiority complex which has bedevilled us for so many seasons.

A cause for more current consternation is the cracks that United have inflicted on the Arsenal's air of invincibility. Suddenly, everyone is talking up Chelsea's chances of administering a fatal blow in the Champions League and the tabloids are backtracking about our premature Premiership coronation. I always knew we were only one defeat away from a media bandwagon waiting to delight in the prospect that we might 'bottle it', with many already reading the Arsenal's last rites.

If I was absolutely shattered on Sunday morning, I imagine our squad must have been more aware of their aching limbs than they've been all season (especially Reyes, after witnessing a slow-motion repeat of Paul Scholes' tackle). Lifting their spirits for Tuesday's game is possibly the most crucial task of Wenger's tenure. If anything, a losing habit has even more momentum than a winning one. With the Scousers and the Toons both hitting a purple patch, there's every possibility that a European exit might be followed by a slump of seismic proportions at the weekend. It could conceivably result in the ultimate anticlimax of the Arsenal's record-breaking season coming to a conclusion without a single piece of silverware to show for all our efforts.

We require a resounding triumph on Tuesday to re-establish the sort of superiority that will frighten the lives out of our Easter weekend opponents. That doesn't mean I won't be delighted with a dodgy 0–0 draw. It's not just that I've been desperate to see the Arsenal play in the Bernabéu these past few years but I am also anxious to make use of our flights to Madrid because I've recently finished the last carton of Camels from the plentiful stock I purchased in Vigo. Being forced to pay five quid for a pack again is far too great a shock to my system!

In fact, I am looking forward (albeit with all due trepidation) to Tuesday night, to discover what sort of mettle this Arsenal side are really made of. Our players are constantly harping on about the best team spirit they've ever experienced. Well, we are about to discover whether it is the genuine Arsenal spirit that's the cause of our success, rather than merely a consequence of it. On the pitch, it will be a night for real men in red and white to stand up and be counted. I only hope that, unlike Saturday, the lummoxes on the terraces can do likewise.

37

Hands up those Gooners who'd give all 17 straight victories over the Blues in return for this one!

Again, there was no escaping the media build-up to the most important London Derby the capital has seen. I don't know about anyone else but after Saturday's Cup exit, there seemed to be a certain sense of inevitability about the outcome. With all the tabloid talk about Ranieri's departure, whatever transpired, it was as if the Tinkerman was sticking two fingers up at all the ponitificating pundits who predicted that he wouldn't play Hasselbaink when, for about the first time this season, he stuck with the same line-up as their last match. In fact, it was ironic that after spending £120-odd million on transfers, the best two Blues on the night were Lampard and Terry.

Many Gooners will have been out of their seats, trying to beat the queues at the break when Jose bundled the ball in the back of the net in the first-half's injury time. Even then, it was obvious that this full-blooded Cup tie was far from over. When Fat Frankie (Lean Lamps) equalised, the momentum was with Chelsea to such an extent that, to my mind, it felt as if it was a case of not if, but when they were going to get the winner. The most annoying thing was that it was mistakes that led to both goals. Many Gooners blamed our goalie for not holding Makelele's shot but I think that's a bit harsh because it was struck with such venom. However, he could have parried somewhere safer than the six-yard box. The saddest thing, in my opinion, was that after Edu had been largely responsible for getting us there with his amazing effort in Vigo and, after forcing his way into first-team contention with such impressive performances in far less crucial matches, it was a crying shame that fatigue or a lack of composure should finally catch up with him on such a big night.

For Chelsea's first, it was his clearance which should have been hit into

Row Z but landed instead at the feet of the Blues midfielder and, three minutes before the final whistle, it was the Brazilian who failed to track Wayne Bridge before the poor man's Ashley Cole finally put the fatal nail in our Champions League coffin. Up until our loss to Man Utd, I was as guilty as every other Gooner of swallowing the hype. Consequently, it was the conviction that at long last this could be our European year which made the result on Tuesday all the harder to take. It's been a long time since I last felt like crying after a football match but instead it was the Blues manager who was left blubbing like a baby on the touchline.

'This is not the end. It is not even the beginning of the end, but it is, perhaps, the end of the beginning' (post to the Arsenal mailing list on the net)
7 April 2004

It's times like this when the mailing list really comes into its own. I came home last night wishing I had a punch-bag to vent my frustrations and exhaust myself on to the point where sleep came, rather than lying there dissecting in my head all the 'if onlys'. Now I'm in a state where I get distracted every now and again, only for the depression to creep back up on me, every time I realise I've just let out a huge sigh. However, in an attempt to put matters in perspective for some, you have to appreciate that there are always those who are worse off.

For example, the poor sap in Madrid responsible for the Morientes loan contract to Monaco, where Real not only continue to pay 60 per cent of his wages but where they made the mistake of neglecting to include a clause preventing him from playing against them. So, in effect, Real paid for their own player to help knock them out of the Champions League – I wonder how secure in his job this fella is feeling this morning?

Or Shane, my missus's 15-year-old nephew, who is likely to have seen his last live Arsenal game for some time. Shane came over from Dublin last week to come to Villa Park with me on Saturday. Róna phoned me on the way home from Birmingham to say that, after our miserable outing to the semi, she had suggested to Shane's ma that they might change his flight home from Monday to Wednesday. Ró was kindly offering to let him go to last night's game in her place. My instinctive response was to express my fear that if this result also didn't go our way, Shane wouldn't be invited back in a hurry.

I've just dropped him at Heathrow this morning and, not being exactly at my most communicative, I'm afraid I was guilty of not making much of an effort to prevent him from going home believing he's a curse! I guess we'll have to try and break the bok by bringing him back for a Cup game against the likes of Leamington Spa.

We'd arranged to go for dinner after the game and I was convinced none of the management or players would be in a mood to show their faces in the restaurant, so I am just relieved and grateful to Pires for turning up. I assume he's far too much of a gentleman to let down family and friends. As always, Le Bob got a round of applause on arrival (perhaps heartier than usual). There was a French journo at our table who commented on how different it would be on the Continent. I guess in Italy, supporters would probably spit at Pires and his food – and that would be his own fans, let alone opposition supporters. I suppose this is one of the reasons the French prefer to play here.

At least this meant that Shane was sorted, with about the only result of his trip. It was a fortunate coincidence that Pires was featured in the poster in the centre of last night's programme. So Shane got to say hello to Bobby as he signed the poster. I guess he was so blown away that we were halfway home before he realised that he didn't have the programme on his person. I sent him running back and luckily it was still on the floor where he'd dropped it. The way our luck had gone that night, I half expected it to have disappeared.

And for a real hard luck story, there is the example of the sports editor of the *Irish Examiner*. Tony is a mad Gooner and, although he was fortunate to be there on that magical night in Milan, he hadn't managed to make it over to Highbury all season. He'd spoken to me a number of times about coming but while the Arsenal hadn't lost a game, I think he was scared of changing our luck. However, it's not every season that you make the last eight in Europe (or at least we don't!), so having secured a couple of tickets for him and the missus, he wasn't going to pass up such an opportunity. I don't for one minute imagine that the press office at the Arsenal would have accommodated him but since he was here with his wife, he didn't bother applying for accreditation.

Tony arranged to dash back to my gaff after the game to type and file his copy for the morning editions. However, because he'd be in a mad rush to make the deadline, he wanted to come around beforehand to set up his laptop and make sure everything was working for fear of discovering a problem when it was too late to resolve it. I met the two of them earlier in the evening outside the Bank of Friendship pub, brought them home and then plugged up his laptop so he could send a test file (they'd just announced the two teams on Sky).

As anyone who has tried to use their Orange mobile phones in this area recently will have discovered, two of the Orange aerial masts have gone down; they haven't been functioning for more than a month. As a result, it is absolute murder trying to make any calls on the mobile when there's a full house at Highbury.

Shane and I had been sitting down in the restaurant for about 30 minutes and had ordered our grub when I received a frantic call from my missus. She'd been trying to ring me for more than half an hour. Deirdre and Tony had come back to our gaff and he'd opened his laptop and found that the machine was completely frozen. He'd been on the phone to his techy geezer at the *Examiner* and Ró had even phoned Shane's dad, who was at work at Dell computers in Ireland, to see if either could assist in sorting it out. They both tried in vain as apparently the hard disc was corrupted (who'd want a Microsoft-operated PC when you could have an Apple – but that's another evangelical story altogether).

Our food was just about to turn up; in fact we'd already been served once (the waitress had grabbed our plates just as I had my fork in my hand and was about to dig in – I was quite put out when she gave them to someone else, saying there'd been a mistake!). I really didn't want to go home because the grub would have been ruined by the time I returned, so I ended up having to explain over the phone, to someone who is even less computer literate than myself, from a busy restaurant, how to plug up my machine (as I'd unplugged the broadband to plug in his laptop) and then how to write his copy on my Apple Mac. Having mercifully got him started, I suggested that one of them call me when he was almost finished so I could nip back and send it.

By this time, Tony had already missed the deadline for the first editions but he had to write up a match report for the later edition because with the sports editor present at Highbury in person, I don't suppose it would look too good if they'd had to use something from the wires. Despite being exhausted after schlepping over from Cork and being even more traumatised than myself about our defeat (with Cork being such a stronghold of United support, he would be going back to face untold stick at work the next day), he had to try to clear his head and write a completely unbiased account on an unfamiliar machine. I felt sorry for his poor sub-editor, who was still waiting for his column in the office, as it was 11.30 by the time we arrived back and Tony was only just finishing.

Finally, there is me. I am not asking for any sympathy but hopefully my misery might make others feel just a little bit better. I am sure I can't be the only Gooner who had presumptuously booked flights to Madrid and who was thinking that last night was absolutely the worst case scenario. While I'd allowed for the possibility that we might not win, it hadn't occurred to me that Monaco might beat Real Madrid. So, if you should know anyone who fancies a trip to Madrid later this month, feel free to put them in touch. Ró has suggested that we might go anyway but I think it would prove too painful. After so many years of waiting for a chance to see the Arsenal play Real in the Bernabéu, I was almost certain that it was our destiny this season.

When Madrid won the first leg 4–2, I thought that I was fairly safe assuming that even if worse came to worst, I could flog the flights to Chelsea fans. Mind you, there must have been a couple of hundred thousand Real fans who also didn't entertain the thought that Monaco would make such an amazing comeback.

However, that is the lesser of the two possible financial losses resulting from our Cup exits. I had a contract lying around the house for a couple of weeks, waiting for me to sign and send back, for the publication of this, my second book, another collection of my diary pieces. I think subconsciously I didn't want to return it for fear that if I hadn't tempted fate's fickle finger already, it would certainly be pointing at me if I put pen to paper and cashed in on the Arsenal's expected success prematurely. But I did have to arrange for the designer of the cover to come up with something for the publishers to put in their catalogue, along with a 300-word précis (and summarising a story where you don't yet know the ending is an impossible task). Honestly folks, what I came up with was very ambiguous. I did my utmost to allow for virtually all possible eventualities and I promise I didn't once dare to mention the dreaded 'T' word.

After Saturday's calamitous FA Cup exit, I received an email asking if I wanted to change the blurb accordingly. I wrote back and explained that I thought it best to wait before making any changes. Right at this moment in time I could be changing it on an almost daily basis with each successive snake-and-ladder ending to this season. I am now wondering whether I'd made a major ricket in not sending the contract back immediately and at least collecting on my advance. The way things are going, the publishers might not be keen to send a cheque at all until they've seen which way the wind blows; by this time next week, there might not be a book. Then again, if (heaven forfend) our season does continue to go completely pear-shaped, perhaps they'd be doing me a favour by pulling it, since it won't exactly be a 'fun' project if I end up having to spend the next six weeks reliving our demise and perhaps the greatest-ever anticlimax in the Arsenal's history!

It is not that surprising after a season where Lady Luck has smiled upon us so consistently but it would seem that both the Arsenal and I have suddenly hit a losing streak. I am glad Shane was my witness, or else I could just imagine the sort of sceptical response to this story. I was in the karsey of the Holiday Inn just north of Villa Park last Saturday and, having read all the footie-related news, my attention turned to an article on the front page of *The Times*. It was about a scientific study which had been done on that afternoon's Grand National, where the results proved that punters are best off putting their money on horses which have run the Aintree course before.

I am sure there will have been a lot of Gooner money on Gunner Welburn that day but this article listed two other horses which were most likely to succeed. I shouted out to Shane to ask who he fancied but he obviously wasn't thinking of a bet on the horse race when he replied, 'A cheese sandwich, please.' It all sounded most scientific to me but I was in no rush to place a bet. Having checked into the hotel that morning, I said to Shane that, all being well, we could have a punt on the race after the match and come back to watch it in the room whilst waiting for the traffic to dissipate.

As it turned out, the last thing I wanted to do was hang around in Birmingham with the sound of, 'Where's your Treble gone?' wafting into our hotel room from celebrating United fans at the bar. We headed straight home and I was glad of the Grand National coverage on the radio because at least it was a welcome distraction from all those 'what if' thoughts.

I am not much of a betting man. With my addictive nature, I really can't afford to get involved as my lack of self-control could prove very dangerous. I have a superstitious rule never to place a bet on the Arsenal but, like millions of others, I might have a biannual punt on the two big horse races. As a result, I have one of those bits of plastic provided by a kindly bookie, in order to make it that much more convenient for you to hand over your hard-earned readies. This should have made it simple for me to place our bets on the phone as we drove back. Unfortunately, it's been so long since I last used this account that my debit card has since been renewed. I suddenly remembered that the same thing had occurred the last time I'd tried to place a bet over the phone. Instead of giving over my new card details, I thought I might save myself a few quid by not bothering. On the odd occasion I fancy a bet, it is usually because I've heard something on the radio or TV which has taken my fancy. I thought that with the additional hassle of having to fish out my debit card and give all the details, I probably wouldn't bother. Which is exactly what happened in this instance. In my depressed state, I just wanted to get home and get this miserable day over with as quickly as possible. I couldn't muster sufficient enthusiasm to make an additional stop, just so I could get even more distressed by throwing my money away on a couple of gee-gees running in a race which is designed for mug punters like myself.

Like all the other Gunners that day, Gunner Welburn didn't come up trumps but you can imagine my horror when the other two horses mentioned in the article, which I intended putting my money on, came in first and second. I couldn't be bothered beforehand but after the race was finished, I was unable to resist pulling into a service station (with the excuse of getting some gas) in order that I might make the afternoon's wind-up complete by pulling out *The Times* and checking that it was in fact these two horses. I must be some kind of masochist but I just had to satisfy my curiosity and confirm that I'd missed out on the consolation of winning a tidy little sum. I suppose it was bloody typical of our disastrous day.

It's said that bad luck comes in threes and, after blowing the FA Cup and the Champions League, I only pray that I can include my Grand National misfortune as part of this triumvirate. Any winnings I might have missed out on will be a paltry price to pay if, contrary to the predictions of many of the doom-mongers, we don't end up 'bottling it'. I wish I could offer you some optimism and I pray that just by stating them here, I am going to guarantee that my pessimistic thoughts will be proved completely wrong (I will be first in the queue at the humble-pie counter), but I said to Ró before last night's game that not only could we not afford to lose, I also believed we needed to do better than to scrape through to the Champions League semis by some fluke.

We've all been guilty of swallowing the hype in recent weeks. As far as the players are concerned, perhaps it's the cumulative effects of the sort of fatigue which only manifests itself the moment our matches go awry. Or could we be asking too much to suggest that they haven't been in the least bit affected by swollen-head syndrome as a result of the sycophantic slavering in the press? Whatever the cause, only those Gooners with opaque rose lenses will refuse to accept that with hindsight the cracks in the Arsenal walls have been apparent for some weeks now – basically, since we slaughtered Pompey. It doesn't say a lot for the rest of the competition that they are the best of the rest but, in the end, all it took were our two greatest domestic rivals to expose these weaknesses.

Watching the Arsenal get beaten at Villa Park will have been all the inspiration Chelsea needed. After they repeated the feat last night, suddenly we are no longer the invincible side we were only four days previous. Considering the woeful way in which we've reacted to exiting European competitions in the past (which might be multiplied in this instance as we were closer than ever to the Champions League crock of gold), it is unlikely that we will strut out on Friday having regained our all-conquering swagger. If we aren't going to experience a déjà vu with our Premiership points cushion disappearing faster than the few remaining games, possibly the biggest factor could prove to be quite how hungry the opposition are for that precious Champions League fourth place.

Unfortunately, both the Scousers and the Toons have finally found some form and one might expect that they will now approach their encounter with this Arsenal side in a completely different fashion compared to those teams we've met in recent weeks. We were getting away without being beaten even when not at our best because of the respect shown to us by many of our recent opponents. The constant hype in the tabloids has ensured that many of the teams we've played have been in absolute awe of us, terrified of the embarrassment Titi is capable of inflicting on them. As a result, they've been dropping off and defending in numbers, allowing us to get away with less frantic and far fewer physical encounters.

Suddenly, the Arsenal are looking vulnerable and, whatever the instructions of their respective managers, psychologically the instinctive approach of our opponents might be entirely different. The principal point that the likes of Liverpool and Newcastle might take from our two defeats is that (in the words of Corporal Jones), 'They don't like it up 'em.' Previously, one would have imagined that subsconsciously the opposition would be going into games focusing on getting away with anything better than a resounding defeat as a good result, whereas we can now expect them to go for it with all guns blazing. If we are going to get anything from the six points available over Easter weekend, and if we are to extend our undefeated record, perhaps our best chance of success is the air of apathy which can often afflict Premiership sides at this stage in the season. The consolation prizes might not be sufficient as a motivating factor when, mentally speaking, many of the mercenary players have already long since hung up their boots.

Against Newcastle, we might benefit from the fact that our match is squeezed between the two legs of the Toons' UEFA Cup quarter-final. However, if we are to return from Tyneside with anything but our tail between our legs, first we have to bounce back against Liverpool in two days' time. If it is down to our manager to lift the players, you wonder who exactly is going to lift Wenger? Arsène tried to put a brave face on matters but his claims that winning the title would make up for all that's fallen by the wayside sounded particularly hollow. You just know how badly he wants the respect he's entitled to and which he can only truly gain from the media in general by winning in Europe.

I suspect Arsène will be expecting his players to have sufficient self-belief to lift themselves for such an important occasion. If the outcome of Friday's game is dependent on our manager delivering an oration full of Churchill-like tub-thumping rhetoric, then we might well be in big trouble. A quote from one of the England players after they lost to Brazil, describing Sven's half-time team talk, reads, 'We wanted Churchill and we got Iain Duncan-Smith.' Well, Wenger might not quite be in that category but I somehow can't picture him inflaming the players' passions with a morale-boosting speech.

Out of curiosity, I just pulled up a page of quotes on the net from the original British bulldog and virtually all of them would be most appropriate under the circumstances. But even if we should end up fighting the Scousers 'on the beaches' on Friday and losing, it will only be a battle and not the war. Right now, if the title was turned into a procession, our Premiership trophy might be slightly tainted because it would be perceived by some as a second-rate consolation prize. Whereas, if we should drop all six points this weekend and the title race is thrown wide open, there would be a silver lining if a resurgent Arsenal came back to triumph out of adversity. I will take Premiership success whatever way it comes and it will save a lot of heartache and stress if we continue on our undefeated course. Yet, it would be bloody typical for the Arsenal to go about it the hard way – and how much sweeter would it be, especially for all those ingrates who had already taken such success for granted.

Recent events have seen our expectations raised to the point where many assumed that we would only have to turn up at White Hart Lane in a couple of weeks for the formality of winning the League on the enemy's turf for the second time in my lifetime. However, with everyone suddenly jumping on the bandwagon to write the Gunners off, now is the time to roll up those red-and-white sleeves and make them all eat their words with a demonstration of true Gooner grit.

38

Premiership: Friday, 9 April (H) Arsenal 4 Liverpool 2 Henry (31, 50, 78), Pires (49)
Premiership: Sunday, 11 April (A) Arsenal 0 Newcastle United 0

Gunners silence all those who thought there was no fight left in this dog as Scousers bear the full brunt of Wenger's wounded animals; battling point against the Barcodes puts White Hart Lane hoedown back on the agenda.

That it should have been Easter when the Gunners served up a reminder for us all to keep the faith was particularly poignant. It was indeed a gift from the Gooner gods as the Arsenal rose from the dead, soaring phoenix-like from the flames of those whose barbs dared to suggest they lacked backbone. But not without the customary fright or two along the way!

I am still not sure whether this was the Gunners back to their very best, or further evidence, in the way the Scousers folded, of the gulf that exists between the Premiership upper echelons and the also-rans. After suffering the agony of seeing the visitors tear the last of our silverware dreams into tatters, with them twice taking the lead, the half-time mood amongst us Gooners has rarely been more melancholy. Yet this was in complete contrast to the ecstasy at the final whistle, after Dartagnan and our most menacing musketeer, with a magical hat-trick, had breathed the life back into what has become a quite remarkable quest for undefeated glory. We were still celebrating Pires putting us back on level terms when Titi conjured up one of the goals of the season, leaving half the Scousers and the whole of Highbury mesmerised with a magical jinking run through the massed ranks of white shirts and then casually curling his second past Dudek. And as if to answer the affront of anyone who dared suggest he would end his sensational season empty-handed, he rounded off his afternoon by completing his hat-trick with the sort of hideously ugly goal (an oxymoron, if ever I heard one) that Henry apparently can't score.

We'd started our Easter weekend praying that a season which had promised so much wasn't going to end up as a repeat of last term's anticlimactic agony. Whereas, by full-time on Friday afternoon, we were full of hope, wondering whether the Kings Road massive might be kind enough to drop the points necessary for a wonderful reprise of '71. There was no better tonic for our Champions League blues than the possibility of our second title triumph on Tottenham's own turf.

It was understandable that, for our last arduous trek of the season and our fifth game in nine days, the leg-weary Gunners were mostly concerned with just getting the job done on Tyneside. Yet, with Wiltord returning for his first Premiership start since October, playing up front alongside Henry and Reyes, unlike many of his managerial counterparts, Wenger wasn't putting any restraints on his side's attacking instincts away from home. However, it was a day for defences to hold sway on a pockmarked surface which was hardly conducive to a precise passing game. Lehmann went some way towards redeeming himself with an immaculate performance, while at the other end of the pitch, the match was summed up by the fact that Sky awarded Woodgate the man of the match award. Wiltord might have gone some way to winning back some Gooner hearts and minds if he hadn't scuffed a good chance before the break but the few decent first-half opportunities petered out later in the game as both teams seemed to settle for a stalemate.

The only advantage to my missus's asthmatic affliction over the years has been that we've been able to suss out the elevators at various grounds around the country. Despite Ró's absence, it felt as if she was there in spirit, as I remembered to avoid a seemingly eternal stairway to our seats in the gods by seeking out some mechanical assistance. Although, I felt more than a little foolish when I realised I was requesting access to the lift amongst the home fans, asking for some sympathy from a steward for my own supposed respiratory problems and I was only standing there blathering away with a fag in my hand! We hadn't failed to score on our travels since Old Trafford in September but that didn't stop us partying away the afternoon, high up in our lofty St James' Park perch. It may only be the UEFA Cup but the Toons' continued involvement entitled them to tease us with, 'There's only one team in Europe'. But with the competition's second-class status, Gooner wags were quick to remind them that there weren't that many people watching the coverage with a chorus of 'Channel Five'.

We're a multi-talented bunch, us Gooners, and after an afternoon of exercising our vocal chords in a stadium where our chants of, 'Where's your famous atmosphere?' were a reminder that Highbury is not alone in suffering in silence, it was time to exercise our brains. You didn't need to be a mathematician to know that we needed nine points to guarantee the Premiership title but, personally, I could have done with Carol Vorderman's assistance in calculating the necessary points permutation for a Premiership title party on Derby day.

Glass Half Full? Our Bleedin' Cup Runneth Over!
12 April 2004

Walking down Elwood Street after the Scousers had been well and truly put to the sword, the North Bank crowd bustling towards the Gunners' boozer were more cacophonous than they've been virtually all season. The din wasn't exactly deafening but the air of merriment amongst the Gooner massive was a sweet sound by contrast to the regular post-match response to our record-breaking undefeated run. So, with the Thierry Henry version of 50 Cent's tune pumping out of the beatboxes of those flogging the Arsenal Away Boys CD, it was great to see and hear some Gooners for once letting their hair down on their way out of Highbury. I certainly wouldn't have advocated our devastating demise in both cups but if defeat is what it really takes to remind more of us to show some appreciation for our amazing run of success, then perhaps we are due some more.

Mercifully, Good Friday was great for us Gooners. We discovered that this team has the strength of character to dig themselves out of the pit of despair with or without the aid of their supporters' vocal shovels. When we went 0–1 down, even some of our more faithful fans began berating the players, distraught at the thought that a once-sensational season was sliding into a silverware-bereft freefall. Fickle Gooner travel plans teetered from 'Bollocks to schlepping to St James' Park!' to 'What time you leaving?' and back again, before being confirmed following Titi's final flourish.

As a long-standing resident of the West Upper, I get a fabulous view of the footie but it is for my regular fix of atmosphere that I attend away games so religiously. I was actually quite looking forward to our

Easter Sunday ascension to Tyneside, knowing that none of the fairweather glory-hunting Gooners would be going. Our expectations of achieving anything in Toon Town had taken such a drastic tumble that it was truly going to be a trip for the 'hail or shine' masochists. Consequently, no matter what transpired on the pitch at St James' Park, I was expecting a somewhat more satisfying sortie than the absolutely shameful shenanigans at Villa Park.

I've long since come to terms with the lousy atmosphere at home games. According to the Highbury Library analogy, I suppose the West Upper must be the Reading Room. Unlike a considerable amount of the Arsenal's apathetic 'spectators', that doesn't mean I've given up completely. Far from it, I regularly come away from THOF completely hoarse, having given full vent to my doughty range of decibels, especially as I've become increasingly frustrated in recent weeks. It's been patently obvious to me that as some of our players hit the wall in the home straight, their engines all but out of petrol and only just about ticking over on fumes alone, we could have a part to play in our role as 'supporters' by helping to haul them over the finishing line. We should be supplying the inspiration to elicit that last rush of adrenalin which can override any feelings of fatigue.

Man Utd are prone to similar levels of apathy from the 60,000 muppets at Old Trafford. It is a problem common to most of our new stadia, where enthusiastic young fans are being priced out of Premiership footie in favour of an increasingly ageing and affluent audience who are far too 'mature' to want to make fools of themselves by expressing their feelings. Yet, to any neutral observers at the semi, it was plainly obvious which side and whose supporters were prepared to sing for their FA Cup supper.

I sometimes wonder if our amazing side doesn't deserve more than an audience which is so averse to expressing their appreciation. If a defeat is truly what it takes to generate some Gooner gratitude, then perhaps our ingrates should sod off to White Hart Lane. Personally, I think it should be obligatory for all Arsenal fans to suffer a dose of Spurs, where indifference on the terraces underlies the lack of spirit on the pitch. We'd learn double-quick to be a little more grateful for our gobsmackingly great Gooner fortune. The cyclical nature of the beautiful game means it's almost inevitable that a time will come when we'll all be wishing we still had something to shout about. I only hope that all those who will be only too quick to express their disapproval don't end up regretting a missed opportunity to show the most incredible team we are ever likely to see tread the hallowed Highbury turf quite how much they mean to us.

If ever there's been a week in football deserving of the 'funny old game' cliché, it's been this one (as in funny peculiar, not ha ha). I feel that the seeds of our sad Champions League exit were sown in the psychological effects of our semi-final defeat at Villa Park. Who knows if United would have gone into this game with quite so much confidence if it wasn't for Saha's late equaliser the previous week. However, as my old man was fond of saying, 'If my granny had balls, she'd have been my granddad.' At least we only choked on our away goal against Chelsea, and not the two- and three-goal leads AC Milan and Real Madrid took into their second legs.

I am not sure if it was a consolation knowing that at least I wouldn't find myself sitting here absolutely bulling as the Blues bilked me out of my long-awaited trip to the Bernabéu and perhaps the chance to pit our wits against Serie A's best in the final – or a wind-up, with football's most prestigious trophy apparently there for the taking after all the favourites have fallen.

Yet it was definitely soul destroying going out of Europe to domestic opponents who've been our doormat for so many seasons. The problem is that, prior to last week, according to the fickle pundits in the media, the Premiership had long since been a foregone conclusion. So, while it was an amazing achievement that we managed to bounce back and raise our spirits sufficiently to roll over Liverpool on Friday, the sense of accomplishment is diminished to some extent because in truth we are only going on to do what is expected of us.

European success, on the other hand, has eluded us for so long now that it's becoming a bit of a Gooner Holy Grail. We might all know our manager is a miracle worker and that he has already written his own chapter in the Arsenal's illustrious history but winning the Champions League is the only way Wenger can really rubber-stamp his reputation alongside Chapman, Shankly, Clough and Fergie in football's hall of fame.

Every season, I set out on this long, arduous and expensive European odyssey, schlepping to strange corners of the Continent, anxiously sitting in front of the computer for the draw of each successive round, hoping I can find Hotzeplotz on the computer and an affordable flight to somewhere in the vicinity. More than any other previous campaign, many of us thought that this might be the season when Arsène finally liberates himself from the burden of the European monkey on his back. After clocking up so many air miles in the fruitless pursuit of this ambition, winning it would come as a welcome relief, if only that I might be able to save a small fortune by being able to forego some of the less-delectable foreign trips in future and stop at home to watch them on the box with all the other sensible Gooners.

With hindsight, it is relatively easy to establish reasons why we won't be going to Gelsenkirchen in May (obviously apart from getting beaten by Chelsea!), all of them related to financial constraints. I can't think of a team that's achieved European Cup success without a world-class keeper between the sticks. Our goal-minder might work out as great value at only £1.5 million but, at the end of the day, you only get what you pay for. You can be sure that whatever the Arsenal would have needed to borrow to afford someone a little higher up the scale of proven international ability, we would have been repaid several times over with all the incidental rewards which go with Champions League success (the World Club Championship, etc.). What's more, at the start of the season, according to virtually all of the pundits, Wenger's skeletal squad was going to struggle to survive the domestic dust-up. While I doubt very much he would have tinkered to the same extent as Ranieri, I am sure Wenger would've been grateful for a few more world-class reserves. They might have ensured that some of our stars were just a little fresher for a more successful finale.

However, by and large, the media has patently neglected to consider the Arsenal's progress during Wenger's tenure from a 'glass half-full' perspective. The Arsenal don't have unlimited access to the King of Spain's coffers nor the deep pockets of a Russian sugar daddy, and they don't have the plc status to issue shares which aren't worth the paper they're printed on. Considering Arsène's net spending is substantially lower than many of our domestic rivals, it is downright astonishing that he has produced one of the greatest teams on this planet. Unlike the plight poor Leeds were left in by O'Leary, our club isn't totally dependent on being successful to stay solvent.

Liverpool's visit last Friday was proof positive of quite how lucky we Gooners are, as it highlighted the gulf in class between Houllier's hotchpotch of hirelings and ours (remember, he inherited the likes of Gerrard and Owen). To avoid any further disappointment in my despondent state, I'd prepared myself for the possibility of a Premiership backlash from our cup exits. I believed we might not be able to lift ourselves and the scent of Arsenal blood might see us blow all six points over Easter. I was already envisaging the silver lining that any gloss which had been taken off the Gunners' title triumph would be restored with the enjoyment of winning after a wide-open climax.

It will be an incredible achievement if we can remain undefeated and suddenly there's an added attraction of perhaps winning the title at White Hart Lane (again). At least without any Cup distractions, Wenger won't be tempted to rest players. My biggest concern is that the closer we come to record-breaking glory, the bigger the hype becomes. As we saw at St James' Park where we'd plainly settled for the draw at the death, there is a danger that the fear of losing might prevent us playing out these last six games at our adventurous best.

39

Premiership: Friday, 16 April (H) Arsenal 5 Leeds United 0 Pires (6), Henry (27, 33 pen, 50, 67)

A repeat of last season, I should coco! 'We're the West Stand, Highbury.' 'Nuff said!

Leeds must have gone in at half-time somewhat shellshocked to be 3–0 down, with the sound of, 'You'll never play here again' and 'Premiership? You're having a larf' as they had actually acquitted themselves quite well. They were lucky last season to catch us on the rebound after we'd just blown the title at Bolton but on this occasion, Wenger's side were positively steaming, more like a woman scorned. Usually, when a referee is kind enough to award us a penalty, the first question on Gooner lips is, 'Who's gonna take it?' However, evidence of the renewed confidence surging throughout the Arsenal squad was demonstrated in the absolute lack of doubt about the taker and the consummate nerve in Titi's cheeky chip down the middle, which would have gone straight into the arms of Robinson if it wasn't for his despairing dive.

It was as if Henry was making a point of dispelling the absurd rumours that he wasn't happy with Reyes as he ran straight over to the touchline to give the Spaniard a big hug. However, it was Thierry's 150th goal for the Gunners (as he became the first person to score four at THOF since Wrighty in '91) which summed up the determination that has dominated our undefeated run. Leaving a trail of Leeds defenders eating his dust, Titi still had the presence of mind to put the ball in the back of the net while in the process of hitting the deck after Kelly had clipped his heels. There are many strikers who would have been more interested in ensuring they were awarded a penalty.

Since I am usually so oblivious to my surroundings, it took someone to point out to me that the front of the North Bank upper tier had been adorned with a banner along part of its length which read, 'WHL '71, Anfield '89' and with Chelsea dropping points to Everton at the Bridge and Man Utd losing at Pompey before the weekend was out, it was looking all the more likely that 'WHL '04' might be added by the time we returned for our next home game against Birmingham.

Hallelujah! The Library's Lambs Finally Let Rip
19 April 2004

Dontcha just love this time of year? As the flora and fauna bursts forth in all its resplendent beauty, with the scent of summer and the promise of long, sunny evenings, spring is well and truly sprung. Meanwhile, the final act of football's annual passion play reaches its climactic conclusion. Sporting junkies like myself are mainlining on a massive overdose of intense action before the silverware-sorting curtain calls signal the coming of the cricket bat. Oh, the agony and the ecstasy of an entire season's worth of sweat and toil condensed into a positively priceless, point-saving goalline clearance, or a single scuffed shot sliding centimetres wide of its mark. It's a time when football's fortunes tend to favour the brave and the bold, and hopefully it's the teams full of no-mark narcissists which get nuked. A viewing prospect made all the more pleasurable from the comfort of my living-room couch, in our privileged position sitting atop an insurmountable Premiership cushion.

When I eventually came to a halt in Highbury Quadrant sometime during the wee hours last week after an exhausting 550-mile round-trip to Toon Town, I pulled up the handbrake and, laughing in the face of my lassitude, I let out a long sigh of satisfaction. The nightmare schlep to Newcastle was the last game involving hard graft on my part (Pompey's a piece of piss by comparison), which meant the end was very nearly nigh. Aside from our date with Harry Redknapp's south-coast coquettes, all our remaining matches are on my doorstep. During the course of another marathon season, I've clocked up countless miles amidst Arsène's army of fanatically faithful foot soldiers. Having paid my supporter's dues, hopefully my reward for services rendered will be the scintillating skills of a relaxing, six-game run-in. Romping to the title at White Hart Lane, condemning Spurs to a relegation struggle, not to mention that momentous undefeated record, could all come as exceedingly good icing on one of Mr Kipling's finest.

Leeds certainly lived up to my billing and our Friday night match made for a reminder of why I love my missus. With double the dogsitting duties due to her son's injured pooch, Róna decided to donate her ticket to the lad who lives in the flat downstairs. Apparently, her heartwarming recompense was the youngster's rollicking reaction, as Jamel literally exploded with joy. She watched the live broadcast on the box, listening to the sound of this season's most exuberant atmosphere wafting through our living-room window, while he got to witness live another glut of goals from the magical feet of the Arsenal's goal machine (although there's nothing mechanical about the maestro's organic grace). As the records accumulate each week, it's becoming harder and harder to find words which really do justice to Henry's dumbfounding feats. He's like a highly strung Lipizzaner (high-stepping) stallion, who leaves dray-horse defenders like Duberry petrified of his unpredictability, not daring to even attempt a tackle lest he be left trailing in Titi's wake when he bolts.

However, Leeds hardly merited the slating they received from some quarters of the press. Depleted resources forced them to resort to the unimaginative likes of Radebe in midfield. As they say, 'nuff said. Nor were the Arsenal entitled to such slavish eulogies from the tabloid sheep. In fact, Leeds impeded the Arsenal's flow to a trickle for the first thirty minutes. Until then, our entire efforts only amounted to two attacks. Unfortunately for the visitors, both ended with Robinson picking the ball out of the onion bag. Avid Arsenal watchers can confirm that, aside from our sensational selection of quicksilver, counter-attacking cameos, the Gunners have struggled to find top gear recently. This actually makes the season's achievements and the margin of our success all the more brilliant. The prospect of how much more there might be to come from this particular side makes me feel positively breathless.

Far from complaining, Friday's encounter was without doubt this season's most enjoyable home match to date. Lishman last scored back-to-back hat-tricks at Highbury in 1951 and I wouldn't be at all surprised if it's been a similarly long time since the West Upper whingers last gave it such enthusiastic wellie! There have been many times when I've listened enviously to the two stands behind the goals serenading each other with alternate choruses of, 'We're the Clock End/We're the North Bank Highbury' with the occasional interjection from the fans seated opposite in the East Stand. For the first time in my living memory, I didn't have to resist the temptation to pipe up with 'I'M the West Stand', as almost everyone around me appeared to enter into the spirit of the competitive alternate choruses, rising to a doughty crescendo which left me pinching myself in utter disbelief. Confirmation indeed – if any was needed – that something very special is coming to pass.

I was concerned that Jamel might think this amazing atmosphere and the sensational skills were an ever-present feature at The Home Of Football. I explained to him that I'd served a 30-year apprenticeship, including many fallow seasons full of mediocrity, for him to be able to enjoy the very best the beautiful game has to offer. It's a difficult enough task trying to evaluate players in different positions but you're on a hiding to nothing when comparing those from another era. Nevertheless, there's absolutely no question that Titi is capable of the most dazzling entertainment I've ever witnessed on a football pitch. It is such a privilege to be in the presence of such greatness that the sight of Gooners genuflecting is no longer such a laughing matter. In crediting his teammates in his post-match interview, we saw what a gracious geezer he is, when an egocentric outlook is often the stock in trade of most star strikers. We must be careful not to put Henry too high up on the 'perfect' pedestal, especially in a week when the England captain has been dashed from a similar perch for displaying the simple human flaws that are forbidden to such heroic icons.

Coincidentally, Ray, my West Upper neighbour, and I have both been laid up the past week (obviously not together) after both of us brought a nasty lurgy back from Newcastle. I certainly could have done with a shot of Jewish penicillin but our second Friday night game of the season forced me to take a rain check on our regular date at my ma's (besides, chicken soup is more of a winter comfort food than the sort of thing she might serve up on a sunny spring evening). As much as I enjoy her food (and her company), Mum appreciates that there is no way I am going to want to sacrifice the Arsenal, especially in such sparkling five-goal form.

However, I sincerely hope regular Friday night football is not another cross for us traditionalists to bear (talk about mixing my metaphors). It is yet another example of the TV tail wagging the football-fixture dog with total disregard for the wishes of the fans, as if it wasn't bad enough already with regular fixtures on Sundays and Mondays leaving us with little excuse to get out of the shopping on a Saturday – a dreadfully chauvinistic crack and far from the truth in our case, since most of our shopping gets done in the middle of the night. I suppose it is a sign of my age that I still believe going to a match at the weekend should mean a 3 p.m. kick-off on a Saturday afternoon. Yet these seem to be the rarity rather than the norm in these days of wall-to-wall TV coverage. And if I am not fond of such an irregular fixture list, living only five minutes' walk from THOF, I can't imagine what a pain it must be for those season-ticket holders who have to arrange to travel from Wales, Yorkshire etc., who can't enjoy a drink because they will be returning home in the wee hours.

For lovers of our sport, like myself, Friday night footie is without doubt the worst example of the beautiful game bending over to accommodate the wishes of the Sky cameras. Continuing with the amorous analogy, the euphoria of our triumph over Leeds must be akin to premature ejaculation (where 'must be' is my way of intimating that it is not a problem I am familiar with!). The entire weekend's footballing pleasures are over in a 90-minute flash on Friday night before the weekend has even started, with none of the usual foreplay involved in the build-up to a match in the weekend papers and the preview on *Football Focus*, that tingle of nervous anticipation as you contemplate your coming performance. The only consolation is that at least we don't have to concern ourselves worrying about whether it was any good for them!

Admittedly, I only saw highlights of the subsequent dispassionate performances last weekend but the apparent lack of incisive play served as a poignant reminder of how much Man Utd and Chelsea must have raised their game against us. My heart goes out to Ró's nephew back in Dublin. With Shane's last pilgrimage having included our two most inauspicious performances of the season, he would have been dead jealous of Jamel. Whereas, with a mouth full of his post-match hot dog, Jamel was only too quick to point out that he's never yet seen the Arsenal lose – chancing his arm perhaps that, with his 'lucky mascot' status, he might wangle a seat at White Hart Lane.

He can join the queue including Uncle Tom Cobbleigh and all the thousands of other Gooners who will be wishing they had one of the gold-dust tickets which will enable them to run the hooligan gauntlet in Tottenham High Road on Sunday. I had to explain to Jamel that my missus's extreme benevolence doesn't quite stretch to her being stark raving bonkers. There are tickets to be found if moolah is no object. Some Spurs fans are attempting to save themselves from the possibility of having to suffer '71 revisited, while seeking solace in perhaps fleecing us Gooners for the entire price of their season-ticket renewals. Hopefully, the laws of karma won't condone it but can you imagine their glee if the result should go against us, knowing that the privilege of being there had just covered their costs for a whole season's worth of footballing pleasures? Although many might disagree about it being a pleasure, and most would protest that, at this point in time, it should be Spurs paying their supporters to suffer the frustrations of following that shower!

40

Premiership: Sunday, 25 April (A) Arsenal 2 Tottenham Hotspur 2 Vieira (3), Pires (35)

A draw will do nicely, thank you, and even our goalie's costly little gaff can't put a dampener on our Championship party.

We were scuttling along Tottenham High Road as I tried to keep tabs on the radio commentary of the 2 p.m. kick-off on Tyneside. I took my O level maths when I was 14 but it was absolutely no practical use when John Terry hit the woodwork in the closing moments. It took commentator Jonathan Pearce to confirm that Chelsea's 2–1 defeat meant we only needed a draw at White Hart Lane to bring the Premiership trophy back to its rightful home.

In some respects, I wished the games had kicked off simultaneously because if the players weren't aware of this fact, they might not have taken their foot off the pedal in the second half to give the poor, deluded Spurs fans the illusion that the final result suggested an even contest. Far more indicative of the difference between the two teams was the way we scythed through their entire side with positively majestic simplicity for Paddy's opener (as the cliché says, 'pure poetry in motion'). I am just glad that we got a wriggle on as we'd hardly had time to take our seats before our corner of White Hart Lane was resounding to the sound of incessant choruses of 'We'll win the League at the sh*thole'.

The thing that amused me most was the thought that when Lehmann eventually gifted Spurs their equaliser, probably the most euphoric moment of their entire season, many of the long-suffering but less-than-faithful home fans must have missed it. They had already long since been heading for the exits in the hope of avoiding the final-whistle ignominy of having to suffer the sight of the Arsenal winning the title on their own turf. And while, at the time, everyone was cursing our goalie's aggressive behaviour because it resulted in ref Halsey awarding Keane a penalty, *replays shown later that night suggested that of our keeper's many misdemeanours this was probably the least clear-cut of them all. Perhaps he felt suitably ashamed that he might have played such a major part in pooping our party which is why he skulked off straight away to join Sol in the dressing-room. Little did he realise that nothing, with the exception of a defeat, was going to prevent us milking this special moment for all it was worth. Even Abramovich, with all his millions of roubles, couldn't put a price on this splendiferous occasion.*

We've Gotta Fight for the Right to Party!
26 April 2004

Only a couple of weeks back, the thought of actually winning the title at White Hart Lane was an outrageous fantasy in the minds of most Gooners. Yet our immediate competitors were shipping points in a manner that suggested they weren't too concerned with putting up a committed fight for the consolation prizes. They had more important fish to fry, like what factor suncream they were going to need on their summer hols. As the day grew nigh, the delicious dream of '71 revisited became a reality.

The media coverage of that magical night 34 years back made for a nostalgic week. I delved into the darkest recesses of my somewhat befuddled brain to add my own reminiscences to the words and pictures in all the papers. Every time I read another tale about the unlucky tens of thousands locked out that night (many with tickets!), I marvel at how my old man managed to shepherd two ten year olds into the ground, through all that mayhem.

I was collected from school with a Spurs-supporting neighbour, whose Dad was working. His memory must have borne the ravages of time far better than mine because it wasn't until I met him again for the first time in many moons after my old man's funeral and we were wallowing in this much-loved anecdote that I was reminded of the facts. If there are some with 'more front than Sainsbury's' then Pop had more chutzpah than Harrods and, arriving at the ground to find the queue for the unreserved tickets stretching right around the block, apparently he went up to the copper closest to the front and spun him a yarn about leaving his place to pick up us kids. I can't believe that those who'd been queueing for hours didn't kick up a fuss when we were promptly placed a few yards from the turnstiles!

What I do recall is the rush when the gates eventually opened and I've no doubt we would have never got in otherwise. I can still picture the old man herding the two of us towards this heaven, his reassuring hands on our shoulders, holding us together as a trident with two tiny prongs. Oh, for those innocent days of unreserved seating, when taking the kids to football wasn't an operation requiring military planning. Even without a ticket, one could invariably bowl up and bung the turnstile operator a few bob.

How times have changed! On TV the other night, comedian Frank Skinner proudly displayed his own innovative season ticket. In this 'chips with everything' era, rather like the credit-card type tickets for the City of Manchester stadium, apparently Skinner gains entry to the Hawthorns by holding up his West Brom wristwatch against a gadget on the door!

For me, nothing highlighted the contrast between the ball game of yesteryear and modern footie better than a wonderful photo reproduced in some of the press. The highly toned physiques of today's superfit professionals bear little resemblance to a somewhat pasty-looking John Radford and Ray Kennedy, celebrating in the dressing-room after their title winning performance, Radford with a well-earned glass of champers and a fag in hand only four days before the Cup final.

Unfortunately, the Arsenal are involved in no such encore this season. However, as bothered as I might be by any regrets that this side could have blown away their opponents in both FA Cup and Champions League finals, I have an inkling that our painful European exit might actually prove a blessing. If we'd managed to sweep the board this season, we'd be lumbered with such a supremely dominant disposition that we would have been left facing the anticlimactic fact that there would be nowhere to go but down next term. Whereas, at least now hopefully any complacent tendencies are less likely because this side still has a big point to prove by validating its peerless pedigree on the European stage. Instead of wondering where we go from here, we Gooners have all this to look forward to.

What's more, we couldn't have wanted for a more palliative poultice for any European headaches than the opportunity to wave our incredible Championship-winning exploits in the faces of forlorn Spurs fans at White Hart Lane. As Sunday approached, Gooners grew more desperate for a ticket to this once-in-a-lifetime (twice even, for the luckier ones amongst us) occasion. In an effort to make the very best of a bad situation, one Spurs pal phoned to let me know his tickets were for sale at £300 a pop. He joked that the money wasn't his motivation but the prospect that his extortion might be reported to the club and they'd do him the favour of banning him for life!

A couple of days later, he told me that he'd been taking flak from another mutual Spurs mate for trying to fleece footie fans. Yet, when the call came from no less than the offspring of one of the Arsenal directors, with an offer of a grand for four tickets, apparently the self-same pseud couldn't pipe up quickly enough to participate in this particularly profitable party. Traditionally, it is the form book which goes out of the window when it comes to local derbies but, in this instance, it was the morals of many Spurs fans, where so much money was involved!

With every distraught tale from a ticketless Gooner, I grew increasingly guilty at our good fortune, feeling the need almost daily to dig our own two tickets to our White Hart Lane Valhalla out of my bag to make sure they hadn't disappeared. I actually spent most of the week in bed with a nasty bug, worrying whether I would be able to make it. Although, even if at death's door, there was no way I was going to be denied such a delectable dream! The many 'wish you better' sentiments expressed by my mates didn't sound particularly insincere but perhaps I was suffering from a surfeit of bad vibes sent by all those hoping to go in my stead.

As Spurs sunk ever deeper into the relegation mire with Saturday's results, my mate with the full wallet must have taken my 'bad karma' warnings to heart. He was grafting Sunday morning and somehow managed to conjure up a ticket for one particularly good cause. However, as a single female, this Gooner gal didn't fancy her chances in the ultimate exercise in self-restraint, standing amidst Spurs' most horrible Park Lane heartland having to keep a lid on the emotions which have built up over the course of an entire season, for fear of seriously injurious consequences from a single imprudent smile.

Mercifully, there was no such need to keep a check on our emotions in the Arsenal seats. As the sun shined, we made plenty of hay by rubbing salt in Spurs' silverware-starved wounds. The competition didn't end when the final whistle blew. It was as though both sets of supporters were trying to see who could celebrate more vociferously. The Spurs fans were more than happy with their point and the fact that we hadn't actually won, especially when on the evidence of the first half it looked like they might be overrun. Still, we certainly weren't going to let our party be pooped because of the relatively meaningless matter of having gifted them a virtual guarantee of Premiership salvation.

All I heard at half-time was the sound of Gooners positively purring over our imperious display. The gulf in class was embarrassingly obvious but invariably the frenetic pace of most north London derbies leaves little time for the pretty stuff and so few could believe our brilliance was being made to look quite so effortless. As a result, it wasn't surprising that we switched off for the second half and attempted to see out the remainder of the match playing on autopilot. After losing five of the last six, I suppose I can't blame Spurs fans for clutching at suspect straws. Yet I found myself laughing out loud listening to the radio en route home and the deluded Lilywhites who phoned in to express their delight at this display.

Necessity might be the mother of invention but it appears that our neighbours' perennial failures have forced Spurs fans to forge their own parallel universe. To my mind, it should have been patently clear to even the most biased Spurs bonehead that the Arsenal could have produced a cricket score if they hadn't pulled stumps at the break. Many of them were deluded into believing that they'd witnessed proof of Spurs' ability to compete with the Premiership's very best. In the place of these poor schmucks, I still would have been outraged that I'd paid good money to watch this bunch of mercenaries, when their minds hadn't been on their game for weeks now. Like many of the players at Man Utd, Chelsea and the majority of others, they were far more focused on where they were going to have fun in the sun, than on the football.

Winning the title with two games to spare in '98, we succumbed to a severe case of 'after the Lord Mayor's show' syndrome. No one was too concerned on the terraces. We were too busy celebrating our way to the first of many Cardiff Cup finals. However, in the future it will be forgotten that we shipped our last six points and so the final table gave a false illusion of a close-run affair. We'll have to wait until Saturday to see if we are to suffer a similar fate and whether a White Hart Lane hangover is set to ruin an incredible undefeated record.

The marvelous ranks of this Arsenal squad are not made up of insensible robots. As a result, it would be downright ridiculous not to expect some slight relaxation after nine long months of nuclear-fuelled tension. Who knows? Having been relieved of the burden of bringing home the Championship bacon, this might just be the unencumbered climate for a beautiful bout of fantasy football. No matter whether they stroll to the finishing line in fine style, or we muddle our way to immortality, it would seem that the lads are more than aware that they are on the verge of an extraordinarily immaculate achievement which might never again be repeated in our lifetime (although, apparently that's what they said about Spurs' Double in '61!). Never mind what Preston did over 100 years ago; their undefeated season involved almost half the amount of matches and, while it seems likely that we might get a crack at the Champions League almost every season, we might never again find ourselves having not been beaten with only four games left to play.

Hopefully, Pompey will be sufficiently clear of the drop come our trip to the south coast and, although on the face of it our two away games appear to offer the biggest threat, my feeling is that if the players are sufficiently focused to overcome Birmingham on Saturday, it will suggest that there is likely to be no sleep until sublimity. There was a clue on Sunday night at the PFA awards as to how much Titi and Patrick were prepared to let their hair down. Apparently, their night out on the lash was limited to making sure that their meals came with the skin and fat removed from the meat!

I just pray that the Arsenal aren't infected by this plague of 'end of seasonitis', where the sight of the finishing post appears to cause almost every other team to flag, to the extent that I feel the faithful fans are being fleeced because of an absolute lack of fervour out on the pitch. It will be interesting to see if Spurs show anywhere near as much enthusiasm in their subsequent outing. I don't doubt that it must be incredibly infuriating for those teams duelling to the death with their rivals to beat the drop when others can evade the Nationwide trap door with a doozie of a game against those overpaid and underworked sides who've been clock-watching for weeks now. I suppose we shouldn't be worried if our lot are still concerned about eating cholesterol-free food instead of binging on booze and fags.

Henry's prior engagement on Sunday as the first-ever player to pick up back-to-back PFA awards meant that he must have split from White Hart Lane pretty quickly. So (with apologies to all those whose pants I've bored off with my much-loved tale), sadly there was no chance of us ending up with Titi in the back of our motor, as we did when the old man gave the winning goalscorer a lift in '71. Still, even without a precious souvenir programme like the one signed by Ray Kennedy, 'To Bernard, who I travelled home with', Sunday was every bit as memorable. The splenetic Spurs fans certainly didn't deserve the courtesy of Sol Campbell's swift exit from the scene and I don't think many of us either noticed nor cared that Lehmann disappeared to hide his shame in the dressing-room. Yet, when the stewards began to cut our Premiership-winning party short, as some lunatic home fans began to lose their heads, I think most of us assumed that was our lot for the afternoon.

When the rest of the stadium had eventually emptied and the stewards began busying themselves, there was a buzz of excitement at the prospect of further festivities. There was a certain illicit pleasure to our own private party at the heart of Tottenham's own (albeit third-rate) temple and, as the players trooped out in sandals and in various states of undress (aided by the pant-pulling antics of the jokers in our pack), I don't think I've ever been happier to have been locked inside a stadium, knowing there'd be disconsolate Spurs fans listening from without to the sort of songs they might be unlikely to sing in their entire lifetimes. It was without doubt the highlight of White Hart Lane 2004.

I've seen my fair share of Arsenal celebrations over the years but even to an old lag like myself there was something special about this particular hootenanny. In certain circumstances, the prearranged post-match merriment with some silverware has seemed a little phoney, the songs somewhat forced, the smiles a little false, as if it was primarily being staged for the press and TV cameras rather than a sincere moment of bonding between players and supporters. Even the most cynical of Gooners must have sensed that special sense of unity present in this squad. There were no fake badge-kissing gestures as there were none needed amongst a 'team' genuinely enjoying one another's company as they savoured their moment in the sun.

Unable to parade the original Premiership trophy around the enemy's turf, we were all very grateful to the good-hearted Spurs steward who retrieved an inflatable replica which was thrown towards the pitch. If it wasn't for this magnanimous act, we wouldn't have enjoyed the scenes of the entire team standing in a semi-circle as each of the players ran towards the fans to do a little party piece as they took it in turns to pick up and celebrate with this pretend trophy. When Ashley Cole did a runner with it and headed towards the centre circle, for one hilarious moment as he stood there throwing a pose, I honestly thought he intended to relieve himself, right there on Tottenham's centre spot. Seeing the pictures afterwards, I realise that he was just savouring the moment.

We might not be consanguineous but Ashley Cole was born in Stepney, grew up in the inner city and has been at the Arsenal since he was a schoolboy. With such credentials, you can't help but feel a special connection with him. The whole team tells us that they appreciate how important it is to their fans to win the League at White Hart Lane but, in addition to Cole, there is only the likes of Ray Parlour, Sol Campbell and Martin Keown who can actually *know* what it means and whose joy can therefore be quite so unconfined as our own. No matter how excited their teammates were, they can't really delight in the knowledge that they have just diddled Spurs-supporting friends, family, the window cleaner or the milkman out of several years worth of 'life wouldn't be worth living'-type teasing if Tottenham had prevailed and had been the one team to ruin our unblemished League record. Thierry Henry might be as sincere as they come in his assertions that he is red and white right through to the core but you still cannot replicate an entire life's worth of sentiment woven into our daily social interaction with the enemy.

The scenes of the players otherwise taking the piss on the Tottenham turf will live with me to my dying day. However, when we'd all had our fill of fun and paid tribute to the man who had masterminded the greatest-ever Arsenal side, we were all left hoping that that particular day wasn't going to come far too prematurely. There remained the small matter of making our way back to our end of the Seven Sisters Road without coming to any serious harm, so we could join in with the hullabaloo around Highbury.

I never fail to be amazed that there are some Spurs folk who fork out more to park their cars each week than some footie fans pay for their entire season ticket. I usually stump up a tenner to leave the motor in the car park which my Spurs mate uses at the top of White Hart Lane (where some pay £15 for a prime pitch near the gate, so they can make a swift exit when they leave the match before the end). On this occasion, we decided to walk a few more yards as I'd spotted a different pitch which was only half that price. As we left the car, realising that we might be kept back after the match whether we had something to celebrate or not, I mentioned that we might be delayed. The bloke reassured me that I didn't have to worry as the gates wouldn't be locked until 7 p.m.

It was only when we were eventually let out of the ground that I glanced at my watch and, seeing that we only had ten minutes to get back to the car, I grew a little concerned. I was sure that there must be other Gooner-mobiles in this car park but the last thing I wanted was to get back to find our car had been corralled for the night. It would be no fun having to extricate ourselves from enemy territory on foot, looking for a cab as we went. It would be hard enough keeping a lid on our emotions on our way back to the car, let alone wiping the smile off our faces all the way home, lest we reveal ourselves to any of the animals who were hanging around hoping for an opportunity to inflict revenge on some innocent Gooner victims.

Not that the Neanderthal Spurs numbskulls would possess the necessary powers of deduction but, personally, I thought we Gooners were easy to spot even without the large grins. It was an unusually warm April afternoon and I immediately recognised those of my own faith as we walked along. We were the only ones dripping with sweat, suffering in the heat, having slipped on a second layer of clothing to cover up any sign of our red and white colours. To our right, there was a large police cordon to segregate us from any remaining Spurs fans on the High Road. Róna and I probably could have slipped through but I thought we might be too conspicuous and I didn't fancy walking right past the main entrance. The police directed the vast majority of Gooners to the left, sending them on a long march to Northumberland Park station. They were masking any apprehension by belting out some triumphant tunes as they disappeared into the distance, making themselves the most obvious targets for Spurs' livid lunatics. Moreover, they were heading in completely the opposite direction to our motor.

Mercifully, we didn't join them as any sense of security in numbers soon proved false when they were attacked en masse. Still, it all went very quiet as we found ourselves virtually alone, trying to get back to the car as quickly as possible. We headed left towards the end of the Park Lane stand and then left again into Worcester Avenue, walking along the length of the East Stand. I'd be lying if I said I wasn't sweating as I circumnavigated the ground gripping Ró's hand, trying to avoid direct eye contact with anyone heading in the opposite direction and doing our utmost not to look too pleased with ourselves. Perhaps Ró didn't fully appreciate the seriousness of our situation, having never before legged it from a rabid mob looking to do serious damage (thankfully). She seemed to think we were perfectly safe because both sides of the entire length of the street were lined with meat wagons. I didn't want to ruin this illusion and spoil her sense of security by pointing out that there wasn't a single copper in any of them, as they were probably all off attempting to protect the main bulk of Gooners heading for the station.

I tried to ease the tension by joking with a bloke who was walking along studying a couple of pages of an A–Z, enquiring, 'Planning your escape route?' Although, at the same time, we crossed to the other side of the road as he couldn't have been more obvious if he'd had a neon Gooner sign and a red arrow pointing at his lack of local knowledge. A few of the faces heading towards us looked to be those of some of the enemy's indignant scum, looking for aggro, and I wondered what I'd do if they started on this bloke. Would I get involved and come to the assistance of a fellow Gooner, or would I bottle it completely and just be grateful that his troubles meant they weren't bothering us?

Thankfully, after turning left again along the Paxton Road end, we were able to blend in with folks leaving a bar. I don't think I have ever been more relieved for the relative sanctuary of a far-less-deserted Tottenham High Road and eventually the safety of the car. Even then, my paranoia was such that, as we headed along White Hart Lane, crawling along a queue of a couple of hundred yards to some traffic lights, with the windows wide open and Ró obliviously reliving the afternoon's event to a pal on her mobile, I had to tell her to pipe down a little so as not to sound quite so delighted with herself. I was afraid a flying fist might come sailing through the open window from a particularly peeved pedestrian!

Returning from Tottenham, I never feel guerrilla manoeuvres are really over until we've managed to get over the Green Lanes border into definite Gooner territory. However, as much as I detest the tension involved in this annual outing down the wrong end of the Seven Sisters Road, I still wouldn't miss it for the world. Yet the one common theme coming from those I've spoken to since is that the dangers of travelling to and from the Lane have become a risk they can live without. As a result, many have said to me that they don't plan on returning in future. It would be a crying shame to think that these Gooners schlep all over the country and the Continent, faithfully following our team, only to be stumped by the shortest trip of the season because of Spurs' slieveens! Although, I guess it's not surprising and I should really be counting my blessings.

Having taken off in the opposite direction, we fortunately managed to avoid the straws which broke the backs of many Gooner camels who'd been directed towards the station by the Old Bill. Apparently, they were ambushed and had to take refuge from a hail of bottles and bricks in a school hall. And there these beleaguered Gooners remained, kicking their heels in darkest Tottenham, bereft of all the fun-filled bedlam at Highbury, extremely relieved to eventually make it back to a red-and-white boozer at 9 p.m. Gooners might be swearing off Spurs for life in the aftermath of such a traumatic incident but I wonder if they'll still be of a similar mind when Derby day rolls around again next season? Evading the 'Forces of Darkness' on a sortie in and out of Spurs territory is always a bit of a nightmare but being there is bound to be bloody brilliant. I've no doubt all the naysayers will be back, absolutely revelling in the opportunity to sing loud and proud as we remind Spurs fans "61 . . . never again', "71 . . . we've done it again' and my particular favourite "71 . . . 2004'!

41

Premiership: Saturday, 1 May (H) Arsenal 0 Birmingham City 0

Sadly, all quiet on the western front and everywhere else at the Library, as yet another 12.30 kick-off for live TV has that 'after the Lord Mayor's show' mood. All that matters now is that magical P 38, L 0 target.

A chorus of, 'By far the greatest team' sung with ever-increasing conviction was about the only homage to the previous week's feats from the Highbury faithful. Sadly, it was hardly the fortissimo performance our Premiership homecoming deserved. With my irreverent hullabaloo, I kept expecting a tap on the shoulder from a Librarian demanding hush. In between the silence and Birmingham's spoiler tactics, Ray, my West Upper neighbour, told me that I'd texted the suggestion that he check out the picture of the pasty-faced Radford and Kennedy in the paper on the very same day that he was heading to a do where Radford was a guest speaker. Apparently, the ex-Arsenal striker had quipped that the picture of him with fag and booze in hand was taken prior to the match at White Hart Lane in '71.

With little of note to contemplate, half-time was spent trying to work out who the 'Daddy' was in the 'Well done Daddy and the team' banner hanging from one of the Clock End's boxes. It must be a reflection on the entertainment that the most-memorable moment occurred a few minutes before the final whistle, when Ray Parlour played a prank on Martin Keown by pretending to strip off as our final sub. The camaraderie in our camp was evident in Keown's response as he jokingly grabbed le guv'nor around the throat.

Immortality Beckons
3 May 2004

With Rona visiting her folks on the Emerald Isle, I was faced with a bit of a dilemma last weekend. As the day looms when the renewals for our two season tickets will drop on the doormat, I dread to think how much more than this year's £3,300 we are going to have to find. The nineteen Premiership home games and seven Cup ties currently work out at over sixty-three quid a match. Considering the amount of times I've tapped my ma for loans on the extremely 'long finger' to ensure our seats are secured for another season, I thought that perhaps she should for once get some value for her extremely favourable terms by accompanying me to Saturday's match.

There is a downside to the Arsenal's incredible undefeated record and the longer it continues, the more it becomes a bit of a millstone for a superstitious sod like myself. Forget the necessity for continued concentration and focus amongst the players, and think of us poor fans. As the weeks and months have passed, I've had to put all the more effort and preparation into making sure that I don't alter any of my pre-match rituals. Then there's also the problem of maintaining the correct dress code. I have to take every precaution to avoid donning the one article of clothing which might cause displeasure to the fickle gods of fate, for fear that I might bear responsibility for the club's eventual downfall.

I carry a shoulder bag to football in which I keep my binoculars, terrace tranny, fruit Polos, a pack of tissues, lipsalve and any other accoutrements which have become an integral part of my 'don't leave home without it' footie kit. Admittedly, lipsalve might be a bit of a nancy-boy item, especially now that winter's on the wane, but there's no way I can leave anything out. A runny nose is another winter annoyance but you only have to be caught short standing in the puddles of some northern pisshole, where the nearest thing to a piece of toilet paper is a tin-foil pie wrapper to know how priceless a pack of tissues can be. As each season gathers momentum, so my bag gains weight because on a winning run, anything that goes in there, remains in there for the duration.

When taking a bottle of water to a game, if I remember in time, I usually try to hide it before the stewards take the top away. I forgot at

White Hart Lane last week and the stewards forced me to pour the contents into a plastic cup. Indignant over such futile restrictions, I felt like asking them what the point was of preventing me from using the bottle of water as an offensive weapon when they've ignored the razor-sharp penknife in my bag? So much for security! The knife wasn't for stabbing Spurs fans – far too good a fate for some of the scum – but a throwback to my days in the theatre. Yet I suppose since it's passed through many an airport X-ray machine unnoticed, even in this Al-Qaeda era, there's no reason why a slovenly steward would spot it. Even with my swarthy, certainly non-Anglo-Saxon appearance, St Mary's has been the only stadium this season where I might not have been able to stroll in with a couple of kilos of Semtex.

Anyway, I soon went off the idea of my ma taking my missus's ticket – not only would she never have forgiven herself if she happened to be present for our first defeat all season but I would have struggled to avoid apportioning blame and tried to pretend it was a mere coincidence. Selling my spare would have been the sensible solution. Although, while I might be more than happy to fork out such fancy prices, I always find myself far too embarrassed to ask for the extortionate face value.

Still, any cash would have been a feeble substitute compared to the kick I get from springing the occasional surprise on our neighbour's lad and seeing his little face light up with the thrill. He's already been the fortunate beneficiary a few times and, as a lucky mascot to date, I didn't dare leave him at home in favour of a paying punter. The money would have definitely felt like filthy lucre if we'd lost. Thankfully, Jamel arrived home just in the nick of time from playing for the prize of a precious football in a five-a-side tournament with his pals. Walking to Highbury with this cock-a-hoop kid bounding along beside me, I was glad my heart had ruled my head. I reminded Jamel that he can return the favour when I'm a hard-up pensioner.

After whooping it up with a handful of Gooners at White Hart Lane, I imagined the fanfare for our heroes' return from the 30,000 home fans present would guarantee a day to remember. I can't stand these early kick-offs. When it comes to watching the Arsenal perform before 3 p.m. I am reminded of one of my old man's corny cracks: a man goes to the doctor to complain that he has to pee at 6 a.m. every morning, and is told not to worry since most folks would love to be so regular. 'Yeh, but the problem is I don't wake up until 8 a.m.!'

Well, at least the Arsenal were sufficiently stirred to produce a couple of first-half moves of sublime quality, as the remainder of our Premiership party fell decidedly flat. With the lack of any real ambition after the break, one could have been forgiven for thinking there'd been a tacit half-time agreement in the tunnel to stage manage a mutually agreeable, scoreless second-half draw. Agreeable to all except the long-suffering fans!

It is a scornful sign of these mercenary times that even amongst teams with something still to play for, far too many of the closing fixtures are soporific farces involving combatants who can't even be bothered to feign some commitment. Since we are paying theatre prices, is a little melodrama involving some goalmouth action too much to ask? If football 'matches' were bound by the Trades Descriptions Act, many clubs would be made bankrupt by fans' demands for refunds for some of these cordial comedies.

If I didn't know better, I would have said that our lot looked like they'd been painting the town red (and white) since securing the Premiership, yet Vieira and Henry were hardly partying on down at the PFA awards. Although, I suppose as the only player ever to receive the recognition of your fellow professionals in successive seasons, if anyone was entitled to a bad day at the office it was Henry. At least Titi didn't distract us from dwelling on our White Hart Lane war stories. Everyone who was at Tottenham seemed to have a terrifying tale to tell of how they escaped enemy territory, except for us. As glad as I was that we were delivered out of the apparent maelstrom without any great dramas, I almost felt a bit guilty that we got straight back to Highbury whilst Ray was stuck in Tottenham past nightfall. No doubt, as the years pass, my story will be suitably embellished to the point where I will eventually be telling folks that I was at the heart of the action, single-handedly saving all the women and kids.

The extent of my traumatic tales from our trips to Tottenham involve having my Wee Willie Winkie Arsenal hat snatched off my head as we walked down the High Road. Some might suggest it was no more than I deserved for wearing such stupid head garb. However, every year I count my blessings when we arrive home unharmed, as I am usually flabbergasted later on hearing accounts of how an elderly lady got smacked in the face, or about some young kids who were set upon. It is bad enough when the name of the beautiful game gets besmirched by those who think that their Saturday afternoon isn't complete without some sort of confrontation with opposition fans. But it is beyond the pale when innocent civilians get caught up in this childish aggro. I might not have been a paragon of virtue as a young pup but it was just this sort of violence which saw me giving live games a miss for many years.

Just as White Hart Lane and Anfield would need to hold ten times their capacities to cope with all those who now claim to have been present in '71 and '89, I imagine the same will prove true in years to come as the number of Gooners purporting to have been present at Spurs last weekend swells to the point where we should have outnumbered them ten to one!

42

Premiership: Tuesday, 4 May (A) Arsenal 1 Portsmouth 1 Reyes (50)
Premiership: Sunday, 9 May (A) Arsenal 1 Fulham 0 Reyes (9)

Another south-coast soaking but with little in the way of compensation on this occasion; a vote of thanks to the Fulham goalie, or else the fancy-dress Gooners might have been left feeling rather foolish.

It was great to see David Bentley given his Premiership debut against Pompey but it was hardly a playing surface conducive to his or the Arsenal's passing game. After the goal glut of our previous FA Cup sortie, Harry Redknapp suggested this Arsenal side could win everything including the Boat Race. However, on the back of five wins in eight, Pompey had the best form in the Premiership. So, there was good reason for more than a few nerves and, for a while there on Tuesday night, the good ship Arsenal looked in danger of sinking.

That was until Reyes bailed us out with his debut goal in the Premiership (hopefully, the first of many), while Jens Lehmann plugged some petrifying holes with his oversized hands. The Arsenal's resilience was there for all to see as we came from behind for the eighth time this season. Personally, I'm glad Pompey retained their Premiership status – not just because it's a relatively easy awayday but because the fans at the dilapidated Fratton Park are a credit to football. Apparently, Henry and Vieira got a standing ovation from the home crowd when they appeared for the pre-match warm-up and, at the end of the game, the entire Pompey faithful rose to applaud Thierry Henry and to express their appreciation of the Arsenal's proper football. Were you watching, Highbury?

Having fun was the order of the day for the fancy dress Gooner hordes at Loftus Road and a big vote of thanks to Van Der Sar because, if it wasn't for a cock-up so early on which registered pretty high even on Lehmann's Richter scale, this match would have been far too nerve-racking for any such niceties. As you would expect in their last home game of the season, the Cottagers weren't going to cave in without a fight and, for much of this match, it was as if the rest of the team had grown so accustomed to relying on our defence that they were leaving our assault on the undefeated record squarely on their shoulders. So, thankfully, while Thierry Henry was hitting wayward shots which were closer to the corner flag than the goalmouth, and which resulted in an ironic chant of 'You'll never play for Fulham', the back four (and Jens) resisted the home side's advances and thereby maintained the party mood.

The shenaningans with the fixture schedule might annoy me but at least armchair Gooners were able to see all of our last seven games, including the finale against Leicester, shown live on the box; although, with the Gunners on autopilot, apart from Leeds and Spurs, they've hardly had much entertainment. They also wouldn't have heard a new version of Chelsea's carefree song. I would happily enlighten all those still unaware of the lyrics, if it wasn't for the possibility of protracted litigation with fairly lean Frankie Lampard's dietician and his teammates' dress designers. Wenger suggested afterwards that our players had yet to appreciate the magnitude of what they were on the verge of achieving and this was confirmed by the casual efforts of some. Yet staunch Gooner citizen Sol Campbell remained a solid rock throughout, steering our defence to its 50th Premiership clean sheet. Now, only 90 minutes lay between us and an outcome which 'Football-wise,' as Arsène put it, 'would mean immortality.'

2004 Never Again?
10 May 2004

It's a pity Fulham are going back to the Cottage next season, as Loftus Road is almost like a home game for many Gooners; I left Highbury 30 minutes before kick-off on Sunday. Admittedly, I started to get a bit panicky whilst stuck in traffic on the Marylebone Road, with the added frustration that my tickets had disappeared in the post for the umpteenth time this season (far be it for me to cast aspersions on the Arsenal box office, or I might never again see another ticket, but the lousy state of the British postal service always seems to be a far-too-convenient excuse).

So, needing to pick up duplicates on the day, I was fretting over whether there would still be anyone there from whom to collect them by the time I arrived. I wasn't the only one worrying. With Ró on babysitting duties for her granddaughter, I'd arranged to let a friend of a friend have my spare ticket. When my phone rang ten minutes before kick-off, I suggested that this person might go and pick up the duplicate tickets to save some time. However, I suddenly realised this might have been a big mistake when I arrived at the ground and found not only could I not get through to her mobile but I didn't have a clue what she looked like.

When the bloke at the Loftus Road box office told me that my tickets had been collected minutes earlier, I immediately began to think the worst. Perhaps my good Samaritan act had backfired and she'd thought sod him, and gone into the ground and switched off her phone. As usual, it turned out that I was panicking for nothing and a few frantic phone calls later, we managed to hook up.

After a quick sprint around the ground and the obligatory frisk at the turnstiles, it was as though our young Spanish starlet had very courteously waited until we were uncomfortably seated before making a monkey out of Van Der Sar. I was grateful that the bars had all been shut, because I would have been gutted to have missed the goal whilst grabbing a slurp of tea on my way in. I was also relieved because I would have felt really guilty to have taken the £30 for this ticket, only for her to have missed the only goal of the game due to my tardiness (mind you, I had warned my mate when I offered the ticket and was informed that she was prepared to risk my 'legendary timekeeping').

The Arsenal have been playing on autopilot since winning the League at White Hart Lane (just in case anyone is unsure where we won the League). I am reminded of another of my old man's cracks about the man who goes into his bank and asks to speak to Mr Williams, the bank manager. The teller informs him, 'I am terribly sorry. Mr Williams, the manager, passed away last week.' The same chap is in and out of the bank several times that day, each time receiving the same response to his request. Eventually, the teller loses patience, and says, 'This is the tenth time you've been told that Mr Williams, the bank manager, passed away last week,' to which he replies, 'Yeh, I know, but I love to hear it!'

So, going 1–0 up after only ten minutes certainly didn't help as far as the spectacle was concerned but it sure eased the tension on our particular terrace. Ever since we finally secured the Premiership title (did I mention that this was at White Hart Lane?), I've been pessimistically expecting our assault on this remarkable record to fall victim to the law of averages. The closer we come to such an incredible achievement, the less anyone gives a stuff about how we actually get there, just that we do. Under normal circumstances, with only a one-goal lead, we would all be on the edge of our seats, fearing we might fall victim to a last-minute sucker punch. On Sunday, however, the comfort of knowing Fulham were two goals away from threatening our undefeated record allowed for a party atmosphere amongst the Gooners behind the goal at Loftus Road.

And all credit to Fulham; unlike many recent opponents, they certainly gave it a go, giving us a much harder ride and displaying a healthy lack of respect. It would have made for a nail-biting ending but personally I wouldn't have minded if their worthy efforts had been rewarded with a goal. What a stunner it would have been if Malbranque's wonderful bicycle kick had been on target – the home fans would have at least been rewarded with something to celebrate in their last home game of the season.

Mind you, it was amusing listening to the Cottagers calling the radio phone-in on the way home, suggesting that this Arsenal side is ridiculously overrated. They might be right to some extent; the Arsenal have rarely produced entire performances that are worthy of the sort of lavish praise received from many of the media sheep, who have been falling over themselves in their scrabble for superlatives. I've no doubt it must be galling to fans who've seen their Fulham side acquit themselves so well (although the 0–0 draw at Highbury in November could just as easily have been a cricket score considering the number of shots we had on their goal) and I would hate the sycophants of the tabloid press to promote such a culture of resentment that the ABAs (Anyone But Arsenal) replace the ABUs. Yet, using Arsène Wenger's analogy, surely Fulham fans aren't quite so deluded as to make comparisons between their south London spouse and our end-of-season Arsenal wife, who came out on Sunday without any make-up?

For most Gooners, these last four games have just been an excuse to continue the party which started at Spurs (after we won the League at White Hart Lane!). As has become traditional for the last away game of the season, our contingent of away fans included a motley assortment of musketeers, spidermen, Austin Powers, Fred Flintstone and Tweety Pie (fortunately, Sylvester the Cat couldn't get a ticket). Thankfully, our seats were at the front of the Upper Tier because I'd completely forgotten the biggest drawback for away fans at QPR's decrepit stadium. Visitors should be warned that if you have the misfortune to be lumbered with a seat beyond the front few rows of the upper tier behind the goal, the close proximity to the pitch means that not only is it virtually impossible to see the goalline below but you are also likely to miss much of the goalmouth action.

Sadly, there wasn't much to miss on Sunday. I don't recall us having a shot on target in the entire second half until young Gael Clichy brought some unbridled enthusiasm onto a pitch where many of his teammates' minds appeared to be already focused on the forthcoming European Championships. Personally, I would prefer it if none of our players had international commitments during the break. I picture myself sweating out the summer, praying that the likes of Sol Campbell doesn't aggravate a groin injury which could have doubtless done with a couple of months' rest. Since injuring his eye, of all things, whilst gaining his first-ever international cap in a friendly for Brazil, Edu hasn't been able to kick a competitive ball for his club!

Perhaps Sunday's celebrations were overshadowed somewhat by the annual shock of our season-ticket renewals. In real terms, the increase is negligible and considering they pay similar prices at the wrong end of the Seven Sisters Road (where we won the League!), I suppose that by comparison our seats are great value. However, this fact is of small comfort when it comes to the task of garnering three and a half grand by June in order to secure another season's worth of footballing pleasures for the two of us (perhaps I should have deleted the bank manager joke).

We've still one more coupon in our precious little red booklets for this season, though. Leicester are likely to want to go down with some of their pride intact but I pray they don't poop Saturday's party. After 3,330 minutes of undefeated League football, it would be absolutely devastating if we faltered against the Foxes in the last ninety. I would settle for a draw now, so that, despite being the sixth time I've seen the Arsenal presented with the most prestigious domestic trophy, the celebratory songs and chants from the post-match festivities and Sunday's parade to the Town Hall will ring out with a unique resonance, knowing that we've witnessed a feat which is unlikely to be repeated again in my lifetime.

43

Premiership: Saturday, 15 May (H) Arsenal 2 Leicester City 1 Henry (47 pen), Vieira (66)

Dickov and his relegated Foxes threaten to do the dirty on us by pooping our party but normal service is resumed in the second half; Islington is turned red and white as a couple of hundred thousand turn out on a scorcher of a Sunday for the Town Hall parade.

Walking round to Highbury on the last day of the Premiership season, there were far more than the usual cluster of ticketless Gooners gathered in Avenell Road, at the end of Elwood Street, stealing snatches of Arsène's interview on the Jumbotron screen inside the ground. I wasn't about to give away my ticket to this historic occasion but I couldn't help feeling some sympathy for the dads who didn't have a hope of getting a precious ticket but who'd just brought their kids down to soak up some of the atmosphere around THOF and feel part of a day which might never again be repeated.

As always, loitering near the corner of Avenell Road and Gillespie Road, were the ever-present collection of shady-looking 'who needs tickets?' pond-scum touts. It is downright farcical that there have been several occasions when I've been in fear of being nicked for merely trying to do someone a massive favour by flogging a spare at face value. Yet the police plainly refuse to take any action about all the extremely conspicuous leeches who live off the fact that, for many of us, our footballing pleasures are positively priceless. Naturally, these lowlifes were taking maximum advantage in this instance by fleecing those folks with deep enough pockets to pay their seriously extortionate prices, or, worse still, the not-so-affluent Gooners who were prepared to fork out whatever it took, simply because they knew there was no question – they just had to be there on the day. Personally, I would have loved to have had it within my power to relieve all of them of their handfuls of tickets, if only to see the misery on their faces and the unbelievable looks of astonishment as I passed them out amongst the envious throng of onlookers peeking through the cracks in the big, red gates, hoping to catch a glimpse of our heroes.

Playing against an already relegated Leicester side, the football match itself on Saturday was merely meant to be the prelude for the official presentation of our Premiership trophy and the resulting celebrations of a feat which many of us never dreamed could be possible. Then again, I suppose we shouldn't really have been surprised to find ourselves having a first-half flutter as the Foxes took the lead on 26 minutes, courtesy of Paul Dickov, the one player who had good reason to try to prove the Gunners wrong in letting him go. As many a tension-ridden Arsenal experience has taught us in the past, it just wouldn't be the Gunners for us to go about anything the easy way.

Besides, it was probably fitting for us to come from behind once again. Forget all the hyperbole of a tabloid media, many of whom wouldn't know good football if it smacked them in the face. Avid Arsenal watchers can confirm that the fabulous feats of Thierry Henry apart, this incredible accomplishment hasn't really been founded on the sort of sensational form we witnessed early last season, where we simply steam-rollered several sides with the sort of panache that was the epitome of 'total football'. There have only been about half a dozen games where I could put my hand on my heart and say that the Arsenal played brilliantly. As for the rest, we've been privileged to watch absolutely breathtaking cameo moments where the Gunners have produced goals whilst playing at their counter-attacking best. By and large, this was small beer compared to the way in which we were so spoilt last season.

Personally, when I look back on the season as a whole, if I had to pinpoint one element which was responsible for an achievement which no other team has managed in the past 115 years, it would be the sort of fortitude seen on Saturday. It's become a rarity in a Premiership where many teams have a tendency to fold, perhaps as a result of the proliferation of players who, win, lose or draw, don't have to worry about their incredibly rich pickings. And no doubt this has been a contributing factor which has made life that much easier for a team who refused to be beaten. Those games where we've managed to rescue a draw or a win by the odd goal, merely as a result of the resolve coursing through the entire Arsenal squad, might not be as pleasing to the eye as the sort of entertaining goalfests we witnessed in Milan and against Leeds. Yet, as far as I am concerned, I am just as proud, if not more so, considering how rare it is in these mercenary times to see that the special Arsenal spirit is alive and flourishing at The Home Of Football.

The Gunners have been fortunate to win twelve championships in their glorious history. This is amazing when you contrast our record with the likes of Chelsea and Spurs, where fans under 50 have never enjoyed the experience (unless they were at White Hart Lane in nappies in '61). Those new to Highbury might find it hard to believe but the cyclical nature of the beautiful game means that we must avoid being blasé because we never know if we are one season away from another silverware wilderness of several years. As a result, I always do my utmost to soak in every last tremendous moment of each memorable triumph.

However, standing there basking in the glory of the post-match celebrations on Saturday, it didn't matter in the least how we'd reached the sixth of the Arsenal's title triumphs in my lifetime; those astounding statistics – P 38 W 26 D 12 L 0 – meant that players, manager and supporters alike, we were all sharing in that special sense that this occasion was absolutely unique. There will be those who might argue that this team is better than any of our previous Championship winners,

Bernard Azulay 249

and others who might agree but who don't think they played to their full potential. I actually think it's an impossible task to compare teams from different eras because the game itself has changed so much.

Nevertheless, I do know that in years to come, no matter what your opinion of how well we performed during the course of this championship, when the historians come to look back at the Arsenal's illustrious track record, this season will stand out above all the previous twelve and most likely above all those that follow. In the pressure-cooker Premiership, where there are no longer any easy games, I think it highly unlikely that another team will endure an entire 38-game season with the same mixture of fortitude and good fortune which will ensure that they are never once punished for the occasional bad day at the office. If winning all 38 is out of the question, then perhaps a European Championship is the only possible improvement. Go on Arsène, follow that!

'We Are Unbeatable'
17 May 2003

What a way to end a football season, with one big blow-out of a blistering weekend, absolutely overdosing on Arsenal euphoria. The play-off match between Palace and Sunderland provided us with a palatable appetiser on Friday night but the Foxes certainly didn't follow their script come Saturday. After Leicester had ad-libbed their way into a one-goal lead, Arsenal fans sat there in absolute astonishment. For the first time since we'd clinched the title (at White Hart Lane!), here was a team who had the downright affront to actually take advantage of the indolent 'New Invincibles', as we dragged our weary way towards immortality.

There were a bizarre few minutes before the break, as the so-called relegation fodder wound down the clock playing keep-ball. The Gunners galloped around on a wild-goose chase, while their opponents stroked it around the park to the accompaniment of an ironic chorus of '*olé*'s' from their faithful fans. Anyone just tuning in to watch the champions would have been inclined to think that the colour on their telly had gone completely kaput. After cruising far too comfortably in fifth gear for the last four games, we'd forgotten the foibles of the Arsenal engine and were crunching our way through the gearbox, frantically fumbling for that crucial lower gear in order to up the revs and roll over the Foxes. At the break, 35,000 Gooners sweated it out, all with the same thought on their minds, 'Surely, we're not going to blow it now?'

Over in the Sky commentary box, George Graham might not have been quite so gutted, since his class of '91 could have kept their spot in the record books, having lost only once during an entire League campaign. But outside the ground, all the opportunistic fly-pitchers must have been planking it. Their investment in an assorted range of 'Undefeated' souvenir T-shirts was in danger of going right up in smoke.

I imagined Martin Keown cajoling his colleagues in the dressing-room. Not only would he have been desperate to ensure that possibly his last competitive game in red and white didn't end in defeat but he was still that one all-important appearance away from his ten-match entitlement to a winners' medal. And if still 0–1 down towards the end, Wenger would have been wanting to sub a somewhat more likely goalscorer on the right wing than Martin. Keown's a big man and I am sure he would have accepted his fate with good grace, ending his career as a Gunner in the same fashion as he'd always played, putting the club's interests first and foremost, even to the point of sacrificing his winners' medal. Yet I've no doubt in such difficult circumstances, none of us would have fancied wearing Wenger's decidedly uncomfortable shoes.

Still, with hindsight, Leicester taking the lead was not only a fillip for the Foxes fans but it also ensured that our last game of the season wasn't a boring procession. It brought home the scale of our achievement to any of the blasé Gooners who'd begun to take this team for granted. So, when normal service was resumed only two minutes into the second half, after Ashley Cole earned his penalty, the whole of the Highbury Library was truly grateful when Titi tucked his spot-kick safely into the corner.

Subsequent to his seven-goal glut, including back-to-back home hat-tricks against Houllier's slipshod Scousers and skint Leeds, Thierry has hardly put a foot right in all four games since winning the League (at White Hart Lane!) and earning the recognition of his fellow players for the second successive season – I almost typed 'peers' automatically but if there's anyone on this planet who is peerless, it is

Henry. So, it was fitting that he finally broke that 30-goal barrier (only the fourth Premiership player to do so). I was shocked when our neighbourhood stats man in the West Upper informed us that you have to go back 56 years to find Ronnie Rooke (remember him well!), the last Arsenal player to bag more than 30 League goals in a season.

Thankfully, Titi's equaliser eased the tension, enabling us to relax a tad and enjoy the occasion but it was only when Paddy put away the second that the party really began. Just like Captain Courageous against Everton back in '98, this was another Tony Adams moment; Dennis spotted Vieira's surging run and dissected their defence with an exquisite pass, before our current captain rounded their keeper with consummate poise. Paddy's rare forays into the penalty area make the likes of Lampard and Gerrard look like positively clumsy schoolboys. He invariably leaves me wishing he'd make such searing runs more regularly. Yet we couldn't have wanted for our heroes to sign off on this majestic season in a more marvellous manner.

After our three-week wait following the mock presentation of an inflatable replica (in case you hadn't noticed – at White Hart Lane!), all that was left was the pomp and pizzazz of the presentation party for the proper silverware. I couldn't help thinking of our poor pooch desperately digging in vain for a hidey-hole under the carpet in the concrete floors of our flat, as the fireworks resonated round the manor with a supersonic boom. Not to mention the poor ground staff, who had to reproduce the pitch from under a great swathe of tickertape and streamer topsoil before the Arsenal Ladies could attempt to clinch their own League and Cup Double, in a title decider which kicked off a couple of hours later. Then again, the ground staff weren't exactly in need of my sympathy. Considering this was the end of the season, the entire pitch was in an unbelievably pristine, snooker-baize-like state, which suggests that they aren't exactly going to be overworked this summer.

We got home just in time to rewind the Sky Plus gadget and savour the post-match high jinks for a second time. For me, the highlights were the sight of the upper tier of the North Bank flexing and bending a good few feet as its occupants bounced up and down in time to *Volaré* ('Vieira'). We've seen it before on the rare occasions the Library has been at its out-of-character liveliest. Apparently, a certain amount of flexibility is built into the structure but it certainly wasn't a place for the faint of heart. I was horrified just watching. Instead of 'raising the roof', it was as though the residents were trying to destroy the deck and drive us all into Ashburton Grove a couple of years early!

On TV, I saw a bemused Arsène Wenger presented with a 'Comical Wenger' T-shirt. These were originally produced as a piss-take of the infamous quote which the media elicited out of him last season and were previously for sale on the Man Utd souvenir page of the Football365 website! As the penny dropped, it was obvious that the irony wasn't lost on Arsène. His face broke into a big, broad grin and he proudly held the T-shirt aloft. These appeared to be the actions of a man who was hurt by the way he'd been portrayed as being arrogant for having made such a ridiculous suggestion, when, in fact, he was only responding to a question about whether he thought such a feat was possible.

What's more, if Wenger actually has any flaws in his character, these are mostly obliterated by his virtues. To accuse such an unpretentious person of arrogance is outrageous in the extreme. I was left wondering whether it was just an amazing coincidence that we should have achieved this incredible undefeated feat only the season after all the scorn he suffered for his mere suggestion that it was feasible? Or have we just witnessed evidence of the fact that, while the proverb suggests it's a dish best served cold, Wenger prefers his plate of revenge not just warm, but piping hot?

We've grown so accustomed to the stock images from Championship- and Cup-winning celebrations over the years, that occasionally they appear far too contrived. In certain standard scenes, where the players are forced to pose until the snappers are sufficiently satiated, it can often seem that some of the more illustrious stars who've been there, done it and bought the T-shirt are making heavy weather of having fun for the benefit of the media and their fans. Call me a miserable old cynic but I sometimes get the feeling from certain players that perhaps their most genuine grin of the day is reserved for when they return to the dressing-room for the 'quick draw' of the mobile to check with their agent on the exact figure for their trophy-winning bonus.

Yet, if there was one thing which was all too apparent from the relaxed atmosphere on the pitch on Saturday and on the open-top buses in yesterday's parade to the Town Hall, it was the obvious affection between this bunch of players. It is a special kinship which is often only seen between companies of soldiers, ballet dancers and all sorts of collective groups who spend more time travelling and training with their colleagues than with their own family. Much like their equivalents in the pop world these days, certain footballers' massive celebrity status ensures that there are similarly enormous egos within the dressing-room, which undoubtedly interfere with the group ethic, resulting in underlying petty jealousies about who has the largest pay packet and who can purchase the most lairy motor. However, in the Highbury dressing-room, it is the players' bodies which need massaging and not their egos.

One might have thought that the best player in the world was entitled to be a bit of an egotistical bugger but Thierry Henry always comes across in interviews as an incredibly humble feller. Like most other groups of artistes, who live in a mollycoddled bubble from an early age, footballers' every need is catered for, and all decision making is taken out of their hands so that they are entirely free to concentrate on their game. As a result, they have a deserved reputation for immaturity. It is perhaps not surprising when you consider that, like Henry VIII, they could quite easily afford to employ someone solely to wipe their backside (and in fact often do, with many agents operating as the modern-day metaphoric equivalent of an arse wipe!).

In the past, the best teams in this country have all required men of Fergie-like strength of character to rule the roost over all the bolshy bantams traditionally found in footie dressing-rooms, to keep a lid on any errant egos and to ensure that only they and their chosen captain are able to bully the young charges. However, the times have been a-changing, drastically, and the balance of power at Premiership football clubs has swung so far in favour of the young professionals that the 'old school' managers have become something of an anathema.

As a child, I can recall having a couple of 'old school' teachers who used to patrol their classrooms like a sergeant-major, invariably with a metal ruler at hand which they would occasionally smash down on a hard surface if someone was talking out of turn. But I don't think I can recall either of them ever having to resort to any cruel (and now illegal!) punishment because they were able to command total obedience merely by means of the authoritative tone of their voice. While I might have found myself doing almost daily detentions for all my dastardly deeds in other classes and for giving lip to the other teachers, for some reason I wouldn't dare to challenge the authority of either of these two teachers. Somehow, they managed to terrify us.

To this day, I can't put my finger on it but we all came into their class one day having experienced a simultaneous revelation. It was as if it had dawned on us collectively, overnight, that there was absolutely no reason for us to have been in their thrall for so many years. In reality, there was nothing to be scared of. En masse, we plucked up courage to defy our two despots. Our Latin teacher had this ancient high-backed wooden chair set on a plinth from where he would stare down disdainfully at his students. Prior to his lesson that day, we loosened all the screws holding his chair together and, as he entered the room, the entire class sat with bated breath, exploding into fits of laughter as his seat of authority imploded on contact. We were on a roll after that and nothing was going to stop us! We set up the French teacher by filling his desk drawer with scores of wasps later that afternoon but unfortunately our anticipatory giggling and the faint buzzing gave the game away.

If I recall correctly, our French lessons were never again quite so lacklustre but there were no long-lasting effects on the teacher. Whereas, a handful of unruly larrikins left our tyrannical Latin teacher on the point of a nervous breakdown. He ended up taking early retirement after a bout of narcolepsy left him spark out every time one of us slammed a desk lid. I certainly didn't come across any tutors like Le Prof during my schooldays.

Perhaps it is due to the fact that Arsène comes from a background where players weren't quite so renowned for their childlike behaviour but his attitude is at completely the other end of the spectrum to those of the 'old school'. On the face of it, it would appear that it is a simple case of Arsène treating his charges as adults that helps to instil in them (in the infamous words of Paul Merson) an 'unbelievable belief'. It was a novel approach but one which many of Wenger's associates have been forced to adopt. In an age when our multimillionaire sportsmen earn the sort of sums which mean they can afford to buy and sell most football clubs and still have sufficient change for a Formula 1 racing team, and with so many Continentals in the dressing-room, players won't suffer being spoken to as callow kids.

Bernard Azulay 255

We Gooners have always been proud of the traditional 'Arsenal spirit': that 'backs to the wall', 'never say die' quality which has seen us snatch many a momentous, last-minute victory from the jaws of a disastrous defeat. However, in an age when players are changing clubs as often as their underpants, even the most sentimental of us Gooners are being somewhat naive to expect all of our superstars to be able to appreciate a century of the Arsenal's tradition. As far as I am concerned, his brief hiatus was a hallucination, and the lionheart likes of Martin Keown, with the blood and guts commitment which is a consequence of a one-club career, are very nearly extinct at the highest level.

Perhaps we've all been fortunate witnesses as Wenger has brought the modern-day equivalent to the party. I don't think there's any weird magic in the way Le Prof promotes an air of mutual respect in his dressing-room; the magic is the chemical reaction which results amongst a squad of players where one senses an equality of excellence that fosters this unshakeable belief in one another's and their own abilities. Arsène may be 'the Don' – '*il capo di tutti capi*' – but he's certainly no dictator. Never was the bonhomie around Highbury more apparent than the amusing incident the other week when Keown playfully pretended to throttle Le Prof on the touchline. Can you imagine Diego Forlan doing likewise with Fergie?!

If there are players in this Arsenal squad who can't possibly fully appreciate the amount of history and tradition which has passed through those famous Marble Halls, no matter; the squad plays for one another, their manager and, although we don't always deserve it, for us, the fans. What's more, they perform with a passion and commitment which is only possible amongst those who have spent sufficient time in the trenches together, rolling their sleeves up and digging themselves out of a defeat, or propping each other up after a wretched result.

All season long, I've maintained my conviction that the multitude of stars at Chelski wouldn't win anything, praying that no matter how many millions Abramovich spent, they couldn't dent my faith in the very foundations of this 'team' sport of ours, certainly not in the marathon of consistency that is the Championship. And even if the Kings Road mercenaries had managed to be the exception which proved the rule over the course of a handful of games necessary to win a Cup competition, I might have expected some of the plastic partying referred to above. While the likes of Mutu and Crespo might have enjoyed the individual glory, there's absolutely no way they could have a true appreciation of their team's achievement, without ever knowing the bitter heartache of an unsuccessful campaign in a Chelsea shirt.

It is ironic because, prior to the bottomless pockets of their Russian revolution last summer, the media were rightly putting Chelsea's best League finish in donkey's years down to the lack of summer spending and the resulting spirit in a stable dressing-room. By contrast, our coming season was already being written off. It was weird that none of the newsfolk had the nous to draw any parallels: with no wonga for Wenger to spend, there wasn't a single outfield Arsenal player who hadn't experienced the previous season's agony: the pain of handing the title to United on a plate. After positively strolling to an 'unassailable' lead with some of the most wonderful football we'd ever seen, we saw all ten points wafting out of a window which was left gaping with an air of complacent arrogance as the Moaners nicked our momentum. What's more, including subs, ten of this squad suffered the Scousers' catastrophic last-minute smash-and-grab at Cardiff three years ago, which was the last time we lost an FA Cup game until Villa Park last month.

It seems the memory of our Owen-imposed misery wasn't strong enough to overcome Man Utd. I set out for Villa Park that day certain that our lot would be as desperate as I was to avenge the exact equivalent fixture five years ago that served as the springboard for United's Treble. Dennis would finally drive away the demons of his missed penalty and there'd be no more nightmares of Ryan Giggs running riot. It wasn't merely fatigue which cost us a fourth successive FA Cup final (with an undoubted victory over Millwall) and, far more importantly, the crucial loss of momentum which saw us crashing out of the Champions League three days later.

Our pitiful support from the Holte End couldn't have helped and who knows what might have happened if we'd sung that name with a little more pride? However, according to my own reasoning, there were only six squad members remaining from that match in '99 and, as a result, perhaps we lacked the collective resolve required to inflict revenge on our somewhat hungrier opponents and their fervent fans. But then, as my missus would say, 'If ifs and ands were pots and pans . . .' There are bound to be a few green-eyed pangs watching Porto playing Monaco in the Champions League final but personally I've no room for regrets in a record-breaking season which is unlikely to ever be repeated.

On the positive side, hopefully youngsters like Kolo, Clichy, Reyes and Aliadière will have found the taste of the two cup defeats sufficiently distasteful that it will fuel their fervor to avoid another one for a good few years. It will be devastating to see the last vestige of our dinosaur defence disappear when Keown finally departs The Home Of Football in order to play out his career on a slightly less elevated stage. But Dennis Bergkamp is determined to stay on for another swansong of a season. Who can blame him, when his incisive bullets are perfectly designed for the brilliance of the rapid fire gunmen around him.

However, these two old bods from the current first team are the only players who'll be entitled to a free bus pass anytime soon and so it all bodes very well for a future which looks very bright red and white. If the bond of this squad's common experiences to date is so evident in the amount of fun they've obviously enjoyed in one another's company this past weekend, we can only imagine what is to come with so much of their careers ahead of the majority of them. It is a positively terrifying thought (for our opponents, at least) that Titi Henry is not yet 27 and, in the opinion of most sages, he hasn't reached his professional peak!

Regular Gooner game-goers this season are only too aware that some of the bandwagon-jumping press plaudits have been a little over the top: the most exquisite examples of our very best football have been produced in brief cameos and the truly great 45-minute performances have been few and far between. Primarily, our historic achievement has been founded on our great team spirit, ably assisted by a particularly mediocre Premiership, where fans of virtually every other team have been heard lamenting their players' lack of commitment. It also has to be said that if the fates didn't favour us too often last term, we've certainly benefited this season from the occasional leg up from Lady Luck. Having only just tickled the fringes of what this team is truly capable of this season, all I can say to the rest is spend what you will this summer, because heaven help you all when we truly hit our stride.

It seems I was far from the only Gooner caught out as a result of procrastinating about buying tickets for Martin Keown's testimonial. It was downright laziness on my part as I could have walked the dog around to the box office any time over the past few weeks, although Treacle is none too keen on heading in the opposite direction when there are squirrels to chase in Clissold Park and it takes a whole heap of muscular determination when our obstinate heffalump decides to dig her heels in. Even when I was told I had better pull my finger out because the box office had nearly sold out, I assumed they were just feeding me a flimsy sales pitch. Then I called again the day after it was announced that Beckham would be playing and the match had sold out.

I tried to kid myself that I wasn't that bothered. It occurred to me that, unlike many of those who would have been glad to avail themselves of a rare opportunity to buy tickets on general sale, I'd been present at every single game of consequence this season (apart from rather expensive, long schleps to Russia and the Ukraine). I am also unsure whether testimonials continue to be morally justifiable for the vast majority of Premiership footballers, who are likely to have more in their bank accounts than most of us will earn in an entire lifetime. Nevertheless, I love the idea of rewarding ever more rare instances of loyalty in some fashion and being able to express my gratitude for a whole decade's worth of earnest endeavour.

There are examples such as the selfless gentleman Niall Quinn, who donated something like a million pounds from his testimonial to charities in Sunderland, Dublin and Calcutta, and the Romanian Gica Popescu, whose farewell match recently raised £170,000 for a children's hospital in his home town (after he'd already spent £1 million of his own money building a football school for kids there). Such occasions are great because they allow every football fan to feel good about themselves. Yet I am not so sure about the recent trend for the extremely vague statements like those made by both Seaman and Keown's testimonial committees that 'a proportion of the receipts will be donated' to various good causes. Unless we're advised of a specific amount or percentage, some might perceive that it is merely a cynical method of hushing up those who would otherwise be harping on about greedy players looking for yet another pay day.

On Saturday, it seemed that every other Gooner had missed out on tickets for the testimonial in a similar fashion to myself. Being on the away ticket scheme, we are all far too used to our tickets just turning up in the post. We aren't in the habit of having to queue at the box office, or test our patience with the tortuous Ticketbastard telephone torture. Many of those whom I spoke to at Highbury seemed to have the hump with Golden Balls Beckham. They were blaming him because, while ticket sales were very healthy prior, it wasn't until Beckham's participation was publicised that overnight the match was a complete sell-out. I mean, who would ever imagine anyone would be mad enough to bid £200 for match tickets auctioned on eBay for a bleedin' testimonial and gawd love him, but we're not talking about the ever-so-charismatic Thierry Henry: it's Martin 'monkey's head' Keown (Spurs fans' cruel words, not my own). As far as I am concerned, Keown's inner beauty shines out through his commitment to the Arsenal cause and he has never looked more attractive since his efforts at Old Trafford left the Man Utd striker with his new 'Ruud van Sh*t Himself' moniker!

I only hope there's no substance to the rumours that there might be wider implications to Beckham's appearance at Highbury at this precise point in his problematical life (I should have his troubles!). I know Freddie Ljungberg was injured at the time but I found his absence from the White Hart Lane hoedown a little weird. Considering our team are purported to be such close pals, I would have thought Freddie wouldn't have wanted to pass on the possibility of participating in our Premiership-winning party (perhaps he had a prior engagement parading around in his Calvins?). Unless looking for one last big pay day at the tail end of their career, you would have thought any player would be mad to leave the Arsenal for the sake of a few thousand quid a week, especially when they are never going to find a team with the Arsenal's chemistry, which is likely to give them so much professional pride. Yet it is no wonder that his White Hart Lane rain check was grist to the mill of the media's transfer speculation about Ljungberg.

Many might think that Beckham would be more than an adequate replacement out on the right. Personally, I can't see the England captain leaving Madrid, unless it is to save his marriage. By Madrid's lofty standards, they've had a lousy season and Beckham will want to stay at least another year so that he won't be perceived as having been unable to cut it on the Continent. Even if he was returning to England, he'd have to subsidise his own wages if he wanted to come to Highbury.

Leaving aside the question of his ability, Beckham is absolutely the last player I'd want coming into our settled dressing-room because all the incidental baggage that he brings is bound to be disruptive. Perhaps Thierry is the exception which proves the rule because usually a large ego is a prerequisite for those who want to reach the very top in their chosen sport. Whether Thierry's is large or small (his ego, not his Va Va Voom!), I certainly wouldn't want it overshadowed by the whole media circus which accompanies this country's tabloid royalty.

As today drew nigh, I would have been absolutely gutted to have missed out on my first and last match of the season at The Home Of Football. As the various edifices of the Ashburton Grove project rise up from nothing, reaching towards the Highbury skyline ever more rapidly, the day will soon come when we start counting down our remaining matches at our beloved old stadium. Without any of Saturday's tension, tonight's event will be one long evening of unmitigated merriment; a celebration of all things Arsenal.

Usually, the caterwaul of the stadium announcer's 'Welcome to Highbury ladies and gentlemen', as it carries a few hundred yards on the wind through our open windows, is a signal for us to get a wriggle on if we're going to make kick-off. Often, I have to tear myself away from the television the moment an interview with Wenger is finished, but with no live coverage tonight, it would have been absolute agony to have been sitting here trying to work out what was happening from the noise emanating from the stadium.

Aside from being directly responsible for inflicting my weekly missives on unsuspecting Arsenal supporters around the planet and my weekly column in the *Irish Examiner*, the benefits of the Arsenal mailing list on the Internet are many and varied. Not only can it prove a summer sanctuary of Arsenal chinwagging (or, more precisely, keyboard tapping) for those suffering from severe withdrawals but it is also an invaluable tool for those either looking for tickets or those passing them on to genuine Gooners.

Until my box office connection suddenly upped and left the job, which I'd assumed he'd adopted for life (leaving me right up kack creek; never mind the missing paddle but in an Arsenal canoe where

I might never again find a spare West Upper seat), I was in the habit of coming to the rescue of all sorts of geographically challenged Gooner strangers on a rare pilgrimage to Highbury, simply because I could. Not that the odd carton of Camel didn't come as a much-welcomed token of their gratitude. Especially if they arrived during a long enough break between Champions League matches for me to have run out of my nicotine haul from Continental trips.

Having met my good pal Yee Ming from Singapore and introduced him to the wonders of the West Upper, I did likewise when a friend of his arrived from South-east Asia to spend a year here studying law. I couldn't believe my luck when I saw Aileen offering a spare ticket for tonight on the mailing list. Actually, she was offering both her tickets, in the hope that someone might swap the two for a single seat at Saturday's game and the subsequent Premiership trophy presentation. Unfortunately for Aileen (and fortunately for me), she was about as likely to find someone willing to make this swap as I am to give up smoking, and so I am extremely grateful that my good karma came back to me or I would have missed out on tonight.

However, if there was anyone on Saturday who felt cheated of more footie and celebratory frolics on Monday night, after toasting our success in the jam-packed hostelries around Highbury, they were able to head back to the ground to watch the women play gratis. Four hours after the men had been presented with the Premiership trophy, the women pipped Fulham to the title with a 3–1 victory which brought the curtain down on the closest run three-horse title race in the history of the women's Premier League. Arsène Wenger, Patrick Vieira and 5,000 other Gooners stayed on to support the women, as the Arsenal Ladies completed the club's substantial haul of silverware spoils by securing the second string to their own League and Cup Double. I was even led to believe that the Under-14s were playing on the pitch after the parade on Sunday.

It seems that whenever the Arsenal travel to the Town Hall on an open-top bus, the weather is guaranteed to be absolutely gorgeous. If there is an omnipotent one overseeing events on this planet, then he/she's got to be a Gooner. They will have been smiling, looking down on a scene where Highbury and its environs became a brightly coloured Goonerville for the day, with everybody dancing in the streets long into the afternoon to the sound of all the beats pumping out of the boozers, where landlords had been canny enough to purchase a copy of the Arsenal Away Boys CD.

It might sound like a scene straight out of the movie *Fever Pitch*, except that I don't recall anyone having to avoid obstreperous drunks, or having to tread carefully along streets littered with bottles, beer cans and horseshit. Thank heavens it all passed off peacefully and, as a result, a wonderful time was had by all.

And now I am going to sign off so I can head round to Highbury for one final singsong in honour of Martin Keown, one of the last of the Galahad Gunners, before breaking for a summer in which I will be dreaming of the three more games needed to beat Nottingham Forest's record and a mere nineteen to eclipse the amazing fifty-eight-match unbeaten run of Baresi's mighty AC Milan side.

Epilogue
There's Only One Keown

Martin Keown's testimonial match: Monday 17 May (H) Arsenal 6 England 0 Cole (17), Aliadière (23, 77), Reyes (53, 58, 66)

A Monday night star-studded tribute to the last of our defensive dinosaurs.

I wouldn't by any means profess to being an expert on the subject and might well be deemed somewhat biased but, in my humble opinion, Freddie Ljungberg is a far more handsome specimen of the human male form than David Beckham. Still, although I might struggle to comprehend the British public's obsession with the England captain and even though I had the hump with all those who'd denied many genuine Gooners tickets by being quicker off the mark, specifically because it presented a rare opportunity to see Golden Balls perform in the flesh, this didn't stop me from feeling sorry for all the Beckham fans on Monday night.

Perhaps the powers that be at Real were punishing him for getting himself sent off in their penultimate match of the season 24 hours earlier. Or with his Golden Balls rapidly losing their sheen, as the Madrid side's season ended with their worst run of results in the club's 102-year history, it might just have been an act of pure spite. Whatever their reasons, Real turned around at the death and refused permission for Beckham to play in Keown's testimonial despite the fact that his red card left him suspended for their last game of the season the following Sunday. There must have been some hectic last-minute negotiations before kick-off because as I headed around to Highbury, I heard the crowd booing as a statement was read out over the PA confirming that Beckham would only be allowed to kick-off the game.

All credit to the England captain. He proved that he's not a man to be pushed around, remaining on the pitch for a whole three minutes, insisting on taking a few touches of the ball before eventually accepting his substitution. So, naturally, by the time I took my seat alongside Aileen, I'd not only missed Beckham's brief appearance but Thierry Henry, Patrick Vieira and Robert Pires were also departing the scene. Instead of disappearing straight after Sunday's celebrations to join a French squad due to play Brazil in a FIFA event three days later, they'd made a point of deciding to stay on just long enough to pay their token respects to Keown.

If it wasn't for Aileen, I wouldn't have been there at all and I am glad one of us was early as I was at least able to spend the next few minutes quizzing her on what I'd missed. Apparently, kick-off was preceded by the presentation of an array of awards. Thierry Henry was presented with the player of the month award for April, the Barclaycard player of the year award and the Golden Boot for his 30 League goals. While Arsène Wenger received all due recognition as the manager of the year with his awards from Barclaycard and the League Managers Association. In this instance, I was left feeling more than a little testy about my infernal tardiness when I discovered that Titi had been presented with his Golden Boot by Ian Wright. I pictured it as a rather poignant moment, as though Wrighty was symbolically passing on the Gooner goalscoring baton to his most-natural successor.

Having replaced the boy Beckham somewhat prematurely, I felt for a decidedly svelte-looking Paul Gascoigne. I very much doubt Gazza was expecting quite such a strenuous evening, whereas Marc

Overmars looked extremely keen to stretch his little legs when he appeared later on. I hadn't noticed his name included in the Arsenal line-up on the back of the programme, yet when Overmars was introduced in the second half, there was absolutely no mistaking who it was haring down the touchline, even though it was a few years since he'd last played at The Home Of Football. The Dutchman has such a distinctive running style, with his stumpy legs pumping up and down like some sort of cartoon character, that when he whooshes past an opponent, you half expect to hear a 'Meep, meep!' I'd forgotten quite how astonishing Overmars' acceleration is and it was plainly evident that he'd lost none of his sparkling pace. Considering his knee trouble has since forced his retirement, I guess we have to consider ourselves privileged to have witnessed one of his last appearances.

It was also no surprise that Sven turned up. I suppose he was there to watch over the six of his Euro 2004 England squad involved in the game. Whereas the attraction for Gooners like myself was that Martin's farewell performance threw up the sort of tantalising match-ups which wet dreams are made of. Apart from a reprise of the double Dutch delight of Bergkamp and Overmars, there was the absolutely intoxicating prospect of a strike partnership of Thierry Henry and Ian Wright. Sadly, we were only treated to a few minutes' tease, as Titi's international commitments forced him off within moments of my arrival. Wrighty also retired before long but this was only so that he could return some time later for the opposite side, playing alongside Shaun Wright-Phillips. I imagine it must have been a real kick for him to play with his stepson. I seem to recall that on a similarly star-studded evening for David Seaman's testimonial, with his enormous personality, Wrighty struggled to avoid stealing the show completely.

I have to admit that it was a rare pleasure to find myself sitting in a West Upper where, instead of the usual sober collection of sadly far-too-staid residents, who are much closer to their pensions than puberty, I was surrounded by the shrill high-pitched screams of several thousand kids whose parents seldom get such an opportunity for a family outing to THOF. Looking around the 38,000 full house, there were hundreds of eager-looking faces, excited at the prospect of picking out the stars they'd only previously seen on their TV screens. Interspersed amongst them there must have been many Gooners like myself who, despite the celebratory mood, couldn't escape the abiding feeling that the evening was tinged with the hint of an 'end of an era' sadness.

During the celebrations at the Town Hall the previous day, the more diffident players might always demur but as tradition demands, they each took their turn at the microphone. It was appropriate that Martin Keown was the last to appear on the balcony (before the women's team squeezed out there en masse). With his wife and two boys in their yellow Arsenal shirts standing by his side, brimming with pride, Martin led a quarter of a million sardine-like Gooners, rammed along the length of Upper Street, in a chorus of, 'There's only one Keown'. There was an air of bemusement in his voice as he announced, 'Everybody else hates me, but you love me!'

Keown's affinity with the Arsenal fans stems from the fact that it is obvious to us all that the Arsenal means as much to him as it does to us. His chivalrous commitment to strain every last sinew in his body in pursuit of the team's cause is sadly becoming something of an anomaly, in a period when players are more concerned with protecting their physical assets than risking health and limbs in the heat of the battle. It is strange to think that pro rata, with the limited amount of time he actually spent on the pitch this season, Keown was probably most responsible for the propagation of the special 'Arsenal spirit' which propelled the side on to establishing their unique place in footballing history.

While the media world was castigating Martin as some kind of uncontrollable monster after his triumphant jostling of Van Nistelrooy at Old Trafford, most Gooners were pleased as Punch. Admittedly, there was the odd stick in the mud at the AGM who raised a voice in protest at such a slur on the Gunners 'good' (??!!) name but, in an age of shameless badge-kissing by mercenary backstabbers, the vast majority of us were absolutely made-up to witness the same depth of feeling from a team member as was felt on the terraces. Who could have imagined that this one 'handbags at dusk' incident, the resulting indignant wrath of the entire media world and the protracted prognostications on the punishment would be the cosmic catalyst for the 'all for one' fervour which probably fuelled our undefeated achievement?

Included in an array of colourful nicknames, Keown has been called 'Rash' because of the way he is all over his opponents, as one of the best man markers in the business. However, in this one rash act of overexuberance, Martin guaranteed that thousands of Gooners would have turned out on Monday, even if we'd been playing Leyton Orient, without a single star name amongst the supporting cast. There may be many who contend that testimonials are superfluous for elite footballers in this day and age, yet such occasions are the sole opportunity for us football fans to express our appreciation to those players who demonstrate the sort of personality traits that are rapidly disappearing from a modern game where a signature on a contract means nothing more than the amount of leverage it provides to the player or the club.

Evidence of the sort of loyalty and commitment we witness every time Martin Keown pulls on an Arsenal shirt is so rare these days that we absolutely must make the most of any opportunity to reward it. Otherwise, what hope is there of clinging on to the last vestiges of such 'one club' allegiances which have traditionally ensured that the British game is so much more intense and passionate than the vast majority of the product seen on the Continent. Yet such sentimental ideals seem all the more out of place when players are now changing clubs in this country almost as frequently as everywhere else. Not to mention examples like Dennis Bergkamp, where after eight years of service to the Arsenal cause, instead of showing their gratitude, sadly the Gunners seemed to try to take advantage of his situation by offering him only a year extension at a third of his salary.

In the programme on Monday night, Martin described how his folks supported the Arsenal as a result of the Irish connection at Highbury during the 1970s (which made Róna happy since, with a name like Keown, she has always sworn that he must be more Irish then English!) and how his determination to play for the Gunners was such that as a lad he travelled down with his sister from Oxford by rail to train at Highbury. It's not quite the romantic 'Roy of the Rovers' tale of Charlie George stepping off the terraces to play for the team he's supported all his life and eventually scoring the winning goal in an FA Cup final. Yet despite Keown not quite being a member of the exclusive 'Islington lad made good' club, there's no mistaking the same sense of 'belonging' – even if he had to don the shirts of Villa and Everton to fully appreciate that he only ever really wanted to play for one club.

As the feelers of the Arsenal's Academy stretch ever further towards the untapped sources of footballing talent in the far-flung corners of this planet and (along with most other top clubs), as a result, our youth team harvest tends to contain the cream of a truly multinational crop, it is sad to think that there is an ever-decreasing potential for the Arsenal production line to create players like George, Keown and Tony Adams, whose very blood runs the red and white of the Arsenal. With Ray Parlour's subsequent departure, Ashley Cole provides the sole connection to this home-grown tradition. If the Gunners are to safeguard the treasure that is the Arsenal spirit, we can only hope that this increasingly rare breed doesn't go the way of the dodo.

Like many Gunners who have gone before him, it's hard to imagine Martin playing for another team. However, his final match in red and white wasn't just significant in the sense that he might be one of the last of his kind, who put club before self. This game brought the curtain down on an entire era: Keown and Parlour were the sole surviving connections to the 'boring, boring Arsenal' of old. Keown himself might not have been immersed in the culture of gambling and boozing which permeated the British game for many years but he and the other defensive dinosaurs were hardly blessed with chameleon-like tendencies; it must have been a massive task for them to adapt from the steak-and-chips regime of old to the pasta and broccoli which were just part of the revolution, as Arsène Wenger introduced the flair-filled Va Va Voom to the musketeers of the Arsenal's new model army.

As it turned out, both sides benefited. Wenger retained the resolute defensive core of the Arsenal's old school and, along with Dixon, Winterburn and Adams, Keown saw his career in the top flight extended, long past the point which might otherwise have been expected. After a decade of defensive solidity, the like of which we might never see again, whoever was to replace this illustrious rearguard was always going to suffer by comparison with our fab back five. As one by one they've each fallen victim to the inevitable swathe of Father Time's scythe, Keown was the last man left standing.

Over the past few seasons, we've witnessed the Arsenal evolve from a team which could once rely on clean sheets and nicking a result by the odd goal, to a side which was able to triumph by outscoring its opponents. This might have guaranteed us an exciting few seasons spent on the edge of our seats but we must be grateful that Keown is signing off just as Sol and Kolo strike up the sort of consistent partnership which has the same impervious solidity that we were once so accustomed to from Keown and his former colleagues.

I'm certain the Irish connection can't be irrelevant but my missus has always had a soft spot for Martin. Personally, I adore his hardman, 'they shall not pass' on-pitch persona but he must undergo a transformation when he dons the Arsenal shirt because in person, you couldn't wish to meet a more humble or gentle soul. Ró's soft spot for Keown developed during our Cup-Winners' Cup conquests of the early 1990s, when we were fortunate to be able to afford to travel on the executive trips to away games in Europe. The principal attraction of these outings was that we were able to travel on the same plane as the team. I forget where we were going but I remember one trip in particular which I believe coincided with the 'bung' scandal.

As a result, 'Cone Man' Stewart Houston was in charge as caretaker manager and as we waited to board the plane, in the absence of the eagle-eyed George 'Gaddafi' Graham, the players were in a particularly playful mood. Keown must have suffered from a dandruff problem because the players were teasing him, calling him 'Snowy' as a bored and childish Ray Parlour sat behind him dropping torn up bits of white paper on his head. As a kind soul who doesn't appreciate cruelty of any kind, Ró pointed this out to an oblivious Keown while we stood queuing to pass through the metal detector. After he'd brushed most of the scraps from his bonce, she asked him to lean forward so she could pick out the remaining bit of paper which was caught in his curly barnet. Keown expressed his gratitude so profusely that he's been a firm favourite of Ró's ever since.

As the last representative of a bygone age of innocence, before interfering agents and middlemen bent the ears of players who would have previously signed any contract put before them, such was their desire to be associated with such a historic club as the Arsenal, Keown had grown on all of us Gooners. Martin had gone from being an unsung hero, who was worried whether we would turn out in sufficient numbers for his testimonial, to a player who spent the last few weeks of the season hearing his name sung repeatedly, merely as he warmed up on the touchline. As he anxiously awaited his last-minute introduction in the final four games of the season, in order that he'd reach the ten-game minimum necessary for him to earn a Championship-winners' medal, it was great that we got an opportunity to show our appreciation in this fashion.

Admittedly, not all of the 38,000 at Highbury on Monday night were there in Martin's honour. Yet no one was disappointed by the entertainment as Ray Parlour put a smile on everyone's faces by pulling Wrighty's shorts down and Jose Reyes sent out an unmitigated message to the manager of the Spanish squad with a spectacular hat-trick which suggested he would be sorely missed in Portugal. Sadly, the Norwich goalie, Robert Green, neglected to follow the script when he instinctively saved not only Keown's penalty but his follow-up shot, resulting in some friendly badinage from behind the goal of, 'That's why you're a centre-half'. I guess it goes too much against the grain for a goalie to resist his natural reactions. Towards the end of the game, it was Arsenal reserve keeper Mark Howard who managed to prevent the evening coming to a perfect conclusion when he kept out probably the best shot Keown has struck for many a moon. After some friendly booing for Howard's contribution, it was time to bid our hero farewell for the last time, as he was substituted just before the final whistle.

You could hear the emotion in Keown's voice as he took the microphone at the end of the game to express his gratitude. He was obviously chuffed with such a huge turn out and as Martin did one last lap of honour around the hallowed turf, the crowd raised the Highbury rafters with one final, hearty rendition of, 'There's only one Keown'. Thanks for the memories Martin.

Arsène Wenger's New Invincibles

Arsenal Football Club 2003–04: Honours and Records

Premiership Champions

First team in the modern era to win the Championship while still unbeaten – *only previously achieved by Preston North End in 1889, whose unbeaten season was 22 games compared to the Arsenal's 38*

First team to remain unbeaten away from home in an entire League campaign on two occasions – *2001–02 and 2003–04*

Longest unbeaten run in the Premiership – *currently 40 games, including 2 games from the previous season. The Arsenal are now 2 games away from equalling Nottingham Forest's all-time record for an unbeaten sequence of 42 games set in 1977–78 and 1978–79 and a mere (!) 14 games from AC Milan's European record of 58.*

Top-flight record for longest unbeaten start to a season – **previous record of 29 held by Leeds (1973–74) and Liverpool (1977–78)**

Longest unbeaten league sequence during a single season – *previously held by Burnley with 30 games (1920–21)*

Fewest defeats in a Premiership season – *previous record of three was set by us in 2001–02, Man Utd (1998–99, 1999–2000) and Chelsea (1998–99)*

Youngest Premiership winner – *Gael Clichy at 18 years and 10 months is the youngest player to win a Premiership medal*

...ll Writers' Association Player of the Season – Thierry Henry

Players' Player of the Season – Thierry Henry

A Premier League Team of the Season – included Lauren, Ashley Cole, **...l** Campbell, Patrick Vieira, Robert Pires, Thierry Henry

Barclaycard Manager of the Year – Arsène Wenger

Barclaycard Manager of the Month – Arsène Wenger (August, February)

League Managers' Association Manager of the Year – Arsène Wenger

League Managers' Association Service to Football Award – Don Howe

Barclaycard Player of the Year – Thierry Henry

Barclaycard Player of the Month – January: Thierry Henry; February: Edu/Dennis Bergkamp; April: Thierry Henry

FIFA World Player of the Year 2003 – 2nd Thierry Henry
Ballon D'Or (European Footballer of the Year) 2003 – 2nd Thierry Henry
French Sportsman of the Year – Thierry Henry
French Footballer of the Year – Thierry Henry
Golden Boot – Thierry Henry (30 League goals)

FA Women's Premier League and FA Cup Double Winners